The
SOUL'S
ALMANAC

The
SOUL'S
ALMANAC

A Year of
Interfaith
Stories,
Prayers,
and Wisdom

AARON ZERAH

JEREMY P. TARCHER/PUTNAM
A MEMBER OF
PENGUIN PUTNAM INC.
NEW YORK

Most Tarcher/Putnam books are available at special quantity discounts for bulk
purchase for sales promotions, premiums, fund-raising, and educational needs.
Special books or book excerpts also can be created to fit specific needs.
For details, write Putnam Special Markets, 375 Hudson Street,
New York, NY 10014.

Jeremy P. Tarcher/Putnam
a member of
Penguin Putnam Inc.
375 Hudson Street
New York, NY 10014
www.penguinputnam.com

Library of Congress Cataloging-in-Publication Data

Zerah, Aaron.
The soul's almanac : a year of interfaith stories, prayers, and wisdom /
Aaron Zerah.
p.   cm.
ISBN 0-87477-934-0
1. Meditations.   2. Devotional calendars.   I. Title.
BL624.5.Z45   1998   98-26471   CIP
291.4'32—dc21

Printed in the United States of America
1   3   5   7   9   10   8   6   4   2

Book design and title page photograph by Deborah Kerner

ACKNOWLEDGMENTS

Gratitude is offered to:

Spirit as it has manifested in so many good teachings and teachers.

Huston Smith, Dhyani Ywahoo, the Dalai Lama, Robert Muller, Joseph Gelberman, and numerous Interfaith pioneers, colleagues, and friends.

Nancy Ellis, literary agent par excellence and a woman of great soul.

Joel Fotinos, David Groff, and all the good people at Tarcher.

My parents, Bronia and Joseph Krause; my brother Steve and nephew Solomon; my mother-in-law, Lillian Peterson; and all my friends for their encouragement and faith.

Becky Luening of Wordrhythm, who with great humor and savoir faire manifested my handwritten manuscript into a living book.

All of you who, by reading and assimilating and sharing this book, participate in the divine act of creativity.

I am dedicating this book to my child of
spirit, Sari Magdala, and to all children of
spirit. Only with the willingness, enthusiasm,
and assistance of Madhuri, my partner,
friend, and wife, was this book birthed.

May its presence in your life, dear ones, move
you to greater dedication to a life of connection and service.

MANY BLESSINGS,
REVEREND AARON ZERAH

INTRODUCTION

Every day is a good day.

So it is revealed in every culture, every faith. What makes a day good?

Appreciation, insight, acquisition of new or increased power, accomplishment and completion, release . . . presence with the reality of the day.

We humans are set up to take life, death, and everything for that matter, day by day. There's something about a day—just long enough to gain wisdom in; just short enough to not overwhelm us with immensity. A day is the perfect unit of and for faith.

Please note that there's an extra, and special, "day" included in *The Soul's Almanac*. It's called "Leap of Faiths" and is found in the February 29 position. You may turn to this page any day for uplifting of spirit and encouragement of faith.

I ask you, dear readers, to apply your faith to the themes, stories and scripture, and contemplations to follow—each blessed day. I ask you to contemplate, that is, to bring your "temple" self, the wise and worshipful one, to these days of faiths.

As you move through this cycle of spirit, may you find refreshment, understanding, and peace.

Blessings on your way.

JANUARY

AIM

Before you climb a tree, you must start at the bottom.

—TRADITIONAL BUJI TRIBAL PROVERB (WEST AFRICA)

Thus, in all interactions the superior person carefully considers the beginning.

—I CHING (CLASSICAL CHINESE TEXT)

The Mullah Nasreddin brought his students to the fair so that they could watch him compete in the archery contest. Before his first shot, the Mullah fixed his cap military style and, assuming a soldier's posture, drew the bow and fired. The arrow missed the target completely, and the crowd roared with derisive laughter. Then he picked up the bow again, this time with little strength, and shot the second arrow. It flew straight, but landed far short of the mark. Again, the onlookers guffawed. For the last of his three allotted shots, Nasreddin nonchalantly turned to face the target, aimed, and let fly. It was a perfect bull's-eye.

The crowd went wild, then fell into a stunned silence. Nasreddin chose the moment to take his prize and indifferently started to walk on. But his students and the astonished throng demanded an explanation. Nasreddin complied and told them, "For the first shot, I was identified with a soldier, face-to-face with the enemy. Fear made the arrow miss. With the second shot, I became like the man who, having failed miserably with the first shot, was so anxious and eager he could not concentrate. He simply had no power."

"And the third shot?" inquired a brave soul. "Who fired that one?"

"That? Oh, that was *me*."

—TRADITIONAL SUFI TALE

CONTEMPLATION

Today is acknowledged as the first day of the year by many of the world's cultures. Yet some people mark the new year at other times and in other seasons.

Any day may be the beginning or renewal of your devotion to spiritual practice. Any day may initiate your turning to real aims. Put all of your true self into achieving those aims, and you may discover, like the old Buddhist Monk Yün-Men, "Every day is a good day!"

GOOD AND BAD

◇

A poor farmer's prize horse disappeared one day, last seen heading for the country of the barbarians. The other farmers, poor like him, knew how much the horse meant to the family and expressed their sympathy. The man's father said only, "How do you know this isn't good fortune?" A few months passed. Lo and behold, the farmer's horse came back, bringing with it another horse, strong and of new stock. The neighbors congratulated the farmer for his good luck. The old farmer was terse. "How do you know this doesn't forebode disaster?" The peasants merely shook their heads and went back to their work. The two horses mated, and soon the family had many fine horses and the family became very rich. The farmer's son, with leisure time now on his hands, took a fancy to riding his beautiful horse, and one day he fell off and broke his hip. Once again came the other farmers to offer condolences and to wish him a quick recovery for his son. The father told them, "How do you know this is not a good thing?" Well, the hip did not heal well, and the son became lame as a result. Some time went by, and the barbarians crossed the frontier. War had begun, and all able-bodied young men were required to fight. Nine out of ten of them died. The young farmer, limp and all, stayed home and alive.

—TRADITIONAL TAOIST TALE

◇

And a certain prince asked him, "Good teacher, what shall I do to inherit everlasting life?" Said Jesus, "Why do you call me good? No one is good but God alone. You know the commandments."

—GOSPEL OF LUKE (CHRISTIAN NEW TESTAMENT)

CONTEMPLATION

On this day, many of us are having second thoughts. Just what were we thinking when we made all those good intentions for the year?

We observe, as the writers of Proverbs did, that misfortune befalls the righteous (even ourselves), and that fortune comes at times to the average person and even those who are powerfully bad. Why not then resign oneself to what seems on the surface of things to be a random process?

Good and bad are not so easily measured. They are an experience, known and felt over a lifetime. At some point, of good and bad there will be no question.

GENIUS

Say, it has been revealed to me that a company of the jinn gave ear. Then they said, "We have indeed heard a Qur'an wonderful, guiding to rectitude. We believe in it, and we will not associate with our Lord anyone. He—exalted by our Lord's majesty!—has not taken to Himself either consort or a son.

"The fool among us spoke against God outrage, and we had thought that men and jinn would never speak against God a lie. But there were certain men of mankind who would take refuge with certain men of the jinn, and they increased them in vileness, and they thought, even as you also thought, that God would never raise up anyone.

"And we stretched toward heaven, but we found it filled with terrible guards and meteors. We would sit there on seats to hear; but any listening now finds a meteor in wait for him. And so we know not whether evil is intended for those in the earth, or whether their Lord intends for them rectitude.

"And some of us are righteous, and some of us are otherwise; we are sects differing. Indeed, we thought that we should never be able to frustrate God in the earth, neither be able to frustrate Him by flight. When we heard the guidance, we believed in it; and whosoever believes in his Lord, he shall fear neither paltriness nor vileness.

"And some of us have surrendered, and some of us have deviated. Those who have surrendered sought rectitude; but as for those who have deviated, they have become firewood for hell."

—QUR'AN (HOLY BOOK OF ISLAM)

CONTEMPLATION

The jinn (source of the word genius) *were, in Islamic cosmology, supernatural beings who, taking on human or other form, dwelled in spirit on the earth. They had the same opportunity as humans to accept God's word or reject it. True genius lies not in the fickle mind, but rather in the heart locked onto God.*

ANIMALS

◇

But ask now the beasts,
and they shall teach thee;
and the fowls of the air,
and they shall tell thee;
Or speak to the earth,
and it shall teach thee;
And the fishes of the sea
shall declare unto thee.

—BOOK OF JOB (HEBREW SCRIPTURES)

◇

Once upon a time all the water in the world was swallowed by a huge frog, and nobody else could get a drop to drink. It was most inconvenient, especially for the fish, who flapped about and gasped on the dry land. So the animals laid their heads together and came to the conclusion that the only way of making the frog disgorge the waters was to tickle his fancy so that he should laugh. Accordingly they gathered before him and cut capers and played pranks that would have caused any ordinary person to die of laughing. But the frog did not even smile. He sat there in gloomy silence, with his great goggle eyes and his swollen cheeks, as grave as a judge. As a last resort, the eel stood up on its tail and wriggled and danced about, twisting itself into the most ridiculous contortions. This was more than even the frog could bear. His features relaxed, and he laughed till the tears ran down his cheeks and the water poured out of his mouth. However, the animals had now got more than they had bargained for, since the waters disgorged by the frog swelled into a great flood in which many people perished. Indeed the whole of mankind would have been drowned, if the pelican had not gone about in a canoe picking up the survivors and so saving their lives.

—TRADITIONAL ABORIGINAL AUSTRALIAN STORY

CONTEMPLATION

Animals have always had a big place in this world. From Adam, who named them, to Noah, who collected them, to Solomon, who understood their secret ways, animals are an important part of what we generally know as our world and our story.

Animals enrich us with their beauty and their uncanny ways of being. Like God, their way is not our way. They are not of our kind; yet we may learn kindness and possibly find salvation in their company.

PRIDE

◆

Once a crow sat in a fig tree with a piece of cheese in its mouth. A fox came under the tree and said, "Noble, handsome, and sweet bird, good, agreeable, and lovely bird, happy indeed is your mate! For you are surely the most beautiful bird in the forest! And if you were to sing, your songs would probably surpass those of all the other birds! Let us see whether your voice matches your fine bearing and plumage."

Hearing this, the crow thought to himself, "I will let him hear my voice, and he will praise me even more!"

So the crow opened his mouth to sing, and the cheese fell to the ground. The fox gobbled it up and continued on his way.

—TRADITIONAL JEWISH TALE

CONTEMPLATION

Yesterday the Zoroastrian holy days of Ghambar Maidyarem concluded. During Ghambar Maidyarem the community shares its food and celebrates the creation of the animals with whom we share this world.

This is not a time for personal pride, nor is it a time for the rich to lord over the poor or the more spiritually knowledgeable to condescend to their fellows.

It's still the beginning of a new year. Soberly look to this day and the year-to-be, and without pride, start again.

LAZINESS

◇

Again, it will be like a man going on a journey, who called his servants and entrusted his property to them. To one he gave five talents of money, to another two talents, and to another one talent, each according to his ability. Then he went on his journey. The man who had received the five talents went at once and put his money to work and gained five more. So also, the one with the two talents gained two more. But the man who had received the one talent went off, dug a hole in the ground, and hid his master's money.

After a long time the master of those servants returned and settled accounts with them. The man who had received the five talents brought the other five. "Master," he said, "you entrusted me with five talents. See, I have gained five more."

His master replied, "Well done, good and faithful servant! You have been faithful with a few things; I will put you in charge of many things. Come and share your master's happiness!"

The man with the two talents also came. "Master," he said, "you entrusted me with two talents. See, I have gained two more."

His master replied, "Well done, good and faithful servant! You have been faithful with a few things; I will put you in charge of many things. Come and share your master's happiness!"

Then the man who had received the one talent came. "Master," he said, "I knew that you are a hard man, harvesting where you have not sown and gathering where you have not scattered seed. So I was afraid and went out and hid your talent in the ground. See, here is what belongs to you."

His master replied, "You wicked, lazy servant! So you knew that I harvest where I have not sown and gather where I have not scattered seed? Well then, you should have put my money on deposit with the bankers, so that when I returned I would have received it back with interest.

"Take the talent from him and give it to the one who has the ten talents. For everyone who has will be given more, and he will have an abundance. Whoever does not have, even what he has will be taken from him. And throw that worthless servant outside, into the darkness, where there will be weeping and gnashing of teeth."

—GOSPEL OF MATTHEW (CHRISTIAN NEW TESTAMENT)

◇

There is no place where one cannot achieve greatness; only the lazy prospers nowhere. There is no place that does not suit me, O God!

—TRADITIONAL YORUBA TRIBAL PROVERB
(WEST AFRICA)

◇

Those who abstain from action while allowing the mind to dwell on sensual pleasure cannot be called sincere aspirants. Action is better than inaction.

—BHAGAVAD GITA (HINDU SACRED TEXT)

CONTEMPLATION

Why was the good master, Jesus, so harsh in the parable of the talents? Or the Hindu Deity Krishna so severe in his instruction to his devotee Arjuna in the Bhagavad Gita? Or indigenous people, like the Yoruba, in warning that no honey can be procured without application of a sharp ax to obtain it? Take heed.

Laziness in any matter is laziness in and of the spirit.

RESURRECTION

Thou shalt come in and go out, thy heart rejoicing, in the favor of the Lord of the Gods, a good burial [being thine] after a venerable old age, when age has come, thou assuming thy place in the coffin, and joining earth on the high ground of the west.

Thou shalt change into a living Ba, and surely thou will have power to obtain bread and water and air; and thou shalt take shape as a heron or swallow, as a falcon or a bittern, whichever you pleasest.

Thou shalt cross in the ferryboat and shalt not turn back, thou shalt sail on the waters of the flood, and thy life shall start afresh. Thy Ba shall not depart from thy corpse, and thy Ba shall become divine with the blessed dead. The perfect Bas shall speak to thee, and thou shalt be an equal amongst them in receiving what is given on earth. Thou shalt have power over water, shalt inhale air, and shalt be surfeited with the desires of thy heart. Thine eyes shall be given to thee so as to see, and thine ears so as to hear, thy mouth speaking, and thy feet walking. Thy arms and thy shoulders shall move for thee, thy flesh shall be firm, thy muscles shall be easy, and thou shalt exult in all thy limbs. Thou shalt examine thy body and find it whole and sound, no ill whatever adhering to thee. Thine own true heart shall be with thee, yea, thou shalt have thy former heart. Thou shalt go up to the sky and shalt penetrate the Netherworld in all forms that thou likes.

—TRADITIONAL EGYPTIAN HYMN

CONTEMPLATION

We view resurrection as a miracle, and so we should.

Still, doesn't it take place every morning when our ba *(spirit) reconnects with our body again? Doesn't it take place within our body itself as old cells die and new, energetic ones are born? Doesn't it take place when we are weary unto death and great music or art revives us?*

Don't rely on a continual spate of spiritually resurrecting experiences; when they occur, cherish them and rejoice.

DISCRIMINATION

◇

Master Tall, as his name implied, was a strapping young man of sixteen years, but he possessed no intelligence. He was sent by his father to the monastery, as were other boys by their fathers, but although he was obedient to the monks and popular with the other lads of the monastery, he learned nothing. It was now time for him to leave the monastery and earn a living, but his father could not get him any employment outside, and he was practically useless on his father's farm. Finally he became a herdsman, caring for his father's three buffaloes. Poor Master Tall found it impossible to distinguish one buffalo from another, and therefore, once he had put his father's buffaloes to pasture, he could not trace them among the buffaloes of other herdsmen. Discovering this failing of Master Tall's, the other herdsmen took advantage of it. They just lay at ease on the grass, playing on their reed pipes or laughing and joking, and whenever they saw a buffalo going astray or wandering onto a piece of farmland, they shouted, "Master Tall, Master Tall, there goes your buffalo!" Master Tall, thinking every buffalo that strayed was his, spent the whole long day chasing and catching the buffaloes. Moreover, when evening came, he had to wait till the other herdsmen had taken away all their buffaloes, leaving behind the three belonging to his father, so that when he arrived home, it was late. This happened for many days, until his anxious father made inquiries and found out the trick played on his son.

So the next day the fond father placed wreaths made of toddy-palm leaves on the horns of his three buffaloes and said, "Now, my son, look at the buffaloes carefully and remember that only a buffalo which has a wreath of toddy-palm leaves around his horns is your responsibility. Do not tire yourself by herding all the buffaloes of the village." That morning, whenever the other herdsmen shouted, "Hey, Master Tall, there goes your animal," Master Tall glanced at the straying buffalo's horns, and if he saw no wreath on its horns, he just sat down and took no further notice. However, by midday Master Tall's secret had been discovered by his companions, who promptly put wreaths of toddy-palm leaves on the horns of their buffaloes too, with the result that poor Master Tall spent the entire afternoon chasing all stray buffaloes. He was late again in reaching home, and to his anxious father, who had been waiting for him at the gate of his house, Master Tall complained, "Father, all was well in the morning, but at midday wreaths of toddy-palm leaves sprouted on the horns of the other buffaloes also."

—TRADITIONAL BURMESE BUDDHIST TALE

CONTEMPLATION

Can you tell which spiritual books and teachings carry the truth? . . . Are you sure?

PACE

The Lord is my pace-setter: I shall not rush.
He makes me stop and rest for quiet intervals.
He provides me with images of stillness
Which restore my serenity.

He leads me in the way of efficiency
Through calmness of mind
And His guidance is peace.
Even though I have a great many things
To accomplish each day,
I will not fret.

For His presence is here.
His timelessness
His all-importance
Will keep me in balance.

He prepares refreshment and renewal in the midst of activity
By anointing my mind with the oil of tranquillity

My cup of joyous energy overflows.
Surely harmony and effectiveness shall be the fruit of my hours,
For I shall walk in the pace of my Lord
And dwell in His house forever.

—PSALM 23 (JAPANESE VERSION)

CONTEMPLATION

As the new year picks up speed, we tend to speed up too, as if we accidentally found ourselves on a racetrack and sucked into the backdraft of the lead car.

To keep the right pace, a pace that is appropriate for you and your life, you must affirm that this is right and possible. Our world today is what Hindu pandits of old would call extremely rajasic—*passion-driven, lustful, and greedy.*

We call it the rat race. But a wise humorist tells it like it is: "Even if you win the rat race, you're still a rat!"

Our object is to be fully human. To do that, a good pace and appropriate timing, in all aspects of our life—from spiritual practice to social interactions—must be developed.

FUNDAMENTALS

◆

Nasreddin and a friend were walking one day when a strange man suddenly confronted them.

He pointed his hand to the sky, knowing that if Nasreddin were a fellow Sufi mystic he would understand this as a sign that, like the sky, one truth embraces all.

Nasreddin's friend, an ordinary man, thought only, "This man is crazy. I hope Nasreddin knows how to protect himself."

Nasreddin immediately reached in his travel-sack, pulled out a rope, and gave it to his friend.

"That's smart," thought the friend. "If this lunatic becomes violent, we can tie him up."

The Sufi got Nasreddin's real message: "Ordinary people seek to obtain truth by techniques as ineffective as trying to reach the sky by climbing a rope."

—TRADITIONAL SUFI TALE

CONTEMPLATION

There's something fundamentally off-base and off-putting about demanding belief in a person or a religious system.

The great ones did not bully in this way; rather they gave their companions and followers time to ripen in their wisdom. Jesus spoke in parables, not in doctrine. Buddha pointed to the moon and the atman (divine consciousness) within, not to himself. Muhammad came to his Meccan friends first with recitation, not with a sword.

This is fundamental—truth is only found where there is acceptance and peace.

FALSE PROPHETS

◇

At last, the people of a certain village managed to capture the rogue who had plagued them. They lashed him to a tree and left him to anguish over his punishment, planning to return after the day's work. The villagers would then toss this rascal into the ocean.

A shepherd, and not a very clever one at that, happened by and asked the bound man how he came to be tied to a tree.

The rogue answered, "I refused to take their money, so these men from the village tied me up here."

"Why did they offer you money, and why didn't you take it?" asked the surprised shepherd.

"Because I am a servant of God," the rogue explained, "and they wanted only to corrupt me."

"Why don't we trade places?" the shepherd recommended. "Then you will be free of these godless men."

So they did.

When the villagers returned after dark, they placed a sack over the captive shepherd's head and heaved him into the ocean.

The next day, what did the astonished villagers see but the rogue himself, strolling into the village with a flock of sheep.

They had to know how all this had come about, and pestered the rogue for clarification.

"There are beneficent beings in the ocean," the rogue calmly put forth, "who reward everyone who drowns in the way I did."

In a moment, all the people ran to the ocean cliff and threw themselves into the sea.

And the rogue had conquered the village.

—TRADITIONAL SUFI TALE

◇

Beware of false prophets, who come to you in sheep's clothing but inwardly are ravenous wolves. You will know them by their fruits.

—GOSPEL OF MATTHEW (CHRISTIAN NEW TESTAMENT)

CONTEMPLATION

The Roman festival of Carmentalia celebrates today the Camanae, the nymphs of prophecy. Their chief, the Goddess Carmentis, used her prophetic power to protect women in childbirth. Huldah, a great Hebrew prophetess, oversaw the rebirth of the Torah, the lost holy book of the Jews, when no one else was sure what it was. False prophets think and speak of themselves. True prophets think and speak of those people and things they wish to preserve.

WRESTLING

That night Jacob got up and took his two wives, his two maidservants, and his eleven sons and crossed the ford of the Jabbok. After he had sent them across the stream, he sent over all his possessions. So Jacob was left alone, and a man wrestled with him till daybreak. When the man saw that he could not overpower him, he touched the socket of Jacob's hip so that his hip was wrenched as he wrestled with the man. Then the man said, "Let me go, for it is daybreak."

But Jacob replied, "I will not let you go unless you bless me."

The man asked him, "What is your name?"

"Jacob," he answered.

Then the man said, "Your name will no longer be Jacob, but Israel, because you have struggled with God and with men and have overcome."

—BOOK OF GENESIS (HEBREW SCRIPTURES)

For we wrestle not against flesh and blood, but against principalities, against powers, against the rulers of the darkness of this world, against spiritual wickedness in high places.

—PAUL'S EPISTLE TO THE EPHESIANS
(CHRISTIAN NEW TESTAMENT)

CONTEMPLATION

By now, some of the personal demons you thought (or more likely wished) would go away and stay away this year have come bumping and crashing into you again.

You're going to have to deal with them. But while you give fair attention to these individual concerns, don't overlook the "spiritual wickedness in high places," in your hometown or in the realm of global religious and political affairs.

You've got to take on all comers.

LIVELIHOOD

This is my defense to those who sit in judgment on me. Don't we have the right to food and drink? Don't we have the right to take a believing wife along with us, as do the other apostles and the Lord's brothers and Cephas? Or is it only I and Barnabas who must work for a living?

Who serves as a soldier at his own expense? Who plants a vineyard and does not eat of its grapes? Who tends a flock and does not drink of the milk? Do I say this merely from a human point of view? Doesn't the Law say the same thing? For it is written in the Law of Moses: "Do not muzzle an ox while it is treading out the grain." Is it about oxen that God is concerned? Surely he says this for us, doesn't he? Yes, this was written for us, because when the plowman plows and the thresher threshes, they ought to do so in the hope of sharing in the harvest. If we have sown spiritual seed among you, is it too much if we reap a material harvest from you? If others have this right of support from you, shouldn't we have it all the more?

But we did not use this right. On the contrary, we put up with anything rather than hinder the gospel of Christ. Don't you know that those who work in the temple get their food from the temple, and those who serve at the altar share in what is offered on the altar?

—PAUL'S FIRST EPISTLE TO THE CORINTHIANS
(CHRISTIAN NEW TESTAMENT)

CONTEMPLATION

Some things you do really well. Do them. The service and products you provide help others to live well in many ways. Provide them.

After all, if God wants, God could do all our jobs. Isn't that so?

Of course, in the Jewish tradition, there's a joke about this:

The rabbi ordered a pair of new pants for the Passover holidays from the village tailor. The tailor, who was very unreliable, took a long time finishing the job. The rabbi was afraid that he would not have the garment ready for the holidays.

On the day before Passover the tailor came running all out of breath to deliver the pants.

The rabbi examined his new garment with a critical eye.

"Thank you for bringing my pants on time," he said. "But tell me, my friend, if it took God only six days to create our vast and complicated world, why did it have to take you six weeks to make this simple pair of pants?"

"But, Rabbi!" murmured the tailor triumphantly. "Just look at the mess God made, and then look at this beautiful pair of pants!"

With such good work, you deserve to make a good living, to have a very beautiful life!

GIVE AND TAKE

Rabbi Shelomo said: "If you want to raise a man from mud and filth, do not think it is enough to keep standing on top and reaching down to him a helping hand. You must go all the way down yourself, down into mud and filth. Then take hold of him with strong hands and pull him and yourself out into the light."

—TRADITIONAL CHASSIDIC JEWISH TEACHING

There was presented to me a papaya,
And I returned for it a beautiful *keu* gem;
Not as a return for it,
But that our friendship might be lasting.

There was presented to me a peach,
And I returned for it a beautiful *yaou* gem;
Not as a return for it,
But that our friendship might be lasting.

There was presented to me a plum,
And I returned for it a beautiful *keu* stone;
Not as a return for it,
But that our friendship might be lasting.

—BOOK OF SONGS (CLASSICAL CONFUCIANIST TEXT)

CONTEMPLATION

There's the tale about a tax man that's to the point of give and take. The man had fallen on train tracks and was unable to get back up safely on the platform by himself. A train was approaching, so a charitable bystander reached down and said, "Give me your hand." The man did not respond. "Give me your hand!" the would-be rescuer now shouted. Still the man did not stir. The train was getting closer. Another man stepped up to the edge, extended his arm, and gently said, "Take my hand," and immediately the man below did and was pulled to safety. "My God," asked the first rescuer of the second, "why didn't he move when I reached down?" "He's a tax man," said the knowledgeable savior. "You said give me your hand. Tax men only know how to take, not to give!"

BECOMING

◇

But to those who did accept him, he gave the right to become children of God . . .

—GOSPEL OF JOHN (CHRISTIAN NEW TESTAMENT)

◇

DISCIPLE: "How can I get out of these contradictions?
That is what I came to ask you."
LAO-TZU: "A moment ago I looked into your eyes.
You are scared to death
Like a child who has lost
Father and Mother.
You have got lost and are trying
To find your way back
To your own true self."

The disciple asked for admittance,
Took a cell, and there
Meditated,
Trying to cultivate qualities
He thought desirable
And get rid of others
Which he disliked.
Despair!

LAO-TZU: "All blocked up!
Tied in knots!
If your obstructions are within yourself,
You cannot destroy them piecemeal.
But you can refuse
To let them take effect.
If they are both inside and outside
Do not try
To hold onto Tao—
Just hope that Tao
Will keep hold of you!"

—WRITINGS OF CHUANG-TZU
(CLASSICAL TAOIST TEACHER)

◇

There is a polish for everything that becomes rusty, and the polish for the heart is the remembrance of God.

—HADITH OF TIRMIDHI (ISLAMIC SACRED SAYINGS)

CONTEMPLATION

In Japan, traditionally on this day, women and men who have reached the age of twenty journey to holy shrines accompanied by their families. There, to the Kami (Divine spirits), the families announce that their children have become adults and pray for health and prosperity for their life to come.

Do not we bless all children in this way, recognizing in them the unlimited potential of becoming? Do we not then bless ourselves, as children of God, in our own becoming?

ACCORD

◇

Heracles was making his way along a narrow road when he saw on the ground an object that looked like an apple. He stepped on it and the object doubled in size. Seeing this, Heracles stamped on it with both feet and hit it with his club. The object then swelled in size until it blocked the road. Heracles threw down his club and gaped in amazement. Athena now appeared and said to him: "Leave that thing alone, dear brother! It is the spirit of argument and discord; if you don't touch it, it does no harm, but if you try to fight with it, it grows as you have seen."

—FABLE OF AESOP (CLASSICAL GREEK)

◇

Let us be united;
Let us speak in harmony;
Let our minds apprehend alike.
Common be our prayer;
Common be the end of our assembly;
Common be our resolution;
Common be our deliberations.
Alike be our feelings;
Unified be our hearts;
Common be our intentions;
Perfect be our unity.

—RIG VEDA (HINDU SACRED TEXT)

CONTEMPLATION

In Christian tradition the journey of the Magi, the first Gentiles to acknowledge Jesus as the Christ-child, is remembered at this time. They came, not only of their own accord, but in accord with each other. There was no contention as to the star and where it led them. No disputes over the gold, frankincense, and myrrh. Only a gift and a blessing.

DESTINY

True reliance is for the servant to pursue his profession and calling in this world, to hold fast unto the Lord, to seek naught but His grace, inasmuch as in His hands is the destiny of all His servants.

—WRITINGS OF BAHÁ'U'LLÁH (BAHÁ'Í FAITH)

A famous Mongol general and his troops had captured a large part of Central Asia. By now his troops were tired and far from home. He wanted to press on to capture the great city of Samarkand which was defended by five times as many soldiers as his own. He felt certain they could win, but the soldiers were reluctant.

Calling them together, they set up a sacred altar and prayed for advice from their gods. At the end of the ceremony, the general took out a large gold coin and said he would now toss it to see what the gods directed. If it came up heads the soldiers would win a great victory.

The toss was indeed heads, and inspired by the gods, the soldiers went on to easily overrun the city.

Afterward a soldier said to the general, "When we have been shown that the gods are with us, nothing can challenge our destiny."

The general laughingly agreed and then showed him the coin, which had a head on both sides.

—CLASSICAL CHINESE TALE

CONTEMPLATION

Fasten yourself to your fixed destination, and you will, with God's help, get there. The wise general's destiny was Samarkand; what's yours?

LIBERTY

. . . Know ye that the embodiment of liberty and its symbol is the animal. That which beseemeth man is submission unto such restraints as will protect him from his own ignorance and guard him against the harm of the mischief-maker. Liberty causeth man to overstep the bounds of propriety and to infringe on the dignity of his station. . . .

. . . The liberty that profiteth you is to be found nowhere except in complete servitude unto God, the Eternal Truth. Whoso hath tasted of its sweetness will refuse to barter it for all the dominion of earth and heaven.

—WRITINGS OF BAHÁ'U'LLÁH (BAHÁ'Í FAITH)

Two men met each other on the road; and each of them had a donkey. Then the men greeted each other: the donkeys also, putting their mouths together, sniffed at each other. And the one man asked his fellow, saying: "We have greeted each other. Why have the donkeys also put their heads together?" The other man answered him: "Do you not know this? The donkeys have sent a strong donkey to the Lord to enter their plaint before him, that is to say, that the Lord should free them from the tyranny of men. Now they ask each other, saying: 'Has the messenger-donkey returned or not?'" And it is said that all donkeys ask each other about this matter by putting their mouths together. By this tale it is seen that every creature longs for liberty.

—TRADITIONAL MENSA TRIBAL TALE (EAST AFRICA)

Now the Lord is that Spirit: and where the Spirit of the Lord is, there is liberty.

But we all, with open face beholding as in a glass the glory of the Lord, are changed into the same image from glory to glory even as by the Spirit of the Lord.

—PAUL'S SECOND EPISTLE TO THE CORINTHIANS
(CHRISTIAN NEW TESTAMENT)

CONTEMPLATION

Martin Luther King, Jr., a strong man, called upon us to fulfill our commitment to liberty for all. This was his dream, his vision. In order to "proclaim liberty throughout the land to all its inhabitants" (as the Bible tells it), Dr. King had first to set his mind free of slavish thoughts and attitudes. Proclaim your liberty today from the particular chains that hold you in bondage. Proclaim liberty in your soul.

UNITY

Happy is the unity of the Sangha.
Happy is the discipline of ones so united.

—DHAMMAPADA (BUDDHIST SACRED TEXT)

How good and how pleasant it is
When brethren dwell as one!
As the dew of Hermon, as the dew
That falls on the mountains of Zion!
For the Lord commanded the blessing—
Life for evermore.

—PSALM 133 (HEBREW SCRIPTURES)

Jesus said, "I shall choose you, one out of a thousand, and two out of
ten thousand, and they shall stand as a single one."

—GOSPEL OF THOMAS
(APOCRYPHAL CHRISTIAN TEACHING)

May the divine Twins create between us and strangers
A unity of hearts.
May we unite in our minds,
Unite in our purposes and
Not fight against the divine spirit
Within us.

—ATHARVA VEDA (HINDU SACRED TEXT)

O contending peoples and kindreds of the earth!
Set your faces toward unity,
and let the radiance of its light shine upon you.

—WRITINGS OF BAHÁ'U'LLÁH (BAHÁ'Í FAITH)

CONTEMPLATION

Everybody wants unity, or do we? The often excruciating discipline, the extraordinary necessity to relinquish prejudice and alienation, the requisite will to abandon habit and embrace obedience to the call to oneness—these are daunting to us.

Yet the light beckons brilliantly and the prospects of happiness are so strong and imminent that—we marry; we join groups, spiritual and otherwise; we pray for harmonious connection!

Here is a beautiful and powerful irony! The one thing that really unites us all is a desire for unity.

PIETY

On a sea journey, an archbishop passed a seemingly deserted island when he viewed three faint figures on the shore. Always eager to promote the faith, he commanded the captain to provide him a small boat with which he could reach the island and the three sinners he was certain to find there.

When the three men saw it was a holy man approaching, they immediately began bowing. Surprised, the archbishop, upon alighting, inquired, "Are you Christians?"

The three men could hardly speak. "We pray to be," they stammered, "but good sir, we are only three hermits who have forgotten what to do or what to say."

"How do you pray, then?" the archbishop asked.

"We say," they uttered haltingly, "Lord have mercy on sinners such as we."

The archbishop was shocked at their ignorance and near blasphemy. "Don't you even know the Lord's Prayer?!"

"We don't remember it," the hermits confessed. "We've been here for so long that we've forgotten. Please," they begged, "please teach it to us."

And to save their souls the archbishop agreed, beginning, "Our Father who art in Heaven . . . ," assuming that the three hermits would understand such a simple and short prayer very quickly. But this was not the case. They needed to go over each part repeatedly and in doing so, it took the entire day before the archbishop was satisfied. His duty done, he departed, and even as he rowed back to the ship, he could see the three hermits practicing the prayer he had taught them so well.

The next day, the ship sailed on, and the archbishop was on the deck again looking out to the horizon. The tiny island of the hermits was no longer visible, but the archbishop nonetheless thought he saw, on the ocean itself, three shapes coming from the very direction of the island. Closer and closer the shapes came to the ship, until the archbishop saw that they were, no doubt about it, the three hermits running on the sea!

"Your Grace," they called out. "Don't be angry with us, but we have forgotten the holy prayer. Could you teach it to us again?"

"Go in peace, my friends," the awestruck archbishop said. "Just pray the way you always do, 'Lord have mercy. . . .' " And they did.

—TRADITIONAL RUSSIAN CHRISTIAN STORY

CONTEMPLATION

Who determines if you are pious? You do.

It is absurd and almost comical how accusations of impiety are hurled across religious lines and even among believers of the same religion. There can be no single formula for a pious life.

Who determines what is pious? You do.

TREES
◆

In the beginning Earth was covered with water. In Sky Land there were people living as they do now on Earth. In the middle of that land was the great Sky Tree. All of the food which the people in that Sky Land ate came from the great tree.

The old chief of that land lived with his wife, whose name was Aataentsic, meaning "Ancient Woman," in their longhouse near the great tree. It came to be that the old chief became sick and nothing could cure him. He grew weaker and weaker until it seemed he would die. Then a dream came to him, and he called Aataentsic to him.

"I have dreamed," he said, "and in my dream I saw how I can be healed. I must be given the fruit that grows at the very top of Sky Tree. You must cut it down and bring that fruit to me."

Aataentsic took her husband's stone ax and went to the great tree. As soon as she struck it, it split in half and toppled over. As it fell, a hole opened in Sky Land and the tree fell through the hole. Aataentsic returned to the place where the old chief waited.

"My husband," she said, "when I cut the tree it split in half and then fell through a great hole. Without the tree there can be no life. I must follow it."

Then, leaving her husband, she went back to the hole in Sky Land and threw herself after the great tree.

As Aataentsic fell, Turtle looked up and saw her. Immediately Turtle called together all the water animals and told them what she had seen.

"What should be done?" Turtle said.

Beaver answered her. "You are the one who saw this happen. Tell us what to do."

"All of you must dive down," Turtle said. "Bring up soil from the bottom, and place it on my back."

Immediately all of the water animals began to dive down and bring up soil. Beaver, Mink, Muskrat, and Otter each brought up pawfuls of wet soil and placed the soil on Turtle's back until they had made an island of great size. When they were through, Aataentsic settled down gently on the new Earth and the pieces of the great tree fell beside her and took root.

—TRADITIONAL HURON TRIBAL TALE (NATIVE AMERICAN)

CONTEMPLATION

Trees are temples. They breathe and meditate for the whole world.

People have worshiped at great trees forever. Buddha was wakened under a tree and Jesus was hung on one until, in a way, he found enlightenment, too.

Celebrate trees, and pray actively for them as you do for yourself. Recite this ancient Hindu prayer:

> *May the ax be far away from you;*
> *May the fire be far away from you;*
> *May there be rain without storm;*
> *Lord of Trees, may you be blessed;*
> *Lord of Trees, may I be blessed.*

WISDOM

◆

Reb Lieb, the son of Sarah, was on his way to his great master, the Mezritcher Maggid. He met a friend on the road.

"What are you going to learn from your rebbe (master)?" the friend asked.

"I'm not going to learn Talmud (holy scriptures)," said Reb Lieb. "I'm going to see the way he ties his shoes."

—TRADITIONAL CHASSIDIC JEWISH ANECDOTE

◆

At this time, the world-honored Dhe serenely arose from meditation and addressed Shariputra: "The wisdom of all the Buddhas is infinitely profound and immeasurable. The portal to this wisdom is difficult to understand and difficult to enter. Neither men of learning nor of realization are able to comprehend it."

—LOTUS SUTRA (BUDDHIST SACRED TEXT)

CONTEMPLATION

Is there a way to wisdom? It dwells in the soul of sages who follow many different ways.

Make and take the opportunity to be in the presence of someone you feel is a holder of wisdom. Watch how this person carries herself or himself. Listen to the timbre of her voice, the roll of his laughter. Sense the bow and flex as she rises, he sits. Wisdom is as wisdom does.

HOME

As they were walking along the road, a man said to him, "I will follow you wherever you go."

Jesus replied, "Foxes have holes and birds of the air have nests, but the Son of Man has no place to lay his head."

He said to another man, "Follow me."

But the man replied, "Lord, first let me go and bury my father."

Jesus said to him, "Let the dead bury their own dead, but you go and proclaim the kingdom of God."

Still another said, "I will follow you, Lord; but first let me go back and say good-bye to my family."

Jesus replied, "No one who puts his hand to the plow and looks back is fit for service in the kingdom of God."

—GOSPEL OF MATTHEW (CHRISTIAN NEW TESTAMENT)

Zeus, who had just married, invited all the animals to his wedding party. Only the Tortoise failed to come. The next day Zeus sought him out and asked: "Why did you not attend my little celebration last night?" "Oh, you know," answered the Tortoise. "There's no place like home!" This reply so angered Zeus that he condemned the Tortoise to carry his home on his back ever after.

—FABLE OF AESOP (CLASSICAL GREEK)

CONTEMPLATION

Mystically oriented Jews try to find the Shekinah, the dwelling place of spirit, on the earth. Dayak tribespeople speak of their dead returning home.

On a day like today, or especially a night like tonight, when the devouring Wolf Moon may be out, it's a terrible time to be homeless. The Tortoise, through his insensitivity, may be condemned to carry his home with him, but at least he has one.

"Home," the poet Robert Frost said, "is the place where, when you have to go there, they have to take you in." This is a literal and spiritual imperative for each of us.

ALIENATION

◆

At first there were no people. Only Mulungu and the decent peaceful beasts were in the world.

One day Chameleon sat weaving a fish trap, and when he had finished he set it in the river. In the morning he pulled the trap, and it was full of fish, which he took home and ate.

He set the trap again. In the morning he pulled it out, and it was empty: no fish.

"Bad luck," he said, and set the trap again.

The next morning when he pulled the trap, he found a little man and woman in it. He had never seen creatures like this.

"What can they be?" he said. "Today I behold the unknown." And he picked up the fish trap and took the two creatures to Mulungu.

"Father," said Chameleon, "see what I have brought."

Mulungu looked. "Take them out of the trap," he said. "Put them down on the earth, and they will grow."

Chameleon did this. And the man and woman grew. They grew until they became as tall as men and women are today.

All the animals watched to see what people would do. They made fire. They rubbed two sticks together in a special way and thus made fire. The fire caught in the bush and roared through the forest, and the animals had to run to escape the flames.

The people caught a buffalo and killed it and roasted it in the fire and ate it. Then next day they did the same thing. Every day they set fires and killed some animal and ate it.

"They are burning up everything!" said Mulungu. "They are killing my people!"

All the beasts ran into the forest as far away from mankind as they could get. Chameleon went into the high trees.

"I'm leaving!" said Mulungu.

He called to Spider. "How do you climb on high?" he said.

"Very nicely," said Spider. And Spider spun a rope for Mulungu, and Mulungu climbed the rope and went to live in the sky.

Thus the gods were driven off the face of the earth by the cruelty of man.

—TRADITIONAL YAO TRIBAL TALE (EAST AFRICA)

CONTEMPLATION

Consider this question the next time you find yourself complaining that so-and-so is ignoring you or not returning calls: "What part did I play in this alienation?"

As with the God Mulungu and the good animals, it usually takes something big to move people to such an alienated position. Act on this immediately. Come forth and face the situation. Mulungu's waiting to hear from you.

JANUARY 25
TRADITION

◇

A man once asked a camel whether he preferred going uphill or downhill.

The camel said: "What is important to me is not the uphill or the downhill—it is the load!"

—TRADITIONAL SUFI ANECDOTE

◇

The pot is a God. The winnowing fan is a God. The stone in the street is a God. The comb is a God. The bowstring is also a God. The bushel is a God and the spouted cup is a God. Gods, Gods, there are so many, there's no place left for a foot. There is only one God. He is our Lord of the meeting rivers.

—BASAVANNA (CLASSICAL HINDU WRITINGS)

CONTEMPLATION

There are so many ways to God. Today they can be found in the library and university. They're proffered on computer networks and the media. They so fill the marketplace that even a graceful seeker cannot help but bump into someone's "God."

What's important, as the camel discovered, is not so much the conditions surrounding what you're carrying but the quality of it.

If the spiritual tradition you carry suits you, then carry it with devotion and pride. Once you've accepted this baggage, you must deliver it.

If you are a camel who is still looking for a tradition to carry, keep yourself in good spiritual condition. If you have chosen to take on multiple sacks (an eclectic mix of traditions), walk steadily and with conviction.

All camels follow an ancient tradition of the desert: When they meet, they nod in friendship and respect. It's something marvelous to be a good camel.

BLAME

◇

There is an old saying: "People will blame you if you say too much; they will blame you if you say too little; they will blame you if you say just enough." No one in this world escapes blame.

There never was and never will be anyone who receives all praise or all blame. But who can blame those who are pure, wise, good, and meditative? They shine like a coin of pure gold. Even the gods praise them, even Brahma the Creator.

—DHAMMAPADA (BUDDHIST SACRED TEXT)

◇

Question: When a shea tree out of water dies, they say it died because of lack of water. What about the tree that has died in the water?

Response: When your child dies, they say he is killed by a witch. But how about a witch's child who dies, who kills it?

—TRADITIONAL WALA TRIBAL TEACHING
(WEST AFRICA)

◇

When an arrow is released from the bow, it may go straight, or it may not, according to what the archer does.

How strange, therefore, that when the arrow flies truly without deviation, it is due to the skill of the archer: but when it goes out of true, it is the arrow which receives the curses!

—WRITINGS OF ATTAR (SUFI MYSTIC AND POET)

CONTEMPLATION

Job was a straight arrow. He did everything right—fed the poor, aided widows, fulfilled his religious obligations—yet when the Great Adversary (known as the Evil One) brought down suffering on Job's head (God had approved this test), whom did Job's good friends blame? Job, of course!

The magnificence of Job's character rests in this: He never blamed anyone, not God, not himself. By staying clear of blaming, he kept his channel to God and God's blessing open.

HELP

◇

Kaishu and his friends were crossing a raging river in heavy rain, and the boat pitched violently. All the master's friends were frightened and lost color, and some of them went so far as to invoke the aid of Avoiokitesvara, the goddess of love. But Kaishu sat calmly in meditation.

When the boat made shore and his friends sighed with relief, Kaishu reprimanded them with the following: "The Zen man is good for nothing if he can't help himself. The goddess must have laughed at your frailty."

—TRADITIONAL ZEN BUDDHIST TALE

◇

And now, may kindly Columba guide you
To be an isle in the sea,
To be a hill on the shore,
To be a star in the night,
To be a staff for the weak.
Amen.

—TRADITIONAL CELTIC PRAYER

CONTEMPLATION

There are days when you feel beyond help—and helping. Today may be one of them.

Help yourself, then. Do something refreshing. Get out of the house if you're always in. Get into the house and your meditation place if you've been out helping others.

You're not required to be an isle in the sea or a star in the night all the time. You'd get washed away or burnt out. Trust yourself. Help is on the way.

REACHING

Nyambe used to dwell on earth but afterward ascended up to heaven on a spider's web. From his post up aloft he said to men, "Worship me." But men said, "Come, let us kill Nyambe." Alarmed at this impious threat, the deity fled to the sky, from which it would seem that he had temporarily descended. So men said, "Come, let us make masts to reach up to heaven." They set up masts and added more masts, joining them one to the other, and they clambered up them. But when they had climbed far up, the masts fell down, and all the men on the masts were killed by the fall. That was the end of them.

—TRADITIONAL A-LOUYI TRIBAL TALE
(SOUTHERN AFRICA)

And the whole earth was of one language, and of one speech.

And it came to pass, as they journeyed from the east, that they found a plain in the land of Shinar; and they dwelt there.

And they said one to another, Go to, let us make brick, and burn them thoroughly. And they had brick for stone, and slime had they for mortar.

And they said, Go to, let us build us a city and a tower, whose top may reach unto heaven; and let us make us a name, lest we be scattered abroad upon the face of the whole earth.

And the Lord came down to see the city and the tower, which the children of men built.

—BOOK OF GENESIS (HEBREW SCRIPTURES)

CONTEMPLATION

It is human nature to reach—for a variety of purposes.

In your reaching for accomplishment, are you killing yourself and the God within through overwork or unethical actions?

You are meant and designed to do great things, and reaching is an integral part of the process.

Build a well-stacked base, strong and balanced, before you climb.

DISCIPLINE

To offer service to the gods, to the good, to the wise, and to your spiritual teacher; purity, honesty, continence, and nonviolence: these are the disciplines of the body. To offer soothing words, to speak truly, kindly, and helpfully, to study the scriptures: these are the disciplines of speech. Calmness, gentleness, silence, self-restraint, and purity: these are the disciplines of the mind.

When these three levels of self-discipline are practiced without attachment to the results, but in a spirit of great faith, the sages call this practice sattvic. Disciplines practiced in order to gain respect, honor, or admiration are rajasic; they are undependable and transitory in their effects. Disciplines practiced to gain power over others, or in the confused belief that to torture oneself is spiritual, are tamasic.

—BHAGAVAD GITA (HINDU SACRED TEXT)

"Revile not, harm not, live by rule restrained;
Of food take little; sleep and sit alone;
Keep thy mind bent upon the higher thought."
Such is the message of awakened ones.

—UDANA (BUDDHIST SACRED TEXT)

CONTEMPLATION

We are like the restless elephant in the Hindu tale. Taken to the marketplace as part of a religious procession, an elephant wandered from stall to stall gorging himself on bananas, coconuts—anything he could stuff into his insatiable belly. When the elephant was given a bamboo rod to hold in its trunk, then and only then did it become disciplined, and it marched straightaway to the temple.

It is not only that we exercise discipline that is important. It is also very important what is the object and focus of our self-disciplined minds. With any good discipline, success leads to success, so every time we forgo indulgence and indiscriminate behavior and hold to the rod of good judgment, we help build our body of discipline. Eventually we become elephants, and as you can imagine, a disciplined elephant is unstoppable.

INDEPENDENCE

◇

Nasreddin was eating a poor man's diet of chickpeas and bread. His neighbor, who also claimed to be a wise man, was living in a grand house and dining on sumptuous meals provided by the emperor himself.

His neighbor told Nasreddin, "If only you would learn to flatter the emperor and be subservient like I do, you would not have to live on chickpeas and bread."

Nasreddin replied, "And if only you would learn to live on chickpeas and bread, like I do, you would not have to flatter and live subservient to the emperor."

—TRADITIONAL SUFI TALE

◇

The perfect man is a spiritual being. Were the ocean itself scorched up, he would not be hot. Were the Milky Way frozen hard, he would not feel cold. Were the mountains to be riven with thunder, and the great deep to be thrown up by storm, he would not tremble in such case; he would mount upon the clouds of heaven and, driving the sun and the moon before him, would pass beyond the limits of this external world, where death and life hold no more victory over man.

—WRITINGS OF CHUANG-TZU
(CLASSICAL TAOIST TEACHER)

CONTEMPLATION

Independence is a state of transcendence. One does not have to scoff at the world and what it offers or be wary of the mighty forces of nature and God seemingly directed our way. Nor should one disdain those still "caught in the trap," for this disdain makes you dependent rather than free.

Go about your way. Nod in understanding to other souls, independent or not. Keep developing your strength of independence.

TOP AND BOTTOM

◇

Two sages of Chelm sat around the synagogue stove on a cold winter day. They debated heatedly over the following question: At which end does a human being grow?

"What a question!" cried one. "Any fool knows that a man grows from his feet up."

"Give me proof," demanded the other.

"Several years ago I bought myself a pair of pants, but they were so long that they trailed on the ground. Now look at them—see how short they've gotten. There's your proof."

"It's just the other way around," maintained the other. "Anyone with eyes in his head can see that man grows from the head. Why, just yesterday I watched a regiment of soldiers on parade, and it was clear as daylight that at the bottom of their feet they all were the same; they differed in size only at the top!"

—TRADITIONAL JEWISH TALE

CONTEMPLATION

When it comes to your growth as a true human being, you want it to happen, as much as possible, everywhere. Near the shores of Lake Galilee, Kabbalists— mystically oriented Jews—prayed to meet the Divine Presence. They wrote:

You must grow again into the image of God both from above and from below. Be as a young tree which is moved by the wind and must stand in heat and cold. In such turmoil, it draws its power to itself above and below and must endure many wind storms and stand in great danger before it can become a tree that bears fruit. In such turmoil the sun's power moves in it, the wild characteristics of the tree are pressed through and tinctured by the sun's power, and by this the tree grows.

FEBRUARY

FIRE

◇

I am the supreme fiery force
That kindles every spark of life:
What I have breathed on will never die,
I order the cycle of things in being;
Hovering round it in sublime flight,
Wisdom lends it rhythmic beauty.

I am divine fiery life
Blazing over the full-ripened grain;
I gleam in the reflection of the waters,
I burn in the sun and moon and stars,
In the breeze I have secret life
Animating all things and lending them cohesion.

—WRITINGS OF HILDEGARD VON BINGEN
(CHRISTIAN MYSTIC AND POET)

◇

As the flame clothes the black, sooty clod in a garment of fire, and re-
leases the heat imprisoned therein, even so does prayer clothe a man in a
garment of holiness, evoke the light and fire implanted within him by his
Maker, illumine his whole being, and unify the Lower and Higher Worlds.

—ZOHAR (CLASSICAL KABBALISTIC JEWISH TEXT)

CONTEMPLATION

*Agni, the God of fire in the Vedic tradition, is known to be the spark of life in
all things. That includes us, too.*

*My God, if that doesn't light your fire, your wood's wet! Get fired up today!
You know exactly what fuels your fire.*

ILLUSION

◇

The Purpose of the one true God, exalted be His glory, in revealing Himself unto men is to lay bare those gems that lie hidden within the mine of their true and inmost selves.

—WRITINGS OF BAHÁ'U'LLÁH (BAHÁ'Í FAITH)

◇

Every being has the Buddha Nature. This is the self. Such a self is, since the very beginning, under cover of innumerable illusions. That is why a man cannot see it. O good man! There was a poor woman who had gold hidden somewhere in her house, but no one knew where it was. But there was a stranger who, by expediency, speaks to the poor woman, "I shall employ you to weed the lawn." The woman answered, "I cannot do it now, but if you show my son where the gold is hidden, I will work for you." The man says, "I know the way; I will show it to your son." The woman replies, "No one in my house, big or small, knows where the gold is hidden. How can you know?" The man then digs out the hidden gold and shows it to the woman. She is glad and begins to respect him. O good man! The same is the case with a man's Buddha Nature. No one can see it. It is like the gold which the poor woman possessed and yet could not locate. I now let people see the Buddha Nature which they possess, but which was hidden by illusions. The Tathagata shows all beings the storehouse of enlightenment, which is the cask of true gold—their Buddha Nature.

—MAHAPARINIRVANA SUTRA
(BUDDHIST SACRED TEXT)

◇

Once upon a time, I, Chuang-tzu, dreamed I was a butterfly, fluttering hither and thither, to all intents and purposes a butterfly. I was conscious only of following my fancies as a butterfly and was unconscious of my individuality as a man. Suddenly I awoke, and there I lay, myself again. Now I do not know whether I was then a man dreaming I was a butterfly, or whether I am now a butterfly dreaming I am a man.

—WRITINGS OF CHUANG-TZU
(CLASSICAL TAOIST TEACHER)

CONTEMPLATION

A haiku asks:

> *Can this truly be,*
> *In winter a butterfly*
> *O, pursuing me?*

Can we be butterflies, ever ready for flight and nectar-sipping? Bejeweled and golden butterflies? We are, we are . . .

STATES

When a jar of salted fish is newly opened,
The flies swarm to it buzzing all around.
When the jar is emptied to the bottom and washed clean,
It is left all alone in its cold desolation.

—WRITINGS OF MASTER I OF KUANG-TE
(BUDDHIST TEACHER)

O Krishna, what is the state of those who disregard the scriptures but still worship with faith?

Every creature is born with faith of some kind, either sattvic, rajasic, or tamasic. Listen, and I will describe each to you.

Those who are sattvic worship the forms of God; those who are rajasic worship power and wealth. Those who are tamasic worship spirits and ghosts. Some invent harsh penances. Motivated by hypocrisy and egotism, they torture their innocent bodies and me who dwells within. Blinded by their strength and passion, they act and think like demons.

The three kinds of faith express themselves in the habits of those who hold them: in the food they like, the work they do, the disciplines they practice, the gifts they give. Listen, and I will describe their different ways.

Sattvic people enjoy food that is mild, tasty, substantial, agreeable, and nourishing, food that promotes health, strength, cheerfulness, and longevity. Rajasic people like food that is salty or bitter, hot, sour, or spicy—food that promotes pain, discomfort, and disease. Tamasic people like overcooked, stale, leftover, and impure food, food that has lost its taste and nutritional value.

The sattvic perform sacrifices with their entire mind fixed on the purpose of the sacrifice. Without thought of reward, they follow the teachings of the scriptures. The rajasic perform sacrifices for the sake of show and the good it will bring them. The tamasic perform sacrifices ignoring both the letter and the spirit. They omit the proper prayers, the proper offerings, the proper food, and the proper faith.

—BHAGAVAD GITA (HINDU SACRED TEXT)

What you do matters. What you eat, how you pray are reflections of your inner state. These signs also determine to a great degree the state of beings who will be drawn to you. Reflect on your dharma, life-calling, and duty. If you are one who has approached or is approaching the appealing state (salted fish), know that the flies are certain to come. Be prepared to offer up at least some of you for consumption. If you don't already have one, a good fly swatter is a very handy thing at times!

When you have emptied yourself of yourself, you will most likely find that the world has left you. This state is too much to bear for most, even passionate friends and devotees. Think of Jesus' abandonment, for example, in the Garden of Gethsemane. Yet what a magnificent state—to be alone, all-one—with holy presence.

ANGEL

◆

It is not to any mortal that God should speak
except by revelation, or from behind a veil,
or that Allah should send a messenger
and reveal whatsoever Allah will.

—QUR'AN (HOLY BOOK OF ISLAM)

◆

O Lord of our prayer, the first of Speech
There is the man who sees, but has not seen Speech
There is the man who hears, but has not heard her
But to another she reveals her lovely form
Like a loving wife, finely robed, to her husband

—RIG VEDA (HINDU SACRED TEXT)

◆

Shan-ku, a scholar, besought his Zen master Huang-lung to show him
the secret shortcut to enlightenment. Huang-lung responded by quoting
Confucius: "My dear students, do you really think I am hiding anything
from you? In fact, I have hidden nothing from you," and then Huang-lung
asked him, "What do you think of these words?"

As Shan-ku searched for an answer, the master interjected: "Not this,
not this!" Shan-ku felt disappointed and very frustrated.

One day he accompanied the master on a walk into a mountainous re-
gion nearby. In the valleys there were a profusion of cinnamon trees in
full bloom. Huang-lung asked, "Do you perceive the fragrance?"

"Yes, I do," Shan-ku said.

The master declared, "You see, I have hidden nothing from you." Then
and there, Shan-ku was enlightened.

—TRADITIONAL ZEN BUDDHIST ANECDOTE

CONTEMPLATION

*The Greeks transformed the Hebrew word and concept of messenger into the
word* angel. *Angelic revelation, like messages and messengers, may come at any
time and in any place.*

*Will you see the fox on the forest path? Will you hear the crow call "Kwah!"
just outside the village? After the story has been told, will you still be waiting
for the one yet to be told?*

FEBRUARY 5
POSITION

◇

Have you not heard of the many skilled men in Ch'i and Lu? Some are clever at working with clay or wood, others with metal or leather; some are good singers or musicians, others good scribes or diviners; some know how to command armies, others to manage ancestral shrines; there is no shortage of any kind of talent. But they cannot give each other positions or tell each other what to do; the men who give them positions lack their knowledge, the men who tell them what to do lack their abilities, yet by these their knowledge and abilities are employed. It is we who employ you administrators; what have you to be conceited about?

—BOOK OF LIEH-TZU (CLASSICAL TAOIST TEXT)

◇

Once a chief minister, in a sudden spirit of renunciation, said, "I don't want to possess anything, I just want to be free." He renounced the world and went to sit in front of a temple. The king went to the minister and inquired, "What is it you have gained by leaving everything to sit here like this?" The minister looked up at the king and replied, "Yesterday I was standing and you were sitting. Today I am sitting and you are standing. That is the first gain."

—TRADITIONAL HINDU TALE

CONTEMPLATION

You may have what the world deems to be a high position. Perhaps you have a large income and hold sway over many people. Do not be smug: Most kings have been forgotten.

You may have what the world deems to be a low position. Perhaps you are underpaid or not paid at all for the work and service you offer. You may officially command no one. Take heart: With rare exceptions, all the great revered souls were either of low birth or brought to a lowly status on their way.

A Hindu sacred book reminds us that we may "realize the Self always to be neither above nor below, nor on either side, not without nor within, but to be eternal and shining beyond the sublime world."

NIGHT AND DAY

◇

I am a monk myself, and the one question I really wanted to ask was, "What is a monk?" Well, I finally did, but for an answer I got a most peculiar question: "Do you mean in the daytime or at night?" Now what could that mean?

When I didn't answer, he picked it up again, "A monk, like everyone else, is a creature of contraction and expansion. During the day he is contracted—behind his cloister walls, dressed in a habit like all the others, doing the routine things you expect a monk to do. At night he expands. The walls cannot contain him. He moves throughout the world and he touches the stars."

"Ah," I thought, "poetry." To bring him down to earth I began to ask, "Well, during the day, in his *real* body . . ."

"Wait," he said, "that's the difference between us and you. You people regularly assume that the contracted state is the real body. It is real, in a sense. But here we tend to start from the other end, the expanded state. The daytime state we refer to as the 'body of fear.' And whereas you tend to judge a monk by his decorum during the day, we tend to measure a monk by the number of persons he touches at night, and the number of stars."

—WRITINGS OF THEOPHANE (CHRISTIAN CONTEMPLATIVE)

◇

My words are tied in one
With the great mountains,
With the great rocks,
With the great trees,
In one with my body
And my heart.

Do you all help me
With supernatural power,
And you, Day
And you, Night!
All of you see me
One with this world!

—TRADITIONAL YOKUTS TRIBAL PRAYER (NATIVE AMERICAN)

CONTEMPLATION

We wish to be spiritually whole, of one piece, with no distinction between our daily lives and our lives of spirit. Constancy! We may be aided by outside forces, yet this constancy must come from within us to be of worth.

FORTUNE

The creatures of Heaven and Earth at times display unusual changes, and these are called wonders. Lesser ones are called ominous portents. The portents always come first and are followed by wonders. Portents are Heaven's warnings, wonders are Heaven's threats. Heaven first sends warnings, and if men do not understand, then it sends wonders to awe them. This is what the Book of Odes means when it says: "We tremble at the awe and the fearfulness of Heaven!" The genesis of all such portents and wonders is a direct result of errors in the state. When the first indications of error begin to appear in the state, Heaven sends forth ominous portents and calamities to warn men and announce the fact. If, in spite of these warnings and announcements, men still do not realize how they have gone wrong, then Heaven sends prodigies and wonders to terrify them. If, after these terrors, men still know no awe or fear, then calamity and misfortune will visit them. From this we may see that the will of Heaven is benevolent, for it has no desire to trap or betray mankind.

If we examine these wonders and portents carefully, we may discern the will of Heaven. The will of Heaven desires us to do certain things, and not to do others. As to those things which Heaven wishes and does not wish, if a man searches within himself, he will surely find warnings of them in his own heart, and if he looks about him at daily affairs, he will find verification of these warnings in the state. Thus we can discern the will of Heaven in these portents and wonders. We should not hate such signs but stand in awe of them, considering that Heaven wishes to repair our faults and save us from our errors. Therefore it takes this way to warn us.

—WRITINGS OF T'UNG CHUNG-SHU
(CONFUCIANIST PHILOSOPHER)

CONTEMPLATION

"Devil's out, Fortune in!" So Japanese, celebrating Setsunbun-sai, shout as they throw beans first into each room of the house and then out the door!

Will such a ritual bring good fortune? In and of itself, no. But if ceremonies such as this or the Chinese attribution of an animal quality (ox, horse, etc.) to each new year brings a greater awareness of signs, wonders, and messages from the divine, then the answer is yes.

The fortunate pay attention.

COMPARISON

Of all the waters of the world, none is as great as the sea. Ten thousand streams flow into it—I have never heard of a time when they stopped—and yet it is never full. The water leaks away at Wei-lu—I have never heard of a time when it didn't—and yet the sea is never empty. Spring or autumn, it never changes. Flood or drought, it takes no notice. It is so much greater than the streams of the Yangtze or the Yellow River that it is impossible to measure the difference. But I have never for this reason prided myself on it. I take my place with Heaven and Earth and receive breath from the yin and yang. I sit here between Heaven and Earth as a little stone or a little tree sits on a huge mountain. Since I can see my own smallness, what reason would I have to pride myself?

Compare the area within the four seas with all that is between Heaven and Earth—is it not like one little anthill in a vast marsh? Compare the Middle Kingdom with the area within the four seas—is it not like one tiny grain in a great storehouse? When we refer to the things of creation, we speak of them as numbering ten thousand—and man is only one of them.

—WRITINGS OF CHUANG-TZU (CLASSICAL TAOIST TEACHER)

CONTEMPLATION

Matched with the scale of nature, what are we?

Perhaps that's why we are so apt at comparing among ourselves. In this Jewish anecdote . . .

A Chassid had heard so much of the sanctity of a certain rabbi that he journeyed all the way from his village to the town where the great rabbi lived.

"What miracles has your rabbi performed?" inquired the visiting Chassid of one of the rabbi's disciples.

"There are miracles and miracles," replied the disciple. "For instance, the people of your town would regard it as a miracle if God should do your rabbi's bidding. We, on the other hand, regard it as a miracle that our rabbi does God's bidding."

If any comparison is valid at all, it's in measuring how obedient you are to God.

IMAGINATION

◇

Once God visited a small Gypsy village, and nobody was there except the *petulengro,* or blacksmith, and his wife. When morning came, the *petulengro*'s wife said to God, "I want to go to heaven when I die."

And God said to her, "You are such a good wife that you can't end up in hell. There's all that crying and suffering there. And as for your husband, because I had such a nice, peaceful night, I'm going to give him the four things that he wants most in his life." So God asked him what he wanted most in life.

The blacksmith answered, "Whatever man I tell to go up in my apple tree, may he never come down until I say so. And whoever I tell to go sit on my mare's blanket, may they never get up unless I tell them to. Whoever goes into my little iron box, may they never come out till I say so. I want my turban with me all my life, and when I sit on it, may no man be able to make me get up."

One day after many years the angel of death came to him and said, "Come with me."

And the Gypsy told him, "Why don't you go up in my apple tree and wait, and I'll be right along."

The angel of death went up in the apple tree, and he couldn't come down. Then the Gypsy said to him, "You let me live another twenty years, and I'll let you come down."

After another twenty years the angel of death came again and said to the Gypsy, "Your time is up."

The Gypsy said, "Let me say good-bye to my children and make things ready for them. You go sit on my mare's blanket."

The angel of death went and sat on the mare's blanket, and he couldn't get up.

And the Gypsy said, "Give me another twenty years to live, and I'll let you get up."

After twenty years the Devil came and said, "Now is your time, you come with *me.*"

"You're so nice," the Gypsy said to the Devil. Then he added, "Let me see you go into that little iron box."

The Devil said, "Oh, I can go in there. No problem."

The iron box became red-hot, and the Devil was trying to get out of it, but the Gypsy put it in the fire, and the Devil fought and fought with him until he had no strength left. And the Gypsy said, "If I let you out, you have to leave me alone all my life."

And the Devil said, "I don't want to see you ever again."

Another twenty years passed, and another angel of death came—the one who judges where you should go—and said to the Gypsy, "Your time has come."

So he took him first to the Devil. And the Devil said, "No, I don't want him here, he's such a bad man, get him out of here, quick!"

And then the angel took the Gypsy to God, who said, "No, I don't want him here, please get him out of here."

And the Gypsy said to God, "Can I see what your big kingdom is like?" The Gypsy opened the door a little bit and looked through the crack, then threw his turban in and sat down, and nobody could get him up off his turban. And that's how the Gypsy went to heaven.

—TRADITIONAL ROM (GYPSY) STORY

CONTEMPLATION

Walt Disney was fired from one of his first jobs because he "lacked imagination." Look where his imagination led him. Look where the Gypsy's imagination took him. Imagine where your God-given imagination may take you!

PREFERENCE

◆

Mencius said, "Fish is what I want; bear's palm is also what I want. If I cannot have both, I would rather take the bear's palm than fish. Life is what I want; dutifulness is also what I want. If I cannot have both, I would rather take dutifulness than life. On the one hand, though life is what I want, there is something I want more than life. That is why I do not cling to life at all costs. On the other hand, though death is what I loathe, there is something I loathe more than death. That is why there are troubles I do not avoid. If there is nothing a man wants more than life, then why should he have scruples about any means, so long as it will serve to keep him alive? If there is nothing a man loathes more than death, then why should he have scruples about any means, so long as it helps him to avoid trouble? Yet there are ways of remaining alive and ways of avoiding death to which a man will not resort. In other words, there are things a man wants more than life and there are also things he loathes more than death. This is an attitude not confined to the moral man but common to all men. The moral man simply never loses it."

—WRITINGS OF MENCIUS (CLASSICAL CHINESE PHILOSOPHER)

CONTEMPLATION

We all have our particular and perhaps peculiar set of likes and dislikes. I adore apricots, and you zucchini. That's natural and morally neutral.

When one's spirituality deepens, however, one realizes that beyond preference there are profound choices far more significant to oneself and our communities. You may enjoy the taste of beef, for example, and prefer to eat it, but what about the health of your heart? What about the rain forests burned to clear grazing space for cattle?

The moral person does not avoid these issues and continually addresses the details of decision.

FEBRUARY 11
FAT

So the children went in and possessed the land, and thou subduedst before them the inhabitants of the land, the Canaanites, and gavest them into their hands, with their kings, and the people of the land, that they might do with them as they would.

And they took strong cities, and a fat land, and possessed houses full of all goods, wells digged, vineyards, and olive yards, and fruit trees in abundance: so they did eat, and were filled, and became fat, and delighted themselves in thy great goodness.

—BOOK OF NEHEMIAH (HEBREW SCRIPTURES)

A hungry jackdaw alighted on the branch of a fig tree, and seeing that the figs were still green, he decided to wait there until they ripened. A fox, fascinated by the jackdaw's long vigil, asked what he was doing, and then said: "Don't fool yourself, my friend. You can feed on hopes, but they won't make you fat!"

—FABLE OF AESOP (CLASSICAL GREEK)

CONTEMPLATION

What happens when one's hopes are fulfilled and all the fat of the land is available for consumption? What then? After the first flush of delighted satiety, the Israelites, Nehemiah observed, no longer "served thee in their kingdom, and in thy great goodness that thou gavest them, and in the large and fat land which thou gavest before them, neither turned they from their wicked works." Being fat is fine. Being fat, arrogant, and ungrateful is merely wasteful.

INDIVIDUATION

◆

Jesus said to her, "I am He who exists from the Undivided. I was given some of the things of my Father."

Salome said, "I am your disciple."

Jesus said to her, "Therefore I say, if he is [undivided] he will be filled with light, but if he is divided, he will be filled with darkness."

—GOSPEL OF THOMAS (CHRISTIAN TEACHING)

◆

The Sixth Patriarch was pursued by the monk Myo as far as Taiyu Mountain. The patriarch, seeing Myo coming, laid the Robe and Bowl [of office] on a rock and said, "This robe represents the faith; it should not be fought over. If you want to take it away, take it now." Myo tried to move it, but it was as heavy as a mountain and would not budge. Faltering and trembling, he cried out, "I came for the Dharma, not for the robe. I beg you, please give me your instruction."

The patriarch said, "Think neither good nor evil. At this very moment, what is the original self of the monk Myo?" At these words, Myo was directly illuminated. His whole body was covered with sweat. He wept and bowed, saying, "Besides the secret words and secret meaning you have just now revealed to me, is there anything else, deeper still?"

The patriarch said, "What I have told you is no secret at all. When you look into your own true self, whatever is deeper is found right there."

—MUMON-KAN (CLASSICAL ZEN BUDDHIST TEXT)

CONTEMPLATION

As Jesus was known to have affirmed that "you are gods" and "the kingdom of heaven is within you," the question arises: Is divinity and a heavenlike state the same for all of us?

Jungian psychology points to individuation, becoming the most of who you are, as an extraordinary aim.

The humble Rabbi Zusya, in his later years, put it this way: "When God speaks to me, He won't ask me, 'Why were you not more like Abraham; why were you not more like Moses?' God will ask, 'Why were you not more like Zusya?'"

COMPANIONSHIP

◈

———— ————	above Ch'ien	The Creative, Heaven
———— ————	below Li	The Clinging, Flame

Here clarity is within and strength without—the character of a peaceful union of men, which, in order to hold together, needs one yielding nature among many firm persons. True fellowship among men must be based upon a concern that is universal. It is not the private interests of the individual that create lasting fellowship among men, but rather the goals of humanity. That is why it is said that fellowship with men in the open succeeds. If unity of this kind prevails, even difficult and dangerous tasks, such as crossing the great water, can be accomplished.

—I CHING (CLASSICAL CHINESE TEXT)

CONTEMPLATION

All of us at times become a little weary with our lot (even Abraham was probably a little relieved when Lot, his nephew, moved). Spiritual companionship can give that little extra spark of life to the tired soul. It may come from something as simple as someone at work noticing that you took care of that little pile of invoices that's been clogging up the department for months. Or it could be a much deeper connection like the one you have with the woman who's taken you under her wing and become your mentor.

Wherever it comes from, you can recognize the special feeling you get from these exchanges. Mary, the mother of Jesus, and her cousin Elizabeth had a special relationship like this. As Luke tells it in the Gospels, Mary, having conceived the Christ-child, soon thereafter hastened to visit Elizabeth at her home in the highlands of Judah. Unbeknownst to Mary, her older and seemingly barren cousin had only months earlier been blessed by the spirit herself. Elizabeth was to be the mother of John the Baptist. When Elizabeth heard Mary's greeting, the baby inside her jumped for joy, and Elizabeth herself was so inspired that she shouted, "Blessings upon you of all women." Mary, too, was caught up in the spirit and said, "My soul magnifies the Lord, and the breath within me has been delighted."

Their sons, John and Jesus, went on to have a unique relationship. True spiritual companions, they both knew very well when to yield and when to hold strong, even with each other.

LOVERS

◇

Love overflows into all things
From out of the depths to above the highest stars
And so love overflows into all best beloved, most loving things.
Because she has given to the highest King
The kiss of peace

—WRITINGS OF HILDEGARD VON BINGEN
(CHRISTIAN MYSTIC AND POET)

◇

The incense in the golden duck is burning out—
She is still waiting behind the embroidered curtains.
In the midst of flute playing and songs,
He returns intoxicated, supported by friends.
The happy adventure of the romantic youth—
His lady alone knows its sweetness.

—WRITINGS OF YUAN-WU
(ZEN BUDDHIST POET)

◇

Seek the Divine with your whole being
I truly love you

No one renders to me service
More precious than this one
Nor will there ever be anyone
Whom I love more on earth.

You will come to me
I promise it to you surely.
I love you.

—BHAGAVAD GITA (HINDU SACRED TEXT)

CONTEMPLATION

We live in sexy bodies. Take a good look around (as if you haven't already), and you'll see a world pulsating with sex and attraction.

Oh, for love! You'll either grab at it in hit-and-miss fashion (most likely suffering equally whether "successful" or not) or come to your senses and desire to be both loved and loving.

This life is a fabulous spiritual romance—and love relationships can be a great part of it. Enjoy!

SEXUALITY

◆

His Augustness, the Male Who Invites, inquired of Her Augustness, the Female Who Invites, "In what manner is your body made?" She replied, "My body in its thriving grows, but there is one part that does not grow together." And His Augustness, the Male Who Invites, said to her: "My body in its thriving also grows, but there is one part that grows in excess. Therefore, would it not seem proper that I should introduce the part of my body in excess into the part of your body that does not grow together, and so procreate?"

Her Augustness, the Female Who Invites, said: "It would be well." And His Augustness, the Male Who Invites, said to her: "Let us go round this August Heavenly Pillar, I and you, and when we shall have come together, let us in august union join our august parts." She agreed . . . and where they met, Her Augustness, the Female Who Invites, said: "Ah! What a fair and lovely youth!" Whereupon His Augustness, the Male Who Invites, said: "Ah! What a fair and lovely maiden!"

—TRADITIONAL SHINTO MYTH

CONTEMPLATION

The story of the world is sex. The deities Izanagi and Izanami engaged in it from the beginning. As spirit-beings they were inherently sexual; so are we.

And we must admit, sex can be divine.

Our designation for a sacred day, holiday, *comes from the Holi festivals in India, where in ancient times sacred sexual intercourse was a vital part of the celebration. The old Germanic word* lust *originally meant "religious joy."*

Some religions therefore have proclaimed sexuality and sexual relations as the highest sacraments of faith. Others have an extreme aversion to sexuality and denounce it as impure and ungodly.

For most of us the middle path between habitual sexual grasping and complete renunciation is best.

MANIFESTATION

◇

Yahweh created me, first-fruits of his fashioning,
before the oldest of his works.
From everlasting, I was firmly set,
from the beginning, before the earth came into being.
The deep was not, when I was born,
nor were the springs with their abounding waters.
Before the mountains were settled,
before the hills, I came to birth;
before he had made the earth, the countryside,
and the first elements of the world.
When he fixed the heavens firm, I was there,
when he drew a circle on the surface of the deep,
when he thickened the clouds above,
when the sources of the deep began to swell,
when he assigned the sea its boundaries
—and the waters will not encroach on the shore—
when he traced the foundations of the earth,
I was beside the master craftsman,
delighting him day after day,
ever at play in his presence,
at play everywhere on his earth,
delighting to be with the children of men.

—BOOK OF PROVERBS (HEBREW SCRIPTURES)

CONTEMPLATION

These are the manifestations of the Divine. At work and at play behind the myriad of possible manifestations is wisdom, wisdom that is bestowed only on the human race. In every way, point by point, we have the potential to bring into creation just as the Divine does.

New and successful designs? Sure! Fruitful and profitable business? Absolutely! Masterworks of art—and a good living? Yes!

Then why are so many of us, especially those devoted to spiritual learning and living, still poor, or unaccomplished in the world, or yet to be discovered and rewarded by the powers that be? Why, with all this awesome potential, spiritual knowledge and attention, haven't we manifested what we want?

There's a gap, a time gap, that's why. The children of the world have an easier time "succeeding" than the children of the light. They are not hindered by moral concerns. They need little or no time off for spiritual practice or journeying. They fit in and manifest more or less an adequate compensation and reward.

Children of the light who wisely keep to the light are sure to be superlative manifestors. When they "take," with the potent leavening Jesus spoke of so often, they make a whole lot of bread!

UNEXPECTED

◇

There was once a deity living among men who wanted to find twelve animals for the zodiac in order to name the years.

He had already placed the dragon, the snake, the tiger, and the hare when the rat and the ox began to quarrel about which was the bigger. Naturally, the body and the appearance of the ox was much larger; when it heard the claims of the rat, it shook its horns and shouted, "Everyone knows that I, the ox, am big and immeasurably strong. How can a rat that only weighs a few pounds dare to compete with me? I call it ridiculous."

The sly and cunning rat merely laughed coldly at the boasts of the ox and said, "Everyone is conceited about his own size and capabilities. That is no standard. We must bend to the judgment of the majority. It is true that I am only a poor little rat, but I will measure myself with you today."

Fearing that the battle of words between the ox and the rat would develop into a serious quarrel, the deity quickly interrupted. "Naturally a rat is not as big as an ox. But since he won't believe it, we must trust to the decision of the crowd. That is the just way to decide. I suggest that you think the matter over and then go out and hear the people's verdict." The ox agreed at once to the suggestion of the deity, since he thought that his victory was assured.

The rat, however, pretended to be in despair and sunk in gloom. He said, "I must be a little bigger before I can appear before the people."

Seeing the rat so disheartened, the ox thought that, whatever happened, the rat would still be much smaller than he, and he agreed to its doubling its size. He himself did not bother, because he was already a hundred times bigger than the rat.

When the rat had grown, they went out into the town. "Look! Never before have I seen such a big rat. It is incredibly big." From the moment they left the house until their return, they heard on all sides exclamations of wonder at the size of the rat; but no one looked at the ox, because people see oxen every day, whereas they had never before seen such a large rat.

The stupid ox had fallen into the rat's trap, but it did not realize that it had been tricked—it merely thought the people had no eyes. Since it had lost, it had no dignity left and had to resign the first place to the rat. From that time the rat became the first animal in the zodiac.

—TRADITIONAL CHINESE TALE

CONTEMPLATION

The strangest and most unexpected things do happen—especially with faith.

David slew Goliath. Lazarus returned from certain death. Mecca was restored to true worship.

In Chinese tradition a new year is beginning. Hasten the unexpected.

MISERLINESS

One day an Arab bedouin journeyed from his desert home to visit the nearby town and its marketplace. In the bazaar, he saw a wonderful pair of boots and made an offer to purchase them. But the shoemaker refused to bargain; it had to be his price. Finally the enraged bedouin stomped out of the shoemaker's shop, shouting, "What you are asking for these boots is what my camel is worth!" and that was not the least of what he said.

The shoemaker was considerably offended by this desert ruffian's insulting behavior and he decided to teach the bedouin a lesson. Seeing that the Arab and his camel had started down the track leading to the desert, the shoemaker picked up the boots and, taking a shortcut, hastened to a spot on the pathway ahead of his adversary. There, he put one of the boots.

The shoemaker went a good distance farther down the trail and deposited the other boot on it. He then hid and awaited the arrival of the bedouin.

When the Arab saw the first boot, he said to himself, "Surely this is one of the shoemaker's fine boots. It looks just like the one I saw in the bazaar. If only there were both boots here, then I'd have the pair of boots for free." But he left the single boot in the sand, for, after all, what good is one boot?

In a while he discovered the second boot, left as well on the desert track. "If I had only taken the first boot when I had the chance," he moaned. And then he thought, "I can still go back for it."

But because he and his camel had traveled quite a way now, the bedouin had to leave the camel on the spot or risk its becoming overtired. And off ran the man to get the first boot.

As soon as he had gone, the shoemaker came out of hiding. He took the bedouin's camel and rode it back to town. The second boot he left just where it had been.

—TRADITIONAL ARABIAN STORY

In vain the foolish man accumulates food. I tell you, truly, it will be his downfall! He gathers to himself neither friend nor comrade. Alone he eats; alone he sits in sin. The plowshare cleaving the soil helps satisfy hunger. The traveler, using his legs, achieves his goal. The priest who speaks surpasses the one who is silent. The friend who gives is better than the miser.

—RIG VEDA (HINDU SACRED TEXT)

CONTEMPLATION

Around this time of year, Icelandic villagers come out of their frigid dwelling-places. They bring with them every bit of remaining food; nothing is spared. This nourishment is then shared among the young and relatively strong—all who have a good chance to survive the few weeks until the land and sea thaw enough and more food can be procured.

The others understand. But they are not left out; the community shares with them, too. Each person's story is told; their lives are honored and blessed with the telling.

You can't be cheap and miserly with spirit. You end up with nothing and no one who cares.

LEADERSHIP

◇

Now three of the thirty captains went down to the rock to David, into the cave of Adullam; and the host of the Philistines encamped in the valley of Rephaim. And David was then in the stronghold, and the Philistines' garrison was then at Bethlehem. And David longed and said, "Oh, that one would give me a drink of water of the well of Bethlehem, that is at the gate!" And the three broke through the host of the Philistines, and drew water out of the well of Bethlehem, that was by the gate, and took it, and brought it to David: but David would not drink of it, but poured out to the Lord, and said, "My God forbid it me, that I should do this thing: shall I drink the blood of these men that have put their lives in jeopardy? For with the jeopardy of their lives they brought it." Therefore he would not drink it.

—FIRST BOOK OF CHRONICLES (HEBREW SCRIPTURES)

CONTEMPLATION

David was a great leader because he did not put himself above his people or reproach. Here he was only a ragged rebel leader; but it is the revered King David who makes this plea:

> *Hear my cry, O God; listen to my prayer.*
> *From the ends of the earth I call to you,*
> *I call as my heart grows faint;*
> *lead me to the rock that is higher than I.*
> *For you have been my refuge,*
> *a strong tower against the foe.*
> *I long to dwell in your tent forever*
> *and take refuge in the shelter of your wings.*
> *For you have heard my vows, O God;*
> *you have given me the heritage of those who fear your name.*
> *Increase the days of the king's life, his years for many generations.*
> *May he be enthroned in God's presence forever;*
> *appoint your love and faithfulness to protect him.*
> *Then will I ever sing praise to your name*
> *and fulfill my vows day after day.*

Let God lead you to the rock that is higher and stronger than you are now.

BRAVERY

Two travelers were making a perilous journey. One was tall and strong, whereas the other was small and weak. They had to pass through, first, a forest full of thieves and robbers and, second, another forest full of tigers and leopards. Single-handed, the Tall Man fought the violent robbers and the ferocious animals while the Small Man merely looked on. Then the two companions had to pass through a long stretch of waterless desert, and when halfway across it, the Small Man lay down on the sand and moaned, "Brother, I can go no farther. So leave me here to die." But the Tall Man pointed toward a clump of trees in the distance and said, "Brother, we must be nearly through the desert, because yonder are some trees. Perhaps they are plum trees, in which case we can quench our thirst by sucking the juice of their plums." Encouraged by these words, the Small Man continued the journey, only to fall down again later, overcome by the heat and thirst.

The Tall Man picked up his exhausted companion and carried him in his arms until they reached the fringe of the desert and came to the trees. As the Tall Man had expected, they were plum trees. The Tall Man swiftly climbed one of the trees, but he found it difficult to pick the plums, as the branches were too thorny and brittle. As he paused aloft the plum tree, the Small Man shouted from below, "You lazy fellow, you cowardly fellow! You call yourself a man, yet you cannot even get a few plums!"

—TRADITIONAL BURMESE BUDDHIST TALE

To see what is right and not to do it is want of courage.

—ANALECTS (CLASSICAL CONFUCIANIST TEXT)

CONTEMPLATION

Bravery is not stupidity. To be brave requires understanding and commitment, not rash behavior. With these criteria, the opportunities to act bravely abound in our everyday life.

A spiritual person cannot be timid. Be a Muhammad today and confront bravely. Be a Joan of Arc today and fight bravely. Be a Mahatma Gandhi today and make peace bravely. Be brave!

APPROPRIATENESS

◇

A fox, while crossing a river, was driven by the stream into a narrow creek and lay there for a long time, trapped.

He was covered with a multitude of horseflies, which had fastened themselves upon him.

It so happened that a hedgehog, wandering in the area, saw the unhappy condition of the fox and called out to him:

"Would you like me to drive away those flies, which are tormenting you so much?"

But the fox begged the hedgehog to do nothing of the sort.

The hedgehog was surprised. "Why not?" it asked.

"Because," replied the fox, "the flies which are sticking on to me now are already full and are not drawing very much more blood. If you were to remove them, a swarm of fresh and hungry ones would descend—and they would not leave a drop of blood in my body!"

—FABLE OF AESOP (CLASSICAL GREEK)

◇

Two monks were each given a golden bowl by the roshi and told to clean them. One monk took his bowl down to the river and washed it out with sand and water. Still not totally satisfied, he scraped and scraped and then got some acid and scraped that bowl till he was satisfied that it could not be anything but perfectly clean.

The other monk sat quietly for a few moments, then with one movement of his hand cleaned his bowl using a soft cloth. They brought their bowls to the roshi.

One shone more than the other, but only one bowl held water.

—TRADITIONAL ZEN BUDDHIST TALE

CONTEMPLATION

Appropriate actions stem from appropriate understanding and sentiment. In modern culture so much real feeling is stifled that we tend to either suppress action or in a devil-may-care rebelliousness do anything we feel is right. The Sufi master Naqshband clarified this for his students more than seven hundred years ago. He said: "When people say 'weep,' they do not mean 'weep always.' When they say 'do not cry,' they do not mean you to be a permanent buffoon."

TOGETHER

◇

▬▬ ▬▬		*above* *K'an*	*The Abysmal, Water*
▬▬ ▬▬			
▬▬ ▬▬		*below* *K'un*	*The Receptive, Earth*

The waters on the surface of the earth flow together wherever they can, as for example in the ocean, where all the rivers come together.

THE JUDGMENT

Holding together brings good fortune.
Inquire of the oracle once again
Whether you possess sublimity, constancy, and perseverance;
Then there is no blame.
Those who are uncertain gradually join.
Whoever comes too late.
Meets with misfortune.

What is required is that we unite with others, in order that all may complement and aid one another through holding together. But such holding together calls for a central figure around whom other persons may unite. To become a center of influence holding people together is a grave matter and fraught with great responsibility. It requires greatness of spirit, consistency, and strength. Therefore let him who wishes to gather others about him ask himself whether he is equal to the undertaking, for anyone attempting the task without a real calling for it only makes confusion worse than if no union at all had taken place.

—I CHING (CLASSICAL CHINESE TEXT)

◇

A thunderclap under the clear blue sky;
all beings on earth open their eyes;
everything under heaven bows together;
Mount Sumeru leaps up and dances.

—WRITINGS OF WU-MEN (CLASSICAL ZEN
BUDDHIST TEACHER AND POET)

CONTEMPLATION

Just as the Hebrew letter Vav joins together words and concepts, including the unutterable holy name of God, so may we, if we're connected to inner spirit, hold spiritual people and groups together. When you have this capacity to influence for good purpose, make the call to others. You may be such a rare person; this may be a rare and fortunate time to bring people together.

STARS

◇

Twelve children were playing together on the grass near their parents' lodges. They decided to play a new game they had made up. They joined hands in a circle and danced in place, singing all the while: "We are dancing. We are dancing."

Their parents listened to this song and saw that the children's feet no longer touched the earth. Amazed and afraid, they ran to stop the children's dancing, but the children were already above their heads, going higher and higher into the sky, singing: "We are dancing. We are dancing."

They went up and up until they disappeared, still holding hands. When they were seen at last, it was as twelve stars in the heavens above their parents' lodges. One was just a little bit out of the circle, and so this star appears a little to one side of the others.

—TRADITIONAL SENECA TRIBAL TALE (NATIVE AMERICAN)

CONTEMPLATION

Stars are a constant explosion of light. So are we.

Many native peoples believe that human life came to earth from the Pleiades or other star groups. And that, once enlightened here, we return home to the heavens and join our relatives there.

How does that happen? You've got to be a star first—to your friends, neighbors, acquaintances, and even strangers who come into your space.

People remember stars. We're still talking about supernovae seen millennia ago whose light was generated millions of years in the past. And the future is full of stars.

FEAR

And I thought over again
My small adventures
As with a shore-wind I drifted out
In my kayak
And thought I was in danger,

My fears,
Those small ones
That I thought so big
For all the vital things
I had to get and to reach

And yet, there is only
One great thing,
The only thing:
To live to see in huts and on journeys
The great day that dawns,
And the light that fills the world.

—TRADITIONAL INUIT TRIBAL SONG (NATIVE AMERICAN)

A snake bit me; I see a worm and I am afraid.

—TRADITIONAL WEST AFRICAN TRIBAL PROVERB

From that which we fear, make us fearless.
O bounteous One, assist us with your aid.
May the atmosphere we breathe
breathe fearlessness into us
fearlessness on earth
and fearlessness in heaven!
May fearlessness surround us
above and below!

May we be without fear
by night and by day!
    Let all the world be my friend!

—ATHARVA VEDA (HINDU SACRED TEXT)

CONTEMPLATION

What a strange combination we are! A tiny worm or problem may terrify us; a voyage into frozen arctic waters or to the stars may be taken with little or no obvious trepidation.

The Yajur Veda, holy scripture of India, reveals the key:

When he knows the *Atman*—the Self, the inner life, who enjoys like a bee the sweetness of the flowers of the senses, the Lord of what was and of what will be—then he goes beyond fear.

STUDY

◇

At fifteen, I set my heart upon learning. At thirty, I had planted my feet upon firm ground. At forty, I no longer suffered from perplexities. At fifty, I knew what were the biddings of Heaven. At sixty, I heard them with a docile ear. At seventy, I could follow the dictates of my own heart, for what I desired no longer overstepped the boundaries of right.

—ANALECTS (CLASSICAL CONFUCIANIST TEXT)

◇

"Since you have done so much studying, there must be much Dharma in your mind."

"Yogin," the man answered, "I have studied a great deal of Dharma, but I am not able to practice what I have learned. Please tell me, are there instructions that will help me to retain what I learn?"

The yogin said there were and gave him the initiation that transfers spiritual power. He then gave him instructions on how to integrate the many themes of the Dharma:

Just as the particles of precious metal
become well-fused by the smith,
so the various things you have studied
must melt together in your mind.

—TRADITIONAL TIBETAN BUDDHIST TALE

◇

And when a company meets together in one of the houses of God to pore over the Book of God and to study it together among themselves, the Shechinah comes down to them and mercy overshadows them, the angels surround them, and God remembers them among them that are His.

—TEACHING OF MUHAMMAD (PROPHET OF ISLAM)

CONTEMPLATION

Study ought to be an aid to the unification of your soul, not an impediment. The story is related in the Zen tradition of a very frustrated student. Hsiang Yen had asked what he felt were all the right questions of his teacher to no avail. He had thoroughly read the Buddhist canon and many additional writings. Still no answers; no enlightenment.

"Of what use is all this study?" he asked himself. "I'll live the life of a simple monk instead."

And he did, forgoing his official studies to farm a small piece of land. One day, turning the soil in preparation to plant some beans, his pitchfork hit a pebble that then struck a bamboo stalk that went "crack" from the blow. The sound enlightened Hsiang Yen.

CYCLES

◆

In a hidden cave lives a woman so old that her face looks a shriveled-up walnut. She has been sitting there for a thousand years or more, working on a blanket strip for her buffalo robe. She is making the strip out of dyed porcupine quills, the way our ancestors did, on this turtle continent. Resting beside her, licking his paws, watching her all the time is Shunka Sapa, a huge black dog. His eyes never wander from the old woman, whose teeth are worn flat, worn down to little stumps, she has used them to flatten so many porcupine quills.

A few steps from where the old woman sits working on her blanket strip, a huge fire is kept going. She lit this fire a thousand or more years ago and has kept it alive ever since. Over the fire hangs a big earthen pot. Inside the big pot, *wojapi* is boiling and bubbling. *Wojapi* is berry soup, good and sweet and red. That soup has been boiling in the pot for a long time, ever since the fire was lit.

Every now and then the old woman gets up to stir the *wojapi* in the huge earthen pot. She is so old and feeble that it takes her a while to get up and hobble over to the fire. The moment her back is turned, the huge black dog starts pulling the porcupine quills out of her blanket strip. This way she never makes any progress, and her quillwork remains forever unfinished. The people used to say that if the old woman ever finishes her blanket strip, then at the very moment that she threads the last porcupine quill to complete the design, the world will come to an end.

—TRADITIONAL LAKOTA TRIBAL STORY
(NATIVE AMERICAN)

CONTEMPLATION

Are we hanging on a thread before the next world cycle begins?

Hindu sages tell of the four ages or Yugas that make up a universal cycle, and purport we are in the last one, the Kali Yuga, the time of greatest darkness in the world. The sacred Purana texts declare that the final days will be known when property confers rank, wealth becomes the only source of virtue, passion the sole bond of union between husband and wife, and falsehood the source of success in life.

Can we face this time? In February, on the night of the new and unseen moon, Hindus perform the rituals of Shivaratri—sacred fires, fasting, and all-night storytelling and worship—to strengthen their wills.

Strengthen yours for the time to come.

REMEDY

It is as if . . . a man had been wounded by an arrow thickly smeared with poison, and his friends and companions, his relatives and kinsfolk, were to procure for him a physician . . . and the sick man were to say, "I will not have this arrow taken out until I have learnt whether the man who wounded me belonged to the warrior caste, or to the Brahmin caste, or to the agricultural caste, or to the menial caste."

Or again he were to say, "I will not have this arrow taken out until I have learnt the name of the man who wounded me, and to what clan he belongs."

Or again he were to say, "I will not have this arrow taken out until I have learnt whether the man who wounded me was tall, or short, or of the middle height."

Or again he were to say, "I will not have this arrow taken out until I have learnt whether the man who wounded me was black, or dusky, or of a yellow skin."

Or again he were to say, "I will not have this arrow taken out until I have learnt whether the man who wounded me was from this or that village, or town, or city."

That man would die, Malunkyaputta, without ever having learned [all] this.

—MAJJHIMA NIKAYA (BUDDHIST SACRED TEXT)

CONTEMPLATION

What if this were not a world of suffering? What if no one got ill, physically or spiritually? What if all that was wished for came to be?

Then perhaps such a foolish and arrogant disdain of offered remedies could be justified. For now, if the remedy for what ails you is there for the taking, take it and swallow.

Afterward, for All that is Holy cares, you can ask all the questions you want.

INSANITY

There was a holy man who lived in a state of ecstasy and spoke to none. Many regarded him as a lunatic. One day, having begged some food in the village, he sat by the side of a dog and began to eat. A crowd gathered around the holy man to witness his strange way of eating. The holy man would put one morsel into his mouth and the next into the dog's, so that the man and dog ate together like two old friends.

Some of the spectators began to laugh at the holy man and called him crazy, until he silenced them by saying, "Why do you laugh? Vishnu is seated with Vishnu. Vishnu is feeding Vishnu. Why do you laugh, O Vishnu? Whatever is, is Vishnu."

—TRADITIONAL HINDU TALE

CONTEMPLATION

Are you insane if you are working for God-realization, or rather might you be considered insane if you are not?

The poor Mullah Nasreddin, out of work as usual, awoke one day and informed his wife, "I no longer will be seeking employment. I work now only for Allah." Not one to be put off easily, she replied, "If that is true, please ask Allah for your back wages." "A good idea," thought Nasreddin, and he proceeded to his back-yard and prayed for a hundred pieces of gold as his just reward. Overhearing him, his well-to-do neighbor decided to play a joke on the simple mullah. He hurriedly put a hundred gold pieces in a sack and, without being seen, threw the sack over the fence at Nasreddin's feet.

The Mullah took the gold, and he and his wife began to spend it. Enough was enough, and the neighbor soon demanded his money back. Nasreddin refused, claiming that the money was a gift of providence. The neighbor became irate and threatened to bring Nasreddin before a judge. After a moment's thought, Nasreddin said, "Let's go right now. But so the court will not be prejudiced against me, lend me a fine robe and a horse so we can appear on an equal footing." The neighbor agreed, and off they went. At the court the neighbor stated his complaint. Then it was Nasreddin's turn. His defense was insanity; Nasreddin claimed that his neighbor was insane! "What is your evidence for this?" the judge inquired. "If you ask the man, he'll say that not only was the money his, but the fine horse I rode here and this very robe I'm wearing, too," Nasreddin said calmly. "But that is indeed so," cried the exasperated neighbor. "Case dismissed," said the judge.

LEAP OF FAITHS

Who was there but an open-armed angel
waiting on the shoreline?
Will they take those first steps,
the mixed multitude, into the Sea of Reeds;
the ones that bring the parting and
safe passage to Sinai and other wonders

Long before, when the earth was but an egg
and women pounding roots to powder
Saw goddess in bird, in birth, in blessed beak,
Worshipped flight and not flight.
In caves as well as cliffs, women and men,
In sacred shape and color, feather and stone,
Bent willow to become place of prayer.

The dark-skinned and the light-skinned
Around the fire, listen now as they always have
To the heart-drum. "It's in this heart,
It's in this heart!" First one, then many.
Clamor, dance, exult, ponder, breathe,
Know. The leap is within you!

MARCH

TRUST

Once a merchant went on a journey. On the eve of the Sabbath, he found himself outside an unfamiliar town.

"To whom can I entrust my money?" he wondered. "I know no one in this town."

Looking around to see that no one was watching, he buried his money under a stump in a field, then went into town to spend the Sabbath. But the man who owned the field saw him bury the money and, as soon as the merchant was gone, dug it up. Two days later, when the man returned for the money, it was no longer there.

The merchant went to King Solomon and complained about the theft.

"Find out who owns the field, and tell him that you buried only part of your money in a secret place. Explain to him that you wish to hide the rest of your money and ask his advice: Should you bury it in the same secret place or in a different place, or should you leave it with a trustworthy person? He will no doubt advise you to bury it in the same place so that he can get his hands on it. Even he will soon realize that if you go to the stump and find the first money missing, you will not want to leave any more there. So he will return the money he stole to the hole under the stump."

The merchant followed Solomon's advice. And as Solomon had predicted, the owner of the field quickly returned the stolen money to its hiding place under the stump, expecting to double his profits this way.

But the merchant outfoxed him. That night he removed all the money and went on his way. And the next morning the thief found only an empty hole under the stump.

—TRADITIONAL JEWISH TALE

CONTEMPLATION

Tomorrow all devout (and able) Bahá'ís begin a nineteen-day period of fasting in preparation for their New Year holiday, Naw Ruz. They have found God as provider and helper to be most trustworthy. What about you?

Ancient Chinese warriors carried swords of such length that the bearer was unable to remove his sword from the scabbard. They traveled in pairs, trusting in their partners to unsheath each other's sword in times of danger.

What about you? Whom do you trust?

WATER

◇

Isaac planted crops in that land and the same year reaped a hundred-fold, because the Lord blessed him. The man became rich, and his wealth continued to grow until he became very wealthy. He had so many flocks and herds and servants that the Philistines envied him. So all the wells that his father's servants had dug in the time of his father Abraham, the Philistines stopped up, filling them with earth.

Then Abimelech said to Isaac, "Move away from us; you have become too powerful for us."

So Isaac moved away from there and encamped in the Valley of Gerar and settled there. Isaac reopened the wells that had been dug in the time of his father, Abraham, which the Philistines had stopped up after Abraham died, and he gave them the same names his father had given them.

Isaac's servants dug in the valley and discovered a well of fresh water there. But the herdsmen of Gerar quarreled with Isaac's herdsmen and said, "The water is ours!" So he named the well Esek, because they disputed with him. Then they dug another well, but they quarreled over that one also; so he named it Sitnah. He moved on from there and dug another well, and no one quarreled over it. He named it Rehoboth, saying, "Now the Lord has given us room, and we will flourish in the land."

From there he went up to Beersheba. That night the Lord appeared to him and said, "I am the God of your father, Abraham. Do not be afraid, for I am with you; I will bless you and will increase the number of your descendants for the sake of my servant Abraham."

Isaac built an altar there and called on the name of the Lord. There he pitched his tent, and there his servants dug a well.

—BOOK OF GENESIS (HEBREW SCRIPTURES)

◇

Spiritual knowledge is like water, it takes the color and shape of the cup. Allah's knowledge is so great, that however much we take, it is like a drop of a huge ocean.

—WRITINGS OF SHAH NAQSHBAND (SUFI MASTER)

CONTEMPLATION

Water, the yin or feminine life energy, has always been highly prized and often fought over.

But a stream, because of its power, or an ocean, because of its immensity, or a well, because of its depth, cannot be taken by force and seized.

This spirit must be gently won by the powers of humility and grace.

CHEATING

◇

Rabbi Safra had some merchandise to sell. When the traders came to buy, he asked ten pieces of gold for it.

"We will give you only five," said the merchants.

When Rabbi Safra refused to sell, they went away.

The following morning they returned while the pious man was at prayer.

"We have returned to offer you seven gold pieces for your goods," they said.

Because he did not wish to interrupt his prayers, Rabbi Safra did not answer. Thinking he was still dissatisfied with their offer, they finally said, "Very well, then, we will give you the ten gold pieces you're asking."

By this time Rabbi Safra had ended his devotions.

"I could not answer you before," he apologized to them, "because prayer and dross do not mix. Know, however, that before even you spoke, I had settled in my mind that I would accept for my merchandise the five gold pieces you offered me yesterday. Therefore, to accept the ten pieces you have offered me now would be to cheat you."

—TRADITIONAL JEWISH TALE

CONTEMPLATION

You can't cheat yourself. When you've made a commitment or promise to advance your spiritual life, you may renege, but this is only an unfortunate act, not an immoral one. When you realize what's at stake, you'll make the promise good again.

PRESERVATION

◇

Agni, preserve us from distress:
consume our enemies, O God,
Eternal, with thy hottest flames.
And, irresistible, be thou a mighty iron fort to us,
with hundred walls for man's defense.
Do thou preserve us, eve and morn, from sorrow,
from the wicked man,
Infallible! by day and night.

—RIG VEDA (HINDU SACRED TEXT)

◇

I will life up mine eyes unto the hills
from whence cometh my help,
My help cometh from the Lord,
which made heaven and earth.
He will not suffer thy foot to be moved: He that keepeth thee will
    not slumber.
Behold, He that keepeth Israel shall neither slumber nor sleep.
The Lord is thy keeper:
the Lord is thy shade upon thy right hand.
The sun shall not smite thee by day,
nor the moon by night.
The Lord shall preserve thee from all evil:
He shall preserve thy soul.
The Lord shall preserve thy going out and thy coming in
from this time forth, and even for evermore.

—PSALM 121 (HEBREW SCRIPTURES)

CONTEMPLATION

Traditionally, as Africans marched forth from their homes each morning, they would stop and make this prayer: "May I (and my people) be kept safe and whole today. May I return this evening as I am this morning." Jews kiss the mezuzah (a sacred object containing holy scripture) at their door for the same purpose.

It is good to remember how fragile we are. Unknown saints and ancestral deities may or may not preserve us, but awareness and gratitude will.

CONFERRING

Chuang-tzu was fishing in the P'u when the prince of Ch'u sent two high officials to ask him to take charge of the administration of the Ch'u state. Chuang-tzu went on fishing and without turning his head said, "I have heard that in Ch'u there is a sacred tortoise which has been dead now some three thousand years. And that the prince keeps his tortoise carefully enclosed in a chest on the altar of his ancestral people. Now would this tortoise rather be dead and have its remains venerated, or be alive and wagging its tail in the mud?"

"It would rather be alive," replied the two officials. . . .

"Begone!" cried Chuang-tzu. "I too will wag my tail in the mud."

—WRITINGS OF CHUANG-TZU
(CLASSICAL TAOIST TEACHER)

For YHVH TZVAOT has conferred, so who will retract it?

—BOOK OF ISAIAH (HEBREW SCRIPTURES)

CONTEMPLATION

In ancient China, tortoise shells were used for ritual divination—a way of holding conference, so to speak, with Heaven. The shells were fired until they cracked, and the patterns then revealed conferred the meaning.

Of course, Chuang-tzu, a good Taoist, saw all this as a bit too forced and preferred to remain aloof from such aggressive (and potentially fatal) conferring.

When real conferring comes, it comes peaceably and with certitude.

All, then, will be furthered.

SIZE

◆

There was once a wicked maharaja who could not bear to think that anyone was his superior. So he summoned all the pandits of the realm, as was the practice on momentous occasions, and put to them this question: "Which of us two is the greater, I or God?"

The pandits shook with fear. Being wise by profession, they asked for time, and then through old habit they clung to their position and their lives. But they were worthy men who would not displease God; they were therefore deep in grief, when the oldest pandit reassured them: "Leave it to me, tomorrow I shall speak with the maharaja."

The next day when the court was gathered, the old man quietly arrived, his hands humbly joined together, his forehead smeared with white ashes; he bowed low and pronounced these words: "O Lord, undoubtedly, you are the greater"—the maharaja twirled his mustaches, which he wore long, and tossed high his head—"You are the greater, king, for you can banish us from your kingdom while God cannot: for truly all is His kingdom and there is nowhere to go outside Him."

—TRADITIONAL HINDU TALE

◆

Allahu Akbar. (God is most great.)

—FROM THE ADHAN (TRADITIONAL MUSLIM
CALL TO PRAYER)

CONTEMPLATION

No matter how great your spiritual achievements, there are those whose accomplishments are greater. No matter how spiritually gifted you may be, there are those whose sizable talents are more precious.

But take heart. There are those who are less advanced and less knowledgeable than you, too. Learn from the greater; help the lesser.

This brings you to God.

CELEBRATION

This is the day the Lord has made.
We will rejoice and be glad in it.

—PSALM 118 (HEBREW SCRIPTURES)

◆

The great sea has set me in motion
Set me adrift
Moving me like a weed in a river

The sky and strong wind
Have moved the spirit inside me
Till I am carried away
Trembling with joy.

—SAYING OF UVAVNUK (SIBERIAN SHAMAN)

◆

The faithful should rejoice without ceasing.

—WRITINGS OF HILDEGARD VON BINGEN
(CHRISTIAN MYSTIC AND POET)

CONTEMPLATION

There are times when, like King David returning from victorious battle for the Lord, one can do nothing but strip off one's clothes and sing and dance ecstatically in celebration. Other times the celebration is a quiet one, inspired by the turning of a star or the face of your beloved. In all instances and circumstances, now is the time.

WOMAN

Woman is the creator of the universe,
the universe is her form;
woman is the foundation of the world,
she is the true form of the body.
Whatever form she takes,
whether the form of a man or a woman,
is the superior form.
In woman is the form of all things,
of all that lives and moves in the world.
There is no jewel rarer than woman,
no condition superior to that of a woman.
There is not, nor has been, nor will be
any destiny to equal that of a woman;
there is no kingdom, no wealth,
to be compared with a woman;
there is not, nor has been, nor will be
any holy place like unto a woman.
There is no prayer to equal a woman.
There is not, nor has been, nor will be
any yoga to compare with a woman,
no mystical formula nor asceticism
to match a woman.
There are not, nor have been, nor will be
any riches more valuable than woman.

—SAKTISANGAMA TANTRA (BUDDHIST SACRED TEXT)

CONTEMPLATION

It's about time that all peoples adopted a new prayer: Thank ____ (fill in the blank: Source, Ultimate Being, the name of the Goddess or God you worship) I was, am, and am to be born a woman!

Today is International Women's Day. It's a great day to start voicing this prayer of praise.

MAN

◇

Kumush, Old Man of the Ancients, went down with his daughter to the underground world of the spirits. It was a beautiful world, reached by one long, steep road. In it were many spirits—as many as all the stars in the sky and all the hairs on all the animals in the world.

When night came, the spirits gathered in a great plain to sing and dance. When daylight came, they returned to their places in the house, lay down, and became dry bones.

After six days and six nights in the land of the spirits, Kumush longed for the sun. He decided to return to the upper world and to take some of the spirits with him to people his world.

With a big basket in hand, he went through the house of the spirits and chose the bones he wished to take.

To all the people created from the bones of the spirits, Kumush said, "You must send certain men to the mountains. There they must ask to be made brave or to be made wise. There, if they ask for it, they will be given the power to help themselves and to help all of you."

Then Kumush named the different kinds of fish and beasts that the people should eat. As he spoke their names, they appeared in the rivers and lakes, on the plains and in the forests. He named the roots and the berries and the plants that the people should eat. He thought, and they appeared.

He divided the work of the people by making this law: "Men shall fish and hunt and fight. Women shall get wood and water, gather berries and dig roots, and cook for their families. This is my law."

So Kumush finished the upper world and his work in it. Then with his daughter he went to the place where the sun rises, at the eastern edge of the world. He traveled along the sun's road until he reached the middle of the sky. There he built a house for himself and his daughter. There they live even today.

—TRADITIONAL MODOC TRIBAL TALE
(NATIVE AMERICAN)

CONTEMPLATION

A man's job has been debated and disputed from the beginning, even in men's societies. Other Native American stories tell of women being the more efficient and powerful of the two groups and laughing at the ridiculous and inept efforts men made to provide for themselves.

Kumush, Old Man of the Ancients, required men to seek bravery or wisdom. How about both?

LOGIC

◇

All their lives the two young brothers had lived in the city behind great stone walls and never saw field nor meadow. But one day they decided to pay a visit to the country.

As they went walking along the road, they saw a farmer at his plowing. They watched him and were puzzled.

"What on earth is he doing that for!" they wondered. "He turns up the earth and leaves deep furrows in it. Why should someone take a smooth piece of land covered with nice green grass and dig it up?"

Later they watched the farmer sowing grains of wheat along the furrows.

"That man must be crazy!" they exclaimed. "He takes good wheat and throws it into the dirt."

"I don't like the country!" said one in disgust. "Only queer people live here."

So he returned to the city.

His brother who remained in the country saw a change take place only several weeks later. The plowed field began to sprout tender green shoots, even more beautiful and fresh than before. This discovery excited him very much. So he wrote to his brother in the city to come at once and see for himself the wonderful change.

—TRADITIONAL JEWISH TALE

◇

If God guides you not into the road,
It will not be disclosed by logic.

Logic is a bondage of forms;
A road that is long and hard.
Leave it for a season. Like Moses
Cast away that staff
And enter for a while "The Valley of Peace."

—MAHMUD SHABISTARI (SUFI MYSTIC AND POET)

CONTEMPLATION

Logic, if overused, is severely limiting, both practically and spiritually. When one understands a situation strictly from a logical point of view, it does not change or transform it, and that's what spirituality is all about. To expect otherwise is illogical.

Here's a joke about such expectations. One winter night a couple has finally fallen asleep. Suddenly the wife wakes up, elbows her husband, and asks plaintively: "Please, dear. Close the window all the way. It's so very cold outside." "And if I shut it," replies the husband, "will it become hot outside?"

HEROES

◆

He came abjectly to his father, Anshar.
As though he were Tiamat thus he addressed him:
"My hand suffices not for me to subdue thee."
Speechless was Anshar as he stared at the ground,
Frowning and shaking his head at Ea.
All the Anunnaki gathered at that place;
Their lips closed tight, they sat in silence.
"No god" (thought they) "can go to battle and,
Facing Tiamat, escape with his life."
Lord Anshar, father of the gods, rose up in grandeur,
And having pondered in his heart, he said to the Anunnaki:
"He whose strength is potent shall be our avenger,
He who is keen in battle, Marduk, the hero!"

—TRADITIONAL BABYLONIAN TALE

CONTEMPLATION

Heroes, including our modern superheroes, vary in both the variety and extent of their powers.

But powers are not what make a hero; it's response. After all, what good is Superman, or Jesus, or Buddha, if he's not there for you when you call upon him?

So it is with you as the hero. First say yes. The battle awaits!

PHILOSOPHY

◇

The Mullah Nasreddin was accosted by a group of young ruffians, who began to throw stones at him. He was taken aback, but quickly gained his wits.

"When you stop," he told the boys, "I'll tell you something really important."

"All right," they agreed, "but none of your philosophizing."

"The Sultan," Nasreddin whispered, "is inviting everyone to an open banquet." When Nasreddin began to describe the fantastic dishes and delightful dancing the boys were sure to find there, they took off.

Nasreddin watched them disappear in the direction of the Sultan's banquet hall. Then, suddenly, he lifted his robes and started running toward it himself.

"It's possible, just possible," he puffed, "that there truly is a banquet there."

—TRADITIONAL SUFI TALE

CONTEMPLATION

In his philosophical masterwork, The City of God, *Saint Augustine describes the plethora of philosophers and philosophical positions in the time of Plato. Twelve sects split to become twenty-four because of some minor (obviously not to the philosophers) dispute. Twenty-four begat forty-eight, and so on: philosophic schools of thought proliferated until there seemed to be as many schools as philosophers.*

And why do we keep inventing more and more philosophies? One just might, as Nasreddin said to himself, turn out to hold truth. Whew!

You don't necessarily require a philosophy of life. But as philosophy means the love of wisdom, it's great to have a life of philosophy.

INTELLIGENCE

◇

Four things on earth are small, yet they are extremely wise: Ants are creatures of little strength, yet they store up their food in the summer; coneys are creatures of little power, yet they make their home in crags; locusts have no king, yet they advance together in ranks; a lizard can be caught with the hand, yet it is found in kings' palaces.

—BOOK OF PROVERBS (HEBREW SCRIPTURES)

◇

A master named Najmaini dismissed a student, saying, "Your loyalty has been tested. I find it so unshakable that you must depart."

The student answered: "I will leave, but I cannot comprehend how loyalty can be a reason for dismissal."

So spoke Najmaini: "For three years we have tested your loyalty. Your devotion to useless knowledge and shallow judgment is complete. That is precisely why you must leave."

—TRADITIONAL SUFI ANECDOTE

◇

How much more foolish are those who depend upon words and seek understanding by their intellect! They try to hit the moon with a stick. They scratch their shoes when their feet itch.

—WRITINGS OF WU-MEN (CLASSICAL ZEN
BUDDHIST TEACHER AND POET)

CONTEMPLATION

Sri Ramakrishna, Indian mystic and teacher, said: "A man cannot comprehend spiritual things with his ordinary intelligence." That's why, King Solomon noted, the four types of animals seemed so wise. Extraordinary intelligence!

The faithful student was dismissed; after three years with the master he still didn't catch on. Extraordinary spiritual stupidity.

A five-year-old was frustrated tying her shoes. "Stupid shoes," she shouted. "Stupid, stupid shoes!" "If you can't tie your shoes," she was asked, "who is stupid and who is smart?"

Stop complaining. Apply your intelligence to spiritual matters especially. The world needs intelligent peace-builders and caregivers more than ever.

ARMAMENT

◆

Once an otter came to King Solomon and complained, "Your majesty, didn't you decree that wild creatures must live in peace together?"

"And who has violated my decree?" demanded the king.

"The weasel," answered the otter. "When I went down to the river to hunt for food, I gave my babies to the weasel to watch over, and it devoured them all. He deserves to die!"

So Solomon summoned the weasel and asked him, "Did you kill the otter's children?"

The weasel replied, "Yes, your majesty, but I didn't do it on purpose. You see, I heard the woodpecker pounding on the war drums, calling me to battle, and as I rushed to fight, I accidentally trampled the otter's children."

So Solomon called the woodpecker and asked him, "Did you summon the weasel to war by thundering on your drum?"

And the woodpecker replied, "I did, my lord, but only because I saw the scorpion sharpening its dagger."

So the king had the scorpion brought before him and said, "Why were you sharpening your dagger?"

The scorpion answered, "Because I saw the tortoise polishing his armor."

The tortoise told the king, "I was only polishing my armor because I saw the crab honing its sword."

And the crab explained, "I was honing my sword because I saw the lobster swinging its javelin."

And when the lobster stood before the king, it said, "I was swinging my javelin because I saw the otter coming down to the water to devour my children."

Then the king turned to the otter and said, "The weasel is not guilty. He who sows death shall reap it."

—TRADITIONAL JEWISH TALE

CONTEMPLATION

There is a purpose for arming oneself—to pierce one's own armor. It is the spiritual coward who blames others and attacks them for their negligence or offensiveness. The true warrior fights the great jihad or holy war against the true enemy.

Hindu sacred teaching instructs us to take as a bow the great weapon of holy scripture, place in it an arrow sharpened by meditation, stretch it with a thought directed to Essence, and . . . let it go right to the mark!

INTERMEDIARY

Moses asked God to guide him to one of God's beloved ones, and a voice answered: "Go to this valley and there you will find one who loves, a chosen one who walks the path."

Moses went and found such a man, dressed in tatters, plagued by insects and other crawling animals. Moses inquired of him: "May I be of service to you?"

The man replied: "Emissary of God, I have thirst. Please bring me a cup of water."

When Moses came back with the water he saw the man was dead. He went to get cloth for a burial sheet and upon his return discovered that the body had been nearly completely devoured by a desert lion.

Moses was sorely distressed and cried out: "O God, the Almighty and All-knowing, you make mud into human beings. Some are lifted to paradise, others are put through torture. One person is happy, another miserable. This is a paradox which no one can understand."

Then Moses heard an inner voice saying, "This man relied on us for drink and then withdrew that faithful reliance. He relied, rather, on you, Moses, for his provision, trusting in you as an intermediary. His was the fault for asking for help from another, when he had been satisfied and content with us."

Your heart attaches itself over and over again to objects. You must know how to keep connected with your original sources.

—TRADITIONAL SUFI TALE

Neither is there any umpire betwixt us.

—BOOK OF JOB (HEBREW SCRIPTURES)

CONTEMPLATION

The road is not the destination. However you get to God is your business, but once you're there, it's God who must be praised, not the means to God.

If your teacher, guru, priest, minister, whatever, proclaims "Worship me"—go. Go to yourself and the direct connection you have established with the Divine.

EFFICIENCY

Seeking to appoint a truly modest man as a judge, the King sent a delegation throughout the land. The Mullah Nasreddin took this as an opportunity. When the King's emissaries, disguised as wayfarers, came to call, they found Nasreddin sitting quietly, his shoulders draped with an old fishing net. Intrigued, they asked, "Why do you wear this fishing net when you are not fishing?"

"So I will always remember that I once was a humble fisherman, even if, Allah be willing, I am bestowed a position of great esteem."

And so it came to be that they appointed Mullah Nasreddin to the high court.

Some time later, one of these officials visited the Mullah's court and, seeing him dressed in fine robes, asked Nasreddin, "Where is your fishing net?"

"Ah," the Mullah-turned-judge replied, "one no longer needs a net when the fish have already been caught."

—TRADITIONAL SUFI TALE

CONTEMPLATION

In our work activities, we understand the necessity for efficiency. No farmer would finish planting and then instead of watering, begin planting again.

So it is with our spiritual lives as well. When you've completed a task or a stage, move on. On occasion, you may want to pause for a moment of self-acknowledgment or celebration of your accomplishments. Good—this, too, is necessary in staying strongly efficient.

LOYALTY

◇

Ukpik, the big owl of the Arctic desert, was in love with Aqilgieq, the little white ptarmigan. However, Aqilgieq already had a husband whom she loved very much.

In a fit of jealousy, Ukpik killed his rival and began to woo Aqilgieq in the hope of winning her heart. But the little ptarmigan cried for her dead husband; she did not love her new suitor and began to sing a song of ridicule:

"Ukpik, go away!
With your big head
And your too large eyes
And your sorry-looking legs—
You are ugly!
Who would want you for a husband?
Who would want for a husband
A being like you?
With big knitted eyebrows,
With lashes that long,
You big dumpy owl,
With no feet and no neck!"

Ukpik, who thought himself handsome, became angry and wanted to shame Aqilgieq in return, and so he sang:
"Eater of owls! Bah!
I shall leave you!"
So saying, he flew away.

—TRADITIONAL INUIT TRIBAL TALE (NATIVE AMERICAN)

CONTEMPLATION

To whom or what are you giving your loyalty? And what are you getting in return?

Personal loyalty is often misplaced because of the fickle nature of one or (often) both of the parties. Watch carefully how those whom you respect (especially spiritual leaders) react to disagreement or desertion. Do they stay loyal to those who leave, or betray them, like Ukpik the unwise owl, with calumny and curses? You be wise; give and profess your loyalty only when you are very certain of it. To do otherwise is fraudulent and potentially very harmful.

MARCH 18
ALL AND EVERYTHING

◇

This holy god, the lord of all the gods, Amen-Râ, the lord of the throne of the two lands, the governor of Apt; the holy soul who came into being in the beginning; the great god who liveth by Maât; the first divine matter which gave birth unto subsequent divine matter! the being through whom every god hath existence; the One who hath made everything which hath come into existence since primeval times when the world was created; the being whose births are hidden, whose evolutions are manifold, and whose growths are unknown; the holy Form, beloved, terrible, and mighty in his risings; the lord of wealth, the power, Khepera who createth every evolution of his existence, except whom at the beginning none other existed; . . . who having made himself [to be seen, caused] all men to live; who saileth over the celestial regions and faileth not; . . . who though an old man shineth in the form of one that is young; . . . who made the heavens and the earth by his will; the greatest of the great, the mightiest of the mighty.

—PAPYRUS OF NESI-KHONSU
(EGYPTIAN SACRED WRITING)

CONTEMPLATION

God, as known in Egypt (Amen-Râ), as known in Polynesia (Ta'aroa), as known in Japan (Amaterasu) . . . is and contains all and everything there is. We know this; now affirm it yourself. Speak this sacred Celtic chant:

I am the wind that breathes upon the sea,
I am the wave on the ocean,
I am the murmur of leaves rustling,
I am the rays of the sun,
I am the beam of the moon and stars,
I am the power of trees growing,
I am the bud breaking into blossom,
I am the movement of the salmon swimming,
I am the courage of the wild boar fighting,

I am the speed of the stag running,
I am the strength of the ox pulling the plow,
I am the size of the mighty oak tree,
And I am the thoughts of all people
Who praise my beauty and grace.

FRUSTRATION

There was a man who desired to have a lion tattooed on his back. He told the tattoo artist what he wanted, but when he felt the first few sticks of the needle, the man began to moan: "You are murdering me. What part of the lion are you putting on?"

"I am doing the lion's tail," said the tattoo artist.

"Then leave off the tail," screamed the client.

The artist began once more. Again the man could not tolerate the needle. "Which part is it now?" he cried. "I just can't take this pain."

Said the tattooist: "It is the lion's ear."

"Let me have a lion without an ear, then." So the tattooist renewed the work. No sooner had the needle pierced the man's skin again than he writhed and shouted: "Which part of the lion are you doing now?"

"This is the lion's belly," the weary tattooist replied.

"I don't want a lion with a belly," said the man.

Distressed and frustrated, the tattoo artist paused and stood still a moment. Then he threw down his instruments and cried: "A lion with no tail, no ear, and no belly? Who could draw a creature like that? Even God did not!"

—WRITINGS OF RUMI (SUFI MYSTIC AND POET)

There are three things that occasion sorrow to a superior man [who is devoted to learning]: If there be any subject of which he has not heard, and he cannot get to hear of it; if he hear of it, and cannot get to learn it; if he have learned it, and cannot get to carry it out in practice.

—BOOK OF RITUAL (CLASSICAL CONFUCIANIST TEXT)

CONTEMPLATION

As he tells it, the Dalai Lama was a very young boy when he had his first gardening experience. He most carefully and assiduously planted his seeds in a well-prepared bed. Satisfied, he returned to his holy abode. The next day he came to see his plants and flowers growing. There was nothing growing. He went back home and came back the following day, expecting to see the new plants growing. There were none. On the third day, seeing that again nothing was there, in frustration the Dalai Lama dug out all the seeds he had placed in the garden.

Now, he laughs and says, "You plant; you water; it blossoms."

DREAM

◇

And Jacob went out from Beer-sheba, and went toward Haran. And he lighted upon a certain place, and tarried there all night, because the sun was set; and he took one of the stones of that place, and put it under his head, and lay down in that place to sleep. And he dreamed, and behold a ladder set up on the earth, and the top of it reached to heaven: and behold the angels of God ascending and descending on it. And, behold, the Lord stood above it, and said, I am the Lord, God of Abraham thy father, and the God of Isaac: the land whereon thou liest, to thee will I give it, and to thy seed; And thy seed shall be as the dust of the earth, and thou shalt spread abroad to the west, and to the east, and to the north, and to the south: and in thee and in thy seed shall all the families of the earth be blessed. And, behold, I am with thee, and will keep thee in all places whither thou goest, and will bring thee again into this land; for I will not leave thee, until I have done that which I have spoken to thee of.

And Jacob awaked out of his sleep, and he said, Surely the Lord is in this place, and I knew it not.

—BOOK OF GENESIS (HEBREW SCRIPTURES)

CONTEMPLATION

Visionary flight occurs for each of us in our dreams. We are then in a world of "reality," sometimes identical to the one we inhabit every day, sometimes vastly different. To many Native Americans, the dream life of the soul was more real and valuable than the mundane, body-inhabited one. Dreams held magical power to heal, to predict good or bad fortune, to provide wise strategies for hunting or battle. Only a fool neglected a dream; the wise did their best to "live out," in the village or forest, their strongest ones. This completed the circle and brought great rewards to both the dreamer and the community. So important were dreams to the Ojibway, who created new ritual dances from them, that "dreams" were even bought and sold. An especially powerful dream was a precious commodity indeed!

All the members of the tribe were encouraged to dream. They were given great support in manifesting their dreams, and if the dream could not be enacted, sadness and disappointment followed. But the wise elders knew that more dreams, maybe even better ones, would come in time.

May grand dreams come to you.

RENEWAL

And may we be those that renew this existence!
O Wise One, and you other Lords, and Righteousness
Bring your alliance
That thoughts may gather where wisdom is faint.

Then shall Evil cease to flourish
While those who have acquired good fame
Shall reap the promised reward
In the blessed dwelling of the Good Mind,
Of the Wise One, and of Righteousness.

—GATHAS (ZOROASTRIAN SACRED TEXT)

Can you let your body become
supple as a newborn child's?
Can you cleanse your inner vision
until you see nothing but the light?

—TAO TE CHING (CLASSICAL TAOIST TEXT)

Be melting snow.
Wash yourself of yourself.

—WRITINGS OF RUMI (SUFI MYSTIC AND POET)

CONTEMPLATION

Refreshment may come with the turning of the seasons.

New, brisk winds may move you about, yet without intention on your part, no renewal of spirit takes root.

Become like a tree. Inside, no matter the season, you are constantly renewing yourself. A tree, then, is always ready for life.

SELF-DECEPTION

Once there was a stupid man who each morning had a difficult time remembering where he had left his clothes the night before. So one day he got a pencil and a piece of paper and wrote down where he was placing each article of clothing. He placed the note next to his bed and thought to himself, "Tomorrow I will have no trouble finding my clothes!"

He awoke the next morning, quite pleased with himself, took the note, and followed it to the letter, finding each piece of clothing exactly where he had set it down. Within a short period of time, he was fully dressed.

Suddenly he was seized with a terrible thought: "But where am I?" he cried. "Where in the world am I?"

He looked everywhere but could not find himself.

"And so," taught Hanokh of Alexander, "so it is with us."

—TRADITIONAL JEWISH TALE

CONTEMPLATION

The biggest fool knows (or should know) that one cannot take care of everything by oneself.

The teacher of esoteric discipline and philosophy George Gurdjieff aimed to disabuse his students of this belief by requiring them to "do" a range of tasks. Could they, for instance, tell even one full truth?

Of course, they could!

But they couldn't really, when it came to it—not a one. Self-deception is so powerful, it takes others to mirror it back to us or we're likely to miss it.

Ask your good friends, if you still think this isn't true.

OCCUPATION

Any man who strives to do his best—
Whether his work be great or small—
Is considered to be doing
The work of a lion.

—WRITINGS OF NAGARJUNA AND SAKYA PANDIT
(BUDDHIST TEACHERS)

Says Philip, "Lord, show us the Father and we will be satisfied."

Says Jesus, "All this time I've been with you and you don't know me, Philip? Whoever has seen me has seen the Father. How can you say, 'Show us the Father'? Don't you believe that I am in the Father and the Father is in me? The things I tell you, I don't say on my own: the Father does His work, remaining in me. Believe me that I am in the Father, and the Father is in me. If you don't believe me, believe my deeds themselves."

—GOSPEL OF JOHN
(CHRISTIAN NEW TESTAMENT)

CONTEMPLATION

Once, it is said, the Buddha was visited by a man and his young daughter who made their living as acrobats. Their occupation was an extremely dangerous one, requiring the young girl to perform twists and flips from her father's shoulders. Their well-being and livelihood literally hung in the balance with each movement. The father cautioned his daughter: "We must take care of each other." "No," responded the youngster, "we must each take care of ourselves. For if you are watchful and remain stable, I will be safe. If I am careful and do my tricks correctly, you will do well also."

The Buddha smiled and agreed that the daughter's statement was both true and wise.

Children, especially wise ones, do not distinguish between the occupations of work and play. If they are doing something they like, they just keep doing it. Time seems to stand still. "Gee, Mom, do I have to come home now?" a child will complain. "Can't I do this just a little longer?"

God meant us to be active. We are here to make the things of this world sacred. It is no wonder that giving up one's life-occupation and retiring is one of the most difficult things a person is asked to do. Most retirees still have sharp minds and skilled hands. They want to keep doing things just as the enthralled child does. And why shouldn't they? No religion forbids work by a willing worker.

In God's universe, everything and everyone has a lifetime occupation.

OPINION

Every afternoon two monks strolled in the garden of the monastery. One day as they were walking along a wooded path, one of the monks asked the other if he thought it would be a pleasant experience to have a cigarette as they took their walk. The other agreed, but they decided they should ask the master of the monastery for his permission.

The next day as they came out for their walk, one of the monks was smoking a cigarette and the other was not. "We agreed to ask the master," said the monk not smoking.

"That is so, and I did," replied the other.

"I asked for permission to smoke and was refused."

"How did you ask?"

"I approached the master and said, 'Master, when I am walking and meditating in the garden is it all right if I smoke a cigarette?' and he said, 'Absolutely not!'"

"You see, my brother, it is in the asking of the question that you were refused. I approached the master and said, 'Master, when I am smoking in the garden, it is all right if I meditate?' and he said, 'Certainly.'"

—TRADITIONAL BUDDHIST TALE

CONTEMPLATION

Today concludes the joyous Hindu spring festival, Holi. Some Hindus dedicate themselves to the Divine Krishna; other Hindus to the God of Pleasure, Kama.

Though of one faith, they have different opinions. If you examine yourself, you'll find you, too, have differing opinions, even on the same subject. It mostly depends on how the matter is presented or who presents it.

This inconsistency may be humorous, but it is inconsistent with an advanced spirituality. Jesus said with conviction, "Make your yes, yes and your no, no."

DIFFERENCE

❖

A monk said, "The Way is one-pointed. All the enlightened beings are on the Way to the one true source. Why do you think that only Lord Buddha can find the road?"

The emperor replied, "Spring rain waters all the plants equally, and yet the flowering branches are long or short."

—KHOA HU (CLASSICAL VIETNAMESE BUDDHIST TEXT)

❖

When it rains, the goats say, "The enemy have beaten us," and they run away and hide themselves; but the sheep say: "Mother has oiled us," and they remain out in the rain.

When the sun burns fiercely, the sheep say, "The enemy have beaten us," and go hide themselves in the shade; but the goats say, "Mother has oiled us," and stay in the sun.

—TRADITIONAL MASAI TRIBAL SAYING (EAST AFRICA)

❖

The hands are alike but in their work they differ. So also, two cows, offspring of a single mother, may yet give differing yields of milk. Even twins are not the same in strength, or kinsmen in bounty.

—RIG VEDA (HINDU SACRED TEXT)

CONTEMPLATION

We're different, and we see things differently. Today, take a good look around you. If you're not already there, go out into the natural world. When we are among fellow humans, we tend to see ourselves as "like them," because the idea of being different carries the risk of ostracization. Up close, we can't help but notice one tree's limbs are bent and another has a doubled trunk. Each cat or cow has a remarkably different coloration and markings.

You, too, then are marked as a different and special being. It's a remarkable and wondrous thing. Rejoice in your difference.

STRENGTH

A man named Ibotite was climbing a tree. The wind blew and split the tree in two. Ibotite fell from the tree and broke his leg. "This tree is very strong," he said, "for from it I have broken my leg."

The tree then spoke. It said, "The wind is stronger than the tree."

The wind said, "No, the hill is stronger, for it blocks the wind." Ibotite was convinced. True strength was the hill's, for it blocked the wind, which split the tree, which broke the leg of Ibotite.

The hill said, "No, it is the mouse which is stronger, for it makes its nest inside the hill.

The mouse spoke of the cat, "who kills mice easily, and quickly, too." So Ibotite then believed the cat to be the strongest.

The cat denied its power, saying that it could be captured by a rope. The rope confessed that it could be cut by iron and that iron was very strong. But iron admitted that the strength of fire melted it.

"So," Ibotite thought, "now I know that fire has real strength." But fire said that water put it out. "It must be water, then, that is strong," Ibotite decided, for water put out fire, which melted iron, which cut the rope, which held the cat, which ate the mouse, which burrowed through the hill, which blocked the wind, which split the tree, which broke the leg of Ibotite.

But water claimed that a boat rode over it and that the boat was destroyed by rock, and that the rock was broken by man, and the man was subdued by a magician, and the magician was overcome by the ordeal of poison, and the ordeal dependent on God, so Ibotite knew at last where is true strength.

For God could triumph over the ordeal, which overcomes the magician, who subdues the man, who breaks the rock, which destroys the canoe, which rides over the water, which puts out fire, which melts iron, which cuts the rope, which holds the cat, which eats the mouse, which burrows into the hill, which blocks the wind, which splits the tree, which breaks the leg of Ibotite.

—TRADITIONAL TRIBAL STORY (EAST AFRICA)

CONTEMPLATION

Just where do you think you are on the chain? It's the application of strength at the right time and place, and for the right effect that's important, not the quantity of it. There are also times not to use strength. An old aikido master who could toss around eight of his best students simultaneously was asked, "If you were accosted by a gunman in an alley, what would you do?" "Run like hell," he replied.

That's strength of mind and character.

VICTORY

◇

Death means the attainment of heaven:
Victory means the enjoyment of the earth.
Therefore, rise up, Arjuna, resolved to fight!
Having made yourself alike in pain and pleasure,
profit and loss, victory and defeat, engage in this
great battle and you will be freed.

—BHAGAVAD GITA (HINDU SACRED TEXT)

◇

The force of arms cannot do what peace does.
If you can gain your desired end with sugar, why use poison?

—SOMADEVA (JAIN SACRED TEXT)

◇

Invincible is the army of the Saints
They ride the horses, chariots, and elephants
Of the understanding of the Divine Path
By conquering their vices, those five robber chiefs,
They find they have conquered the whole world.

—ADI GRANTH (SIKH SACRED TEXT)

CONTEMPLATION

After leading Muslim forces to a victorious occupation of then-pagan Mecca, Muhammad, near the end of his life, is said to have held this conquest to be of lesser importance. The greater jihad (or holy war), he told the faithful, is "the struggle against the lower self." Muhammad was a gentle man, who offered the sweet water of peace even to his sworn enemies, but he did what he had to do. Like Muhammad, we can commit to victory and be confident in its manifestation.

FISH

◇

One day, while hunting, two brothers stumbled on a magic fish hidden in a tree. The older brother was cautious, but the younger brother had a great hunger in his belly. He grasped the fish and ran home with it in great haste. There he immediately cooked and greedily devoured the magic fish.

By the next day, the young man had himself become a fish. Soon other people came to fish from the magic pond, but the voracious hunter-turned-fish would have none of that. He turned into a great bear and killed a member of each fishing party. A council was called and decided that if the bear lived, the people would be destroyed. Three men were chosen to kill the bear, but they failed and never returned. Finally, the elder brother went to kill what his brother had become. He could not do so, but because he pursued the bear so doggedly, the bear, exhausted, agreed to leave his homeland. Once the bear had gone, the fish were plentiful again and the people prospered.

—TRADITIONAL SENECA TRIBAL TALE (NATIVE AMERICAN)

◇

The master fished with a line, but not with a net.

—ANALECTS (CLASSICAL CONFUCIANIST TEXT)

CONTEMPLATION

Just who is being caught anyway? Fishing involves a certain responsibility. In our world, fish stocks of many major species have been seriously depleted by competitive commercial overfishing. Now, in order to have an adequate fish supply, we have to make extraordinary scientifically supported efforts to reestablish these varieties in the seas. We have to stop fishing altogether in certain places and create a network of man-made fish farms instead.

Isn't it better to reflect, like the older brother and Confucius, at the beginning?

MATTER

◆

A rich Chassid once came to Dov Baer, the Maggid of Mezritch, and asked for his blessing.

"How do you eat each day?" asked the Maggid.

"With great simplicity," answered the rich man. "I eat only dry bread with a little salt."

"Dry bread and salt!" exclaimed the Maggid. "Why don't you treat yourself to meat and wine since you are so wealthy?"

The Maggid continued to chastise the man until he promised to start eating a more expensive diet.

After he had left, the Maggid's disciples asked him, "What difference does it make whether he eats dry bread or meat?"

"It matters a great deal," answered the Maggid. "If he is used to rich foods, then he will understand that a poor man must at least have a dry crust with a little salt. But if he is only used to dry bread and salt, he will imagine that the poor can content themselves with stones."

—TRADITIONAL CHASSIDIC JEWISH TALE

CONTEMPLATION

It matters what you do—particularly with the material things given into your hands. Many believe that they can be profligate with their wealth and possessions or, on the other hand, terribly self-denying and have their spiritual life remain unaffected.

This is not so. The Catholic mystic Angelus Silesius put it this way: "I matter as much to God as He does to me; I need him to maintain his being, as he does mine."

MARCH 30
MOVEMENT

◇

After this there was a feast of the Jews; and Jesus went up to Jerusalem. Now there is at Jerusalem by the sheep market a pool, which is called in the Hebrew tongue Bethesda, having five porches. In these lay a great multitude of impotent folk, of blind, halt, withered, waiting for the moving of the water. For an angel went down at a certain season into the pool, and troubled the water: whosoever then first after the troubling of the water stepped in was made whole of whatsoever disease he had. And a certain man was there, which had an infirmity thirty and eight years. When Jesus saw him lie, and knew that he had been now a long time in that case, he saith unto him, "Wilt thou be made whole?" The impotent man answered him, "Sir, I have no man, when the water is troubled, to put me into the pool: but while I am coming, another steppeth down before me." Jesus saith unto him, "Rise, take up thy bed, and walk." And immediately the man was made whole, and took up his bed, and walked: and on the same day was the sabbath.

The Jews therefore said unto him that was cured, "It is the sabbath day: it is not lawful for thee to carry thy bed." He answered them, "He that made me whole, the same said unto me, 'Take up thy bed, and walk.'" Then asked they him, "What man is that which said unto thee, 'Take up thy bed, and walk'?" And he that was healed wist not who it was: for Jesus had conveyed himself away, a multitude being in that place.

—GOSPEL OF JOHN (CHRISTIAN NEW TESTAMENT)

CONTEMPLATION

Jesus moved—a lot! When the waters needed stirring, so to speak, to get the lame man up and moving or to get his disciples going on their initial missionary excursions, Jesus moved on it and quickly moved on.

So much impetus was generated in the Jesus movement in just two years!

You may be moved internally by a great desire or externally by personal or world events. Resolve to act on these impulses of your soul.

OPPOSITES

◇

Two other men, both criminals, were also led out with him to be ex-ecuted. When they came to the place called the Skull, there they cruci-fied him, along with the criminals—one on his right, the other on his left. Jesus said, "Father forgive them, for they do not know what they are doing." And they divided up his clothes by casting lots.

The people stood watching, and the rulers even sneered at him. They said, "He saved others; let him save himself if he is the Christ of God, the Chosen One."

The soldiers also came up and mocked him. They offered him wine vinegar and said, "If you are the king of the Jews, save yourself."

There was a written notice above him, which read: This is the King of the Jews.

One of the criminals who hung there hurled insults at him: "Aren't you the Christ? Save yourself and us!"

But the other criminal rebuked him. "Don't you fear God," he said, "since you are under the same sentence? We are punished justly, for we are getting what our deeds deserve. But this man has done nothing wrong."

Then he said, "Jesus, remember me when you come into your kingdom."

Jesus answered him, "I tell you the truth, today you will be with me in paradise."

—GOSPEL OF LUKE (CHRISTIAN NEW TESTAMENT)

CONTEMPLATION

On one side, the cynical criminal; on the other, the faithful one. Below, the mocking Roman soldiers; above, the accepting ruler of the universe. Oppo-sites—and in the middle of it all, Jesus. Just like us.

Jesus described himself just prior to his crucifixion as "a green tree" and wondered, "If men do these things when the tree is green, what will happen when it's dry?"

In this world, most people think in terms of opposites and opposition. Like a fresh green tree, maintain your flexibility; you will need it.

APRIL

FOOL

One day Akbar lamented to Birbal, "As emperor, I am allowed to meet only wise and learned men. Show me the ten greatest fools in the kingdom." Birbal brought him a collection of morons, figures typical of a fool in Indian literature: the first man, riding a horse, carried a bundle of firewood on his head, reasoning that the burden would be too heavy for the horse if he placed it on the saddle; another was found looking at night for a ring he had lost, searching not where he dropped it in the dark under a tree, but in a nearby clearing where the light was better. Birbal brought eight such simpletons to the king who soon reminded him that he had asked for ten. "There are ten," the trickster laughed, "including you and me—the two biggest fools of all—you for giving me such a ludicrous order, and me for obeying it!"

—TRADITIONAL HINDU TALE

Because the foolishness of God is wiser than men.

—PAUL'S FIRST EPISTLE TO THE CORINTHIANS
(CHRISTIAN NEW TESTAMENT)

CONTEMPLATION

Basically, there are two kinds of fools—fools for the world and fools for God. Nabal was the first kind. In the Old Testament, Nabal was the rich man who stupidly refused to give food to David's starving army. He spurned David's demands and then celebrated his "victory" that very night by eating and drinking to such excess that he died. When David returned, intent on destroying Nabal (and surely he would have done so), he found Nabal's wife Abigail glad to be rid of such a fool and ready to leave with the king-to-be. Nabal, the preeminently practical businessman, lost his wealth, his wife, and his life all in one day. The Hebrew name Nabal means "a fool"; it indicates someone who's got his head so caught up in the practical "reality" of things that he becomes impractical.

David, on the other hand, was a fool for God. When God granted victory to the Israelites over the Philistines, the kingly David sang out praises and, virtually naked, danced in foolish abandonment. The Holy Ark was returned! Michal, David's first wife, watched her foolish husband with haughty disgust. "I will dance like a fool on such a day," he declared, and danced on. The name David means "beloved of God."

IDENTIFICATION

◇

All of a sudden, the wise Mullah Nasreddin simply did not know who he was. He was in an unfamiliar city, but nevertheless he bolted into the bazaar in hopes of finding someone who knew him. Alas, there was no one who recognized him.

He burst into the first and closest shop, a bakery.

The baker asked, "May I be of service to you?" Yet Nasreddin was silent in response.

"Some bread, or maybe a sweetcake?" persisted the baker.

Nasreddin spoke: "I've got something to ask you first. Did you see me enter your bakery?"

"Yes, of course."

"Before today, had you ever seen me?" Nasreddin inquired.

"No, never."

"Then how," asked Nasreddin, "are you so sure it's me?"

—TRADITIONAL SUFI TALE

◇

A monk made a portrait of his master, Chao-chou, and presented it to him. Chao-chou responded, "If it is a true image of me, then you may kill me. If it is not, you ought to burn it."

—TRADITIONAL ZEN BUDDHIST ANECDOTE

CONTEMPLATION

Are you the image you or—God help us—others have of you? What then is your image of the Divine and your relationship?

Commenting on the scriptural verse, "I stood between the Lord and you," Chassidic rabbi Mikhal of Zlotchov said: "The 'I' stands between God and us. When a man says 'I' and encroaches upon the word of his Maker, he puts a wall between himself and God. But he who offers his 'I'—there is nothing between him and his Maker." Remove this unnecessary barrier; put up a blessed mirror instead.

APRIL 3
PLACE

◆

Blessed is the spot, and the house,
and the place, and the city,
and the heart, and the mountain,
and the refuge, and the cave,
and the valley, and the land,
and the sea, and the island,
and the meadow where mention
of God hath been made,
and His praise glorified.

—WRITINGS OF BAHÁ'U'LLÁH (BAHÁ'Í FAITH)

◆

When I conceived of Thee, O Mazda, as the very First and the Last, as
the most Adorable One, as the Father of the Good Thought, as the Creator of Truth and Right, as the Lord Judge of our actions in life, then I
made a place for Thee in my very eyes.

—GATHAS (ZOROASTRIAN SACRED TEXT)

CONTEMPLATION

*Today a great portion of the world's people are immigrants or refugees—or the
descendants of such. Many indigenous people have been forcibly displaced from
their native lands.*

*Is it any wonder, although generations may have passed since your people
found a new homeland, that you still feel out of place and out of sorts at times?*

There is no instant cure for this. An additional period of acculturation may help.

*The only proof against this discomfort is to find and make a place with the
Divine a present reality. If this means turning or returning to your ancestral
faith, do so. If it means accepting and adopting a new tradition or traditions,
do that.*

*When the Yogi Poondyswami was asked why he sat for ten years at a holy
shrine in India, he replied, "Mind absorbed in God; no place to go."*

PRESENCE

◇

In the year that King Uzziah died, I saw the Lord seated on a throne, high and exalted, and the train of his robe filled the temple. Above him were seraphs, each with six wings: With two wings they covered their faces, with two they covered their feet, and with two they were flying. And they were calling to one another:

"Holy, holy, holy is the Lord Almighty;
the whole earth is full of his glory."

At the sound of their voices the doorposts and thresholds shook, and the temple was filled with smoke.

"Woe to me!" I cried. "I am ruined! For I am a man of unclean lips, and I live among a people of unclean lips, and my eyes have seen the King, the Lord Almighty."

Then one of the seraphs flew to me with a live coal in his hand, which he had taken with tongs from the altar. With it he touched my mouth and said, "See, this has touched your lips; your guilt is taken away, and your sin atoned for."

Then I heard the voice of the Lord saying, "Whom shall I send? And who will go for us?"

And I said, "Here am I. Send me!"

—BOOK OF ISAIAH (HEBREW SCRIPTURES)

◇

Yang-shan asked a monk, "Where have you come from?"
The monk said, "Lu Mountain."
Yang-shan asked, "Did you go to Five Elders Peak?"
The monk said, "I didn't visit there."
Yang-shan said, "Then you didn't go to the mountain at all."

—TRADITIONAL ZEN BUDDHIST ANECDOTE

CONTEMPLATION

Moses went to the top of Mount Sinai. How do we know? When confronted by the presence of Spirit in the burning bush, Moses answered, "I am here."

Wherever you are, be present.

When working, work. When eating, be aware of the grains and particles that constitute your food. When meditating, let your thoughts be present, too, so that they can freely go their way. When making love, look in your partner's eyes and see your present self. When playing, watch the ball.

TALENT

◇

A stag came to a pool and, after drinking his fill, paused to contemplate his image in the still water. The sight of his antlers in all their sturdy splendor filled him with pride, but his legs struck him as a sorry sight, frail and scrawny. While he was thus absorbed in his thoughts, a lion suddenly burst upon him. The stag took flight and quickly outdistanced the lion—for a stag's strength is in his legs, whereas a lion's is in his heart. As long as he kept to the open ground, he continued to outrun his pursuer, but when he entered a thick forest, his antlers caught in the branches, and the lion gradually overtook him. As he was about to be killed, the stag lamented to himself: "How strange is fate! Those pitiable legs of mine almost saved me, and my noble antlers have proved my undoing!"

—FABLE OF AESOP (CLASSIC GREEK)

CONTEMPLATION

Poor deer! Like us, he mistook his real talents for the more obvious ones.

In Jesus' time a talent was a heavy, extraordinarily valuable weight of silver or gold. In his parable of the talents, Jesus castigates the ones who did little or nothing with them and praises the steward who invested his.

This is a sound principle of spiritual growth. If you have a grand talent and you now know it, you must become invested in its development, refinement, and use.

ADVICE

A certain man caught a bird in a trap. The bird says, "Sir, you have eaten many cows and sheep in your life, and you're still hungry. The little bit of meat on my bones won't satisfy you either. If you let me go, I'll give you three pieces of wisdom. One I'll say standing on your hand. One on your roof. And one I'll speak from the limb of that tree."

The man was interested. He freed the bird and let it stand on his hand. "Number one: Do not believe an absurdity, no matter who says it."

The bird flew and lit on the man's roof. "Number two: Do not grieve over what is past. It's over. Never regret what has happened."

"By the way," the bird continued, "in my body there's a huge pearl weighing as much as ten copper coins. It was meant to be the inheritance of you and your children, but now you've lost it. You could have owned the largest pearl in existence, but evidently it was not meant to be."

The man started wailing like a woman in childbirth. The bird, "Didn't I just say, *Don't grieve for what's in the past?* And also, *Don't believe an absurdity?* My entire body doesn't weigh as much as ten copper coins. How could I have a pearl that heavy inside me?"

The man came to his senses. "All right. Tell me number three."

"Yes. You've made such good use of the first two!"

Don't give advice to someone who's groggy and falling asleep. Don't throw seeds on the sand. Some torn places cannot be patched.

—WRITINGS OF RUMI (SUFI MYSTIC AND POET)

Why tell animals living in the water to drink?

—TRADITIONAL WEST AFRICAN PROVERB

CONTEMPLATION

There's a beautiful paradox about advice: The one who really needs advice rarely asks and generally doesn't listen even after soliciting or begging for it. Mark Twain, noted American author, hit the nail on the head with this piece of humorous advice: "Never try to teach a pig to sing. It wastes your time and annoys the pig."

If you really are seeking advice, don't be a pig. Be humble and responsible.

SOLITUDE

◇

Saraha married a fifteen-year-old house girl, left his home, and went into another land. He settled in a solitary place, where he practiced the Dharma while the girl went out begging for his food. One time he asked her to prepare some radishes for him. She mixed some radishes in yogurt and took them to him, but he was sitting in meditation, so she went away without disturbing him.

Saraha remained uninterruptedly in meditation for twelve years. When he finally arose, he asked, "Where are my radishes?" The serving girl replied, "How could I keep them? You have not arisen from meditational trance for twelve years. It is now spring, and there are no radishes." Saraha then said to the girl, "I will go to the mountains to meditate." But the girl replied, "A solitary body does not mean solitude. The best solitude is the mind far away from names and conceptions. You have been meditating for twelve years, yet you have not cut off the idea of radishes. What good will it do to go to the mountains?"

—TRADITIONAL TIBETAN BUDDHIST TALE

◇

I have seen nothing more conducive to righteousness than solitude. He who is alone sees nothing but God, and if he sees nothing but God, nothing moves him but the will of God.

—TRADITIONAL SUFI TEACHING

CONTEMPLATION

The renowned Zen Buddhist teacher D. T. Suzuki spoke of "walking the universe in royal solitude." If in solitude you are consecrated in thought and deed, then by all means seek it.

If in solitude you think of radishes and other such things, then you need to question whether solitude is for you just an avoidance of reality.

APRIL 8
TABOOS

◇

Before the Meamei sisters left the earth, they went into the mountains and made springs of water to feed the rivers, so that there would be water for men and women for all time. A young hunter, Karambal, was sorrowful when he heard the Meamei sisters were leaving because he had fallen in love with one of them. When he found the girl alone one day, he carried her off to be his wife. But the others sisters sent cold wintry weather to the earth to force the hunter to release their sister. After this they made their departure into the sky in search of summer, to melt the snow and ice.

It is at summertime every year that they appear, bringing the hot days with them. After the hot weather they travel far to the west, and winter comes to remind men that it is wrong to carry off women who belong to a totem that is forbidden them.

After his experience with the Meamei, Karambal went in search of another wife. He thought he had learned his lesson and was determined to choose one of the right totem. When he found the woman he wanted, he was again unfortunate, for she was already married to a great warrior whose name was Bullabogabun. With soft words Karambal induced the woman to leave her husband and go away with him.

Their life together was short and sweet. Bullabogabun followed their tracks and speedily overtook them. Karambal's love was less than his fear. Abandoning the woman, he climbed a tall tree that grew near the camp and hid in the branches. Bullabogabun saw him crouched there and lit a fire at the base of the tree. The branches caught fire, and then the trunk, which blazed like the torch of a giant in the midst of the plain. Karambal was borne up by the hungry flames and rode on them into the sky, close to the Seven Sisters. Forgetting all that he had learned, he still pursues them through the sky—Karambal, who became the star Aldebaran, the pursuer.

—TRADITIONAL ABORIGINAL AUSTRALIAN STORY

CONTEMPLATION

Every culture posits that punishment will follow when taboos are broken.

Taboos are meant to ensure personal and tribal purity and harmony, but sometimes the only way to accomplish these are by not following convention.

Jesus broke numerous taboos, social and religious. He talked to tax collectors and associated with women (often of dubious repute), Samaritans, and Romans. His followers harvested pinches of wheat berries (God forbid) on the Sabbath, and Jesus himself healed on these holiest of days.

In his place, what would you do?

RUNNING

On a road among the eastern hills a Burmese traveler heard a Hillman shouting out his ware, which happened to be rice. But as he was shouting in his own language, the Burmese traveler did not understand and asked, "What is it? What is it?" The Hillman of course knew Burmese, but like most Hillmen, he spoke it with a twang. To enlighten the Burmese stranger, he shouted the Burmese word for rice.

The Burmese word for rice was *sunn,* but because of his twang, it sounded like *sinn,* which meant "elephant." So the Burmese traveler thought that the Hillman was warning him of an approaching wild elephant, and he started to run as fast as he could. The Hillman, although perplexed at the Burman's behavior, ran behind him. The sun was hot, and the road was rough. About an hour later the two arrived at a village, and both fell down in a swoon through sheer exhaustion.

After the two strangers had been nursed back to consciousness, the villagers asked, "Why did you come running so hard? Did robbers waylay you, or did some wild animal chase you?" "This Hillman here warned me of an approaching wild elephant," explained the Burman. The Hillman looked at his fellow runner with amazement and denied that he had ever given such a warning. "Then why did you run?" the villagers asked. "It was quite simple," replied the Hillman. "I ran because he ran."

—TRADITIONAL BURMESE BUDDHIST TALE

Farmers hurry to keep up with the seasons, merchants run after profit, craftsmen chase new skills, officials hunt power; the pressure of their circumstances makes this so. But farmers meet with both water and drought, merchants with both gain and loss, craftsmen with both success and failure, officials with both good luck and ill; destiny makes this so.

—BOOK OF LIEH-TZU (CLASSICAL TAOIST TEXT)

CONTEMPLATION

Just exactly what is it we are running after? Ah . . . maybe that's the problem.

If we are to run, it ought to be, Saint Thomas à Kempis declared, "flying, running, and rejoicing" into a life of spirit. What a glorious prize!

APRIL 10

SERVING

◇

A Chassid complained to Rabbi Wolf that certain persons were turning night into day, playing cards. "That is good," said the zaddik. "Like all people they want to serve God and don't know how. But now they are learning to stay awake and persist in doing something. When they have become perfect in this, all they need to do is turn to God—and what excellent servants they will make for him then!"

—TRADITIONAL CHASSIDIC JEWISH ANECDOTE

◇

All of creation is a servant of God.

—SAYING OF MUHAMMAD (PROPHET OF ISLAM)

CONTEMPLATION

Whose interests are you serving if, once you have turned to serving God, you indiscriminately throw yourself into the world of the needy?

You can't help everyone, and in fact you can't help anyone who is unreceptive or antagonistic.

Krishna, God on earth to devoted Hindus, knew this well from his experience here. His guidance on serving:

Do not share this wisdom with anyone who lacks in devotion or self-control, lacks the desire to learn, or scoffs at me. Those who teach this supreme mystery of the Gita to all who love me perform the greatest act of love; they will come to me without doubt. No one can render me more devoted service; no one on earth can be more dear to me.

BELIEF

◇

In the holy city of Safed lived one of the Lamed-Vav-Tzaddikim, one of the thirty-six secret saints. He was very poor, but he shared his crust with those who were even poorer than he. Yet he wished to disguise his virtue so that no one might say he was good and cause him to fall into the error of self-righteousness.

As the Passover holidays came near, this meek saint fell gravely ill and was no longer able to earn his crust. His wife and children now suffered hunger. And since they were proud, no one knew of their plight. But the saint consoled his household, "Have faith in God—He raises up the fallen!"

No one in Safed knew of the holy man's trials except Rabbi Isaac Luria, "The Holy Lion," the Master of the secret wisdom of the Kabbalah. With wanderer's staff in hand and a knapsack on his back, he went forth to aid the hidden saint.

"Sholom aleichem!" the traveler greeted him.

"Aleichem sholom!" answered the saint. "Are you looking for someone?"

"No, but I'm in trouble," sighed the stranger. "I have no place to spend the holy Passover."

"I've nothing to give you, but you're welcome to stay with me," answered the saint.

The traveler was grateful and rejoiced in his good fortune.

"Here are a hundred dinar," he said to the saint. "Prepare the Passover feast!"

"What is your name?" asked the hidden saint in amazement.

"Rabbi Nissim they call me," the stranger replied.

On the first night of Passover, the saint sat down to read the Seder service that tells of the liberation of the Jews from their bondage in Egypt, but he would not begin without the stranger, who had not returned yet from the synagogue. He waited and waited, but in vain. Rabbi Nissim seemed to have disappeared. Suddenly, in a flash of illumination, the identity of the stranger became clear to him. No doubt the good Lord had sent an angel from Heaven to help him in his need!

Yet neither he nor anyone else knew that this Rabbi Nissim (Miracles) was none other than The Holy Lion, the Ari himself.

—TRADITIONAL JEWISH TALE

◇

Believe nothing because a wise man said it,
Believe nothing because it is generally held.
Believe nothing because it is written.
Believe nothing because it is said to be divine.
Believe nothing because someone else believes it.
But believe only what you yourself judge to be true.

—TEACHING OF THE BUDDHA

CONTEMPLATION

There is great power in belief. Consider this Chassidic Jewish joke:

A disciple once was boasting rapturously before strangers about his rabbi:

"My rabbi, long life to him! He fasts every single day except, of course, on the Sabbath day and on holidays."

"What a lie!" mocked a cynic. "I myself have seen your rabbi eating on weekdays!"

"What do you know about my rabbi?" the faithful disciple snorted disdainfully. "My rabbi is a saint and very modest in his piety. If he eats, it is only to hide from others the fact that he is fasting!"

To have the power to bring miracles, belief must be connected to experience and knowledge of the soul.

FRIENDS

◇

A bird in a secluded grove sings like a flute.
Willows sway gracefully with their golden threads.
The mountain valley grows the quieter as the clouds return.
A breeze brings along the fragrance of the apricot flowers.
For a whole day I have sat here encompassed by peace,
Till my mind is cleansed in and out of all cares and idle thoughts.
I wish to tell you how I feel, but words fail me.
If you come to this grove, we can compare notes.

—WRITINGS OF FA-YEN (ZEN BUDDHIST
TEACHER AND POET)

◇

It is because one antelope will blow the dust from the other's eye that two antelopes walk together.

—TRADITIONAL AKAN TRIBAL PROVERB (WEST AFRICA)

◇

All jealousies have vanished in the society of the Saints.
All are my friends now, there being no enemy or stranger.

—ADI GRANTH (SIKH SACRED TEXT)

CONTEMPLATION

Two peasants, Ivan and Boris, the oldest and dearest of friends, were drinking in a tavern one night, when Ivan, who had been drinking far more heavily, turned to his friend and asked, "Do you love me?"

"Of course, I love you," Boris answered.

"But do you love me?" Ivan asked again.

"You know I love you," Boris told him.

Now Ivan pleaded with his friend: "Do you love me?"

"Yes, yes," Boris said. "I love you."

Ivan broke into tears. "If you really love me, you'd know what was wrong with me!"

Go, meet your friend today.

WILLINGNESS

◇

Possessing worlds multiple quenches not the rage of avarice and
desire.
A thousand million feats of intellect bring not emancipation.
How then to be true to the Creator?
Through obedience to His Ordinance and Will.

—ADI GRANTH (SIKH SACRED TEXT)

◇

The poor Mullah Nasreddin had been saving his money for a long time
to buy a new shirt. At last he had enough, and full of excitement, he went
to the tailor's shop to place his order. The tailor took the Mullah's meas-
urements and, that completed, told him: "Come back in a week and—
Insh'allah, as God wills it—your shirt will be done and waiting for you."

Nasreddin, keeping to this agreement, returned, to the hour, one week
later, and asked for his new shirt. "Something has come up," the tailor informed the poor Mullah. "Your shirt is not yet finished, but—*Insh'allah,*
as God wills it—tomorrow your shirt will be ready."

Nasreddin dutifully returned the next day. "I'm sorry, Mullah," the
tailor apologized, "but it's still not quite done. Try again tomorrow
and—*Insh'allah,* as God wills it—it will be ready."

"How long then will it take," Nasreddin inquired this time, "if you
leave Allah out of it altogether?"

—TRADITIONAL SUFI TALE

CONTEMPLATION

*Whose will is it anyway? Most, perhaps all, of us have experienced a time of
grace, when everything we wish to have happen does. It may have been on the
basketball court, where every pass made it to the receptive hands of a teammate
and the most improbable shots went in for scores. Or at work, you call up about
that deal you've pitched for months, and a newly assigned manager, who just
loves it, answers.*

*It seems like luck or Divine intervention. On reflection, didn't you use your
will—strongly and powerfully—to practice those extra minutes or to make
that last attempt to conclude the deal? You were willing—so God is with those
of willing spirit.*

RESPONSIBILITY

◆

"You see, the kingdom of the skies is like a certain landowner who went out with the dawn to hire workers for his vineyard. After agreeing with the workers on a drachma a day, he sent them off to his vineyard. And going out around nine o'clock he saw others standing around the marketplace idle and said to them, 'You go off to my vineyard, too, and I will pay you what is reasonable,' and they went. Going out around noon and three, he did the same.

"Around five o'clock he went out and found others standing and said to them, 'Why are you standing here all day with nothing to do?'

"They said to him: 'Nobody hired us.'

"He said to them, 'You go off to my vineyard, too.'

"So when it got late, the owner of the vineyard said to his foreman: 'Call the workers and pay them their wages going from last to first.' And the ones from five o'clock came forward and received a drachma apiece. And when the first ones came forward, they thought they'd get more, but they got a drachma, too.

"On receiving it, they started grumbling at the landowner, saying, 'These last ones worked one hour, and you make them equal to us who bore the burden and the heat of the day!'

"But he answered one of them, saying, 'I'm not cheating you, pal. Didn't you agree with me on a drachma? Take what's yours and go your way.'"

—GOSPEL OF MATTHEW (CHRISTIAN NEW TESTAMENT)

CONTEMPLATION

Surely this boss was acting irresponsibly, wasn't he, in bestowing an equal amount even to those to whom he had made no promise? Yet as the vineyard owner was later to point out, he had the ability to respond (responsibility) to his circumstances as he chose. Having violated no laws or covenants, he was free to act.

Similarly, the latecomers acted responsibly by being present and ready for hire and fulfilling their commitment to work the rest of the day. They, too, were then able to receive their pay.

Responsibility has nothing to do, then, with position or timing. It's about presence and integrity.

HALLOWED

The great Tao flows everywhere.
All things are born from it,
yet it doesn't create them.
It pours itself into its work,
yet it makes no claim.
It nourishes infinite worlds,
yet it doesn't hold on to them.
Since it is merged with all things
and hidden in their hearts,
it can be called humble.
Since all things vanish into it
and it alone endures,
it can be called great.
It isn't aware of its greatness;
thus it is truly great.

—TAO TE CHING (CLASSICAL TAOIST TEXT)

May the road rise to meet you,
May the wind be always at your back,
May the sun shine warm upon your face,
The rains fall soft upon your fields,
And until we meet again, may
God hold you in the hollow of his hand.

—TRADITIONAL CELTIC BLESSING (IRELAND)

CONTEMPLATION

Today is a fine day, a very fine day indeed. The sun may be shining or not, yet wherever you are, you can sense loveliness and a certain confidence in the world today.

It is a good day to venture forth or to stay home. A sweet day to frolic with friends or to spend the whole day meditating.

In Hebrew there is a phrase for a day like today—Hakol B'Seder. It means all is in divine order. And so it is.

TERRITORY

Behold, my brothers, the spring has come;
The earth has received the embraces of the sun
And we shall soon see the results of that love!

Every seed is awakened and so has all animal life.
It is through this mysterious power that we too have our being
And we therefore yield to our neighbors,
Even our animal neighbors,
The same right as ourselves, to inhabit this land.

—TEACHING OF SITTING BULL (NATIVE AMERICAN)

CONTEMPLATION

To native people, the land they live in is holy, sacred, imbued with God-ness. The Lakota, the people of Chief Sitting Bull, call this Wakan. So powerful is Wakan that ancestral spirits, like Sitting Bull's, when they do return, return to their own land.

Yet when the white peoples came to Turtle Island (the Americas), with very few exceptions they were welcomed and given free rein in the new territories. Even now, after a five-hundred-year holocaust, many Native Americans are allowing non-natives into what had been exclusively their own spiritual territory.

Why?

Sitting Bull said that all creatures have a right to inhabit this lovely land. When you close off territory, you miss out on things of great beauty and worth.

APRIL 17

ANGER

◇

The fly cannot be driven away by getting angry at it.

—TRADITIONAL IDOMA TRIBAL WISDOM (WEST AFRICA)

◇

And he says to the fellow with the withered hand, "Come in the middle here." And he says to them, "Which is allowed on the Sabbath: doing good, or doing evil? Saving lives, or killing?" They are silent. And looking around at them in a fury, grief-stricken at the stoniness of their hearts, he says to the fellow, "Reach out your hand."

—GOSPEL OF MARK (CHRISTIAN NEW TESTAMENT)

◇

Why, sir, do you get angry at someone
Who is angry with you?
What are you going to gain by it?
How is he going to lose by it?
Your physical anger brings dishonor on yourself:
Your mental anger disturbs your thinking.
How can the fire in your house burn the neighbor's house
Without engulfing your own?

—BASAVANNA (CLASSICAL HINDU WRITINGS)

CONTEMPLATION

Is it okay to get angry? Jesus did. He cursed the unfruitful fig tree; he tongue-lashed the hypocritical ultra-religionists of his day; and let's not forget he whipped and chased the corrupt wheeler-dealers right out of the Temple! How do we reconcile this with his and so many other divine teachings on the inefficacy and blasphemy of anger? It's all about time and place. Remember the Temple.

RIDING AN ASS

◇

Nasreddin and his donkey were riding along the path when something startled the donkey. All of a sudden, the donkey was galloping at break-neck speed.

Some of Nasreddin's friends, astonished to see him speeding past, cried out, "Where are you going so fast, Nasreddin?"

"Don't ask me," he shouted back. "Ask my donkey!"

—TRADITIONAL SUFI TALE

◇

Two diseases in connection with the practice of Zen: "The first is to ride an ass in search of the ass. The second is to ride the ass and refuse to dismount."

—WRITINGS OF CH'ING-YÜAN (ZEN BUDDHIST TEACHER)

◇

And when they got close to Jerusalem and came to Bethphage on Mount Olive, at that point Jesus sent off two of his students, saying to them, "Go on into the village ahead of you, and right away you'll come upon a donkey tied up and her foal with her. Untie them, and bring them to me. And if anyone says anything to you, you'll say, 'The master needs these,' and they'll send them right back with you." This happened so as to fulfill what was spoken by the prophet:

Tell your daughter Zion,
Here comes your king,
Gently, mounted on donkey-back,
And on its foal, the beast of burden's son.

—GOSPEL OF MATTHEW (CHRISTIAN NEW TESTAMENT)

CONTEMPLATION

In ancient times (and even in some places today), an ass or donkey was, for most people, the only available and affordable means of transportation and con-veyance.

Spiritually speaking, this describes the limited options and choices people had in terms of religion or practice. If the "spiritual vehicle" of your locality took you, out of control and willy-nilly (like the unfortunate Nasreddin) in a direction you had no desire to go, well, that was just the nature of the beast.

Extraordinary people (like Jesus or aged Zen monks) with extraordinary wills could get off the ass they were riding, gain perspective, and if required, find and train a new one.

We are lucky. There are lots of asses to ride; there is a growing body of information about their qualities; and there are many expert riders offering instruction.

Steadfast and devoted, the right ass will always get you there.

KARMA

◆

A man went out to cut wood; he tried the trees as he passed along, but they were all bad; so he climbed up a rock, and at last he saw a good tree. So then he took a rock and rolled it down from under the tree; the rock rolled down, and went into a bush, and disturbed a duiker. The duiker ran and got into a bush. A buffalo happened to be lying in the bush. The buffalo ran away, for it was afraid of the duiker. The buffalo met a man who was hunting, and it killed him. But when people saw the vultures, they ran, and found the man dead. They did not know what had killed him. So then they stood and asked one another, "What was this man killed by?"

Then they saw a hoofprint. "A fine hoofprint of a buffalo! When the buffalo went out to kill the man, where did it come from?" They followed it by the hoofprint; they found it came out of a bush. They said, "When the buffalo came out of the bush, what disturbed it?" They looked for what had disturbed it. They saw the hoofprint of the duiker. They asked one another, "When the duiker went to disturb the buffalo, where did it come from?" and they followed it also by the hoofprint; they said: "The duiker came out of this bush. But when the duiker went to come out of this bush, what disturbed it?"

They saw the rock; they said, "This rock, when it went to disturb the duiker, where did it come from?" They said, "This rock came from those rocks." They followed it up and said, "What pushed this rock?" They found the rock had come from under a tree. They said, "Oh! It was a man who moved the rock, in cutting down this tree." And so then they went and said: "Whatever did that man want? There were plenty of trees; he went and disturbed things that were lying still."

—TRADITIONAL ISWANA TRIBAL TALE
(SOUTHERN AFRICA)

CONTEMPLATION

Traditionally Hindus understand there to be three kinds of karma. They don't just cavalierly say, as we sometimes do in the West when something bad happens, "Well, that's just your karma," or "You must have bad karma." The first form of karma is samchit; this is what we carry into a new life as a result of actions in

previous incarnations on earth. Samchit creates for each person a predisposi-
tion to have desires for certain types of things in life. The second type, pararab-
dha karma, also is from the past. This karma determines a person's nature and
talents; it is our fate to be born as a particular personality in a particular time
and place. Thirdly, there is agami. This is karma which has nothing to do with
the past. This "now karma" means that our present actions, every single one of
them, will bear fruit, sweet or sour, at some future moment.

A traditional Buddhist tale gets right to the point:

> The Buddha in his travels encountered a Jain, whose practice consisted of standing still on one leg. The Buddha asked him, "Would you tell me why you are doing this? What will this practice of standing on one leg do for you?"
>
> The Jain replied, "Through this practice I am working out my karma, it will free me of all past karma."
>
> The Buddha asked him, "How much have you worked out so far?" The Jain replied, "I could not say." The Buddha then asked, "How much karma do you still have left to work out?" The Jain again replied, "I do not know." Lastly the Buddha asked him, "But how will you know when you have finished working out your karma?" The Jain could only answer again, "This I do not know."
>
> At this reply the Buddha spoke to him, saying, "It is time for you to set aside this practice and to understand the path to the end of suffering. It lies within the truth of each moment, here and now."

PRIORITIZATION

◆

Seek first the Kingdom, and all else will be added to you.

—GOSPEL OF LUKE (CHRISTIAN NEW TESTAMENT)

◆

Once there was a man who was not only a very pious Jew, he was also a most devoted Kabbalist. Over the years he had increased his studies of sacred texts, his prayers, and holy invocations to the point where they occupied virtually the whole day. This poor man slept only a few hours each night, for he was certain not to miss either of the especially holy times for prayer to the Almighty, midnight and dawn. With all this he expected to be showered with blessings, but instead he waxed poorer and poorer and found it difficult to support his family, even in the most meager way. With his wife's encouragement, he went to see his teacher, a Kabbalistic master, known for his great wisdom.

The rabbi heard the man's story and asked only, "What do you do the first thing in the morning?" The man answered truthfully: "I wash and purify myself for morning prayers. I prepare my ritual garments properly so as to make sure I am right before my God." And so he spoke, describing how he completed the morning prayers so righteously that it was well into the day before he began work, taking care of his animals and other tasks.

The rabbi said only, "Feed your chickens," and with that ended the meeting.

The poor man spent many a day pondering the mystical meaning of his rabbi's instructions, "Feed your chickens." Deciding it could only mean that he had been lacking in truly nourishing his soul and that he needed to pray even more, he did just that. And of course, his affairs (if it was possible) took a turn even more for the worse.

In desperation he returned to the rabbi and told the master of his woes. Once again the rabbi simply said, "Feed your chickens."

On the way home, the good man received a revelation—a divine revelation. The rabbi meant exactly what he said: "Feed your chickens"—the actual, real chickens his family kept to both eat and sell for profit.

The next morning he fed the chickens the very first thing, and from then on he prospered in all ways.

—TRADITIONAL JEWISH TALE

CONTEMPLATION

Don't follow anyone's rules! They may be fine for a particular individual or even in general for an entire religious community. Only you, in your heart, know what comes first. Right now.

"Amen," the completion to many prayers, means "so be it." Not "so was it" or "so it will be." When you are with what is your highest priority, acting on it, this is a heavenly state of being.

BIRTHING

◇

That the father and mother give birth to him from mutual desire, so that he is born from the womb, let this be known as his physical birth. But that birth which is given, according to the ordinance, through the Savitri, by the preceptor who has mastered the Vedas, that is the true birth, the unaging and immortal.

—MANU DHARMA SASTRAS (HINDU SACRED TEXT)

◇

Then they moved on from Bethel. While they were still some distance from Ephrath, Rachel began to give birth and had great difficulty. And as she was having great difficulty in childbirth, the midwife said to her, "Don't be afraid, for you have another son." As she breathed her last— for she was dying—she named her son Ben-Oni. But his father named him Benjamin.

So Rachel died and was buried on the way to Ephrath (that is, Bethlehem). Over her tomb Jacob set up a pillar, and to this day that pillar marks Rachel's tomb.

—BOOK OF GENESIS (HEBREW SCRIPTURES)

CONTEMPLATION

Birthing is a most glorious thing! Astrophysicists, Native Americans, and Egyptians alike claim we are born of star-matter. The hieroglyph for the God Amun signified the sun in the pregnant belly of the mother.

Yet as blessed as birthing is, it is accompanied by risk. Don't take your own spiritual labors and birthing nonchalantly. Just as you do when a mother is pregnant with child, you take great care and choose wisely the setting for any and all upcoming birthings.

APRIL 22
EARTH

◇

The earth is the Lord's and the fullness thereof.

—PSALM 24 (HEBREW SCRIPTURES)

◇

They gave sacrifice to the East,
The East said, "Give it to the West,"
The West said, "Give it to God,"
God said, "Give it to the Earth, for Earth is senior."

—TRADITIONAL IDOMA TRIBAL PRAYER (WEST AFRICA)

◇

The solid sky
The cloudy sky
The good sky
The straight sky

The earth produces herbs
The herbs cause us to live
They cause long life
They cause us to be happy.

The good life,
May it prevail with the air
May it increase
May it be straight to the end.

Sweet Medicine's earth is good.
Sweet Medicine's earth is complete.
Sweet Medicine's earth follows the eternal ways.
Sweet Medicine's earth is washed and flows.

—SONG OF TIS-TSIS-TAS / TRADITIONAL CHEYENNE
(NATIVE AMERICAN)

CONTEMPLATION

Today, many of us rarely touch the earth. How can we, sitting all day in a chair in a tall building?

Go to the earth. Bend down and place your hands on her. Take your shoes off, as Moses did on Mount Sinai, and feel this ground as holy ground, your holy ground.

Is this not sweet?

DRAGON

◇

And I saw an angel coming down out of heaven, having the key to the Abyss and holding in his hand a great chain. He seized the dragon, that ancient serpent, who is the devil, or Satan, and bound him for a thousand years. He threw him into the Abyss, and locked and sealed it over him, to keep him from deceiving the nations anymore until the thousand years were ended. After that, he must be set free for a short time.

—BOOK OF REVELATION (CHRISTIAN NEW TESTAMENT)

◇

And the parched ground shall become a pool and the thirsty land springs of water: in the habitation of dragons, where each lay, shall be grass with reeds and rushes.

—BOOK OF ISAIAH (HEBREW SCRIPTURES)

CONTEMPLATION

You can't keep a good dragon down forever. The dragon in you, the large wild, terrible creature whose lair is the cave of your soul, will have its way eventually.

The Tsalagi (Cherokee) saw their dragons as protectors. Certainly they are powerful beasts. Let yours out for regular exercise. It just might turn out to be an ally.

DIVERSITY

◆

The Magician had made the world but felt that something was missing. Then it came to him that what he wanted on this earth was some beings like himself, not just animals. "How will I make them?" he thought. First he built himself a *horno,* an oven. Then he took some clay and formed it into a shape like himself.

After a while the Magician said, "He must be ready now." He took the image and breathed on it, whereupon it came to life. "Why don't you stand up?" said Man Maker. "What's wrong with you?" The creature barked and wagged its tail. "Ah, oh my, Coyote has tricked me," he said. "Coyote changed my being into an animal like himself.

So Man Maker tried again. "They should be companions to each other," he thought. "I shouldn't make just one." He shaped some humans who were rather like himself and identical with each other in every part.

"What's wrong here?" Man Maker was thinking. Then he saw. "Oh my, that won't do. How can they increase?" So he pulled a little between the legs of one image, saying, "Ah, that's much better." With his fingernail he made a crack in the other image. He put some pleasant feeling in them somewhere. "Ah, now it's good. Now they'll be able to do all the necessary things." He put them in the *horno* to bake.

"They're done now," Coyote told him. So Man Maker took them out and made them come to life.

"Oh my, what's wrong?" he said. "They're underdone; they're not brown enough. They don't belong here—they belong across the water someplace." He scowled at Coyote.

So the Magician tried again, making a pair like the last one and placing them in the oven.

"No, they aren't done yet," said Coyote. "You don't want them to come out too light again; leave them in a little longer."

"Well, all right," replied Man Maker. They waited, and then he took them out. "Oh my. What's wrong? These are overdone. They're burned too dark." He put them aside. "Maybe I can use them some other place across the water. They don't belong here."

For the fourth time Man Maker placed his images inside the oven.

This time the Magician did not listen to Coyote but took them out when he himself thought they were done. He made them come to life, and the two beings walked around, talked, laughed, and behaved in a seemly fashion. They were neither underdone nor overdone.

"These are exactly right," said Man Maker. "They are beautiful."

—TRADITIONAL PIMA TRIBAL STORY (NATIVE AMERICAN)

CONTEMPLATION

Bahá'u'lláh, the messenger of the Bahá'í faith, addressed humankind thusly: "Ye are all leaves of one tree and the fruits of one branch." Yet so many diverse colors to these leaves, so many diverse tastes to these fruits. Ain't diversity grand?

CONSIDERATION

One day the ruler of heaven had some important business in a distant part of his realm, which would keep him busy for three days. He therefore transferred all his duties to the old mother of heaven and asked her to look after everything in his absence. "But for these three days you must grant man's every wish," he warned her. The mother of heaven smilingly nodded in agreement.

She left her palace, mounted a cloud, and traveled everywhere to attend to the wishes of men. As she was passing a river, she heard a man say, "Heavenly Father, send wind. If a wind blows, I can sail away." She ordered the wind to blow and went on her way.

Soon she arrived at a large orchard where she heard someone calling, "Heavenly Father, please tell the wind to stop. If it goes on any longer, all my pears will fall." This was too much for the mother of heaven, and she returned to her palace.

The next morning she set off again and heard an old voice saying, "Heavenly Father, send rain. If it rains, I can sow my beans." She sent a heavy rain, which lasted all day.

But in the evening on her way home, she heard a young girl say with a sigh, "Heavenly Father, please send fine weather. Otherwise all the ginger I am drying will rot." The mother of heaven could bear it no longer, and with a groan she returned to her palace. During the third day she kept to her room.

In the evening the ruler of heaven returned from his journey, and she told him all that had happened and begged him to forgive her. He said generously, "It isn't very difficult. You must send a strong wind to blow on the rivers, and a gentle breeze on the pears. Rain must fall during the night in order to sow beans, and the sun shine during the day to dry the ginger."

The mother of heaven understood at once, but asked with a smile, "Why didn't you tell me before?"

—TRADITIONAL CHINESE TALE

CONTEMPLATION

We are taught as children to be considerate of others. This, we are told, will please them and keep us out of trouble. It does neither.

In your spiritual life, it serves you well to be reflective, but it is a disservice to be considerate and especially obsequious in meeting others' alleged needs. Take care of yourself.

POTENCY

A man, dining at an inn, placed an order for boiled eggs. The owner brought the bill himself—ten gold pieces.

The diner immediately protested that this was an unheard-of price for a few boiled eggs.

The sly innkeeper responded, "If I had kept the eggs, instead of serving them to you, they would have become chickens, and these chickens in their time would produce more chickens, and these in turn would beget more, and these untold thousands of chickens are far more valuable than the measly ten gold coins I am billing you."

The diner took his case to court before Nasreddin, the judge. Nasreddin often convened his court in his home, for he claimed that "justice is found in life," and so that is where the diner and the innkeeper put forth their arguments.

After listening to the two adversaries, Nasreddin took some grain seeds and boiled them for a few minutes. Then he took the seeds out to his garden and, one by one, planted them.

"Whatever are you doing?" the two men asked.

"I am planting these grain seeds," replied Nasreddin, "so that they will grow and bear more grain seeds."

"How can seeds that have been boiled grow and produce more?" the innkeeper scoffed.

"That is exactly this court's opinion," Nasreddin declared. "The decision is made."

—TRADITIONAL SUFI TALE

CONTEMPLATION

Some spiritual adepts, especially those who have achieved a certain advancement, go off half-cocked; they have wild imaginings of glorious states of being and consequent adoration.

Don't mistake accomplishment with potency. Just because you can do something at an initial level—say, for example, sit still for an hour—does not mean that you will become an ascended master.

Take your spiritual life one moment, one day at a time. Be a good spiritual egg.

EVANESCENCE

The past flies away,
coming months and years do not exist:
Only the pinprick of this moment
belongs to us.

We decorate this speck of a moment—time—
by calling it a flowing river or a stream.

But often I find myself alone
in a desert wilderness,
straining to catch the faint echo of
unfamiliar sounds.

—WRITINGS OF MAHMUD SHABISTARI
(SUFI MYSTIC AND POET)

Could it be true we live on earth?
On earth forever?

Just one brief instant here.

Even the finest stones begin to split,
even gold is tarnished,
even precious bird-plumes
shrivel like a cough.

Just one brief instant here.

—NEZAHUALCOYOTL
(TRADITIONAL AZTEC TEACHING)

CONTEMPLATION

What makes cherry blossoms so beautiful is how briefly they last. Butterflies, too, come and go quickly in our view.

Just for a moment
An orange butterfly waves
From yellow rose-tip.

When one has no regret, evanescence creates meaning.

FLOWERING

◇

As a garland-maker chooses the right flowers, choose the well-taught path of Dharma, and go beyond the realms of death and of the gods.

Like a lovely flower, full of color but lacking in fragrance, are the words of those who do not practice what they preach. Like a lovely flower full of color and fragrance are the words of those who practice what they preach.

The scent of flowers or sandalwood cannot travel against the wind; but the fragrance of the good spreads everywhere. Neither sandalwood nor the *tagara* flower, neither lotus nor jasmine, can come near the fragrance of the good.

Faint is the scent of sandalwood or the *tagara,* but the fragrance of the good rises high to reach the gods.

—DHAMMAPADA (BUDDHIST SACRED TEXT)

CONTEMPLATION

Korah and many of the Israelite princes, disgruntled at what they perceived to be the exclusive leadership of Moses and Aaron, confronted them. What made Aaron so special that he was High Priest, lording over the other tribal leaders?

Moses said, "Let's put this to a test." Each tribal leader, Aaron included, was to bring his staff to the tent of reckoning, to be left there overnight.

Behold! Almond flowers, the next day, sprang from the head of one staff only—Aaron's. Sweet almond flowers grow not from bitterness, but from goodness and service.

APRIL 29
POVERTY

◇

I have naught but my destitution
To plead for me with Thee.
And in my poverty I put forward that destitution as my plea.
I have no power save to knock at Thy door,
And if I be turned away, at what door shall I knock?
Or on whom shall I call, crying his name,
If Thy generosity is refused to Thy destitute one?
Far be it from Thy generosity to drive the disobedient one to
    despair!
Generosity is more freehanded than that.
In lowly wretchedness I have come to Thy door,
Knowing that degradation there finds help.
In full abandon I put my trust in Thee,
Stretching out my hands to Thee, a pleading beggar.

—TRADITIONAL SUFI PRAYER

◇

But if you will not know yourselves, you dwell in poverty and it is you
who are that poverty.

—GOSPEL OF THOMAS (APOCRYPHAL CHRISTIAN TEACHING)

CONTEMPLATION

Want a rich life? The prophet Muhammad declared, "Poverty is my glory." He knew well enough that a declaration of spiritual bankruptcy before God not only was honest self-evaluation but also initiated a pathway to God's mercy and generosity.

We are spiritually ignorant and irresponsible when we make worldly poverty an exemplary virtue. If we are all poor, who then will help the poor? To be charitable—this, too, God wants of us.

BETRAYAL

◆

In the spring, at the time when kings go off to war, David sent Joab out with the king's men and the whole Israelite army. They destroyed the Ammonites and besieged Rabbah. But David remained in Jerusalem.

One evening David got up from his bed and walked around on the roof of the palace. From the roof he saw a woman bathing. The woman was very beautiful, and David sent someone to find out about her. The man said, "Isn't this Bathsheba, the daughter of Eliam and the wife of Uriah the Hittite?" Then David sent messengers to get her. She came to him, and he slept with her. (She had purified herself from her uncleanness.) Then she went back home. The woman conceived and sent word to David, saying, "I am pregnant."

So David sent this word to Joab: "Send me Uriah the Hittite." And Joab sent him to David. When Uriah came to him, David asked him how Joab was, how the soldiers were, and how the war was going. Then David said to Uriah, "Go down to your house and wash your feet." So Uriah left the palace, and a gift from the king was sent after him. But Uriah slept at the entrance to the palace with all his master's servants and did not go down to his house.

When David was told, "Uriah did not go home," he asked him, "Haven't you just come from a distance? Why didn't you go home?"

Uriah said to David, "The ark and Israel and Judah are staying in tents, and my master Joab and my lord's men are camped in the open fields. How could I go to my house to eat and drink and lie with my wife? As surely as you live, I will not do such a thing!"

Then David said to him, "Stay here one more day, and tomorrow I will send you back." So Uriah remained in Jerusalem that day and the next. At David's invitation, he ate and drank with him, and David made him drunk. But in the evening Uriah went out to sleep on his mat among his master's servants; he did not go home.

In the morning David wrote a letter to Joab and sent it with Uriah. In it he wrote, "Put Uriah in the front line where the fighting is the fiercest. Then withdraw from him so he will be struck down and die."

—SECOND BOOK OF SAMUEL (HEBREW SCRIPTURES)

CONTEMPLATION

How innocently this story begins: "In the spring . . ." All the parties in this drama of betrayal—King David, Bathsheba, Uriah—were originally innocent, yet only Uriah remained so. It is all too easy to fall into acts of betrayal, and betrayal leads to more betrayal. You are not immune, from either the possibility or the consequences. Just as King David handed over Uriah to death (and Bathsheba complied), so was their newborn baby son given into God's hands in death—the beginning of a legacy of bloodshed in the royal family.

MAY

GLORY

◇

Glory be to that God who is in the fire, who is in the waters, who is in the plants and trees, who is in all things in this vast creation. Unto that Spirit be glory and glory.

—SVETASVATARA UPANISHAD (HINDU SACRED TEXT)

◇

Now when Solomon had made an end of praying, the fire came down from heaven, and consumed the burnt-offering and the sacrifices; and the glory of the Lord filled the house. And the priests could not enter into the house of the Lord, because the glory of the Lord had filled the Lord's house. And when all the children of Israel saw how the fire came down, and the glory of the Lord upon the house, they bowed themselves with their faces to the ground upon the pavement, and worshipped, and praised the Lord, saying, For he is good; for his mercy endureth forever.

—SECOND BOOK OF CHRONICLES (HEBREW SCRIPTURES)

CONTEMPLATION

A glorious day today, for dancing around the Maypole, for calling on the Divine Spirit, like Moses, like Solomon, to show you the glory!

May your heart, your house, your world be filled with glory!

REPUTATION

◇

At the royal court, wise men of the realm convened to judge the Mullah Nasreddin. His crime: challenging the authority of the state itself by badmouthing the King's most illustrious courtiers—his philosophers, logicians, and lawyers. Nasreddin had confessed calling these men "ignorant, mixed up, unclear, and indecisive."

The King allowed Nasreddin to speak first. "May paper and writing instruments be brought to the court chamber," Nasreddin requested. The King so ordered. "Give them to each of the first seven wise men," Nasreddin said, and this also was done.

"Without consulting or comparing," Nasreddin continued, "let each one answer this single question: 'What is bread?'"

They did, and when the papers were given to the King, he read the answers of the seven wise men.

"Bread is a food."

"Bread is a combination of flour and water," explained the next.

"Bread is a gift of God," put forth the third.

"Dough that has been baked."

"Mutable, relative to how you mean the word 'bread,'" replied the fifth.

"A substance that provides nutrition."

"Nobody really knows," the seventh and last confessed.

"When this group of wise men can conclude what bread is," Nasreddin declared, "then it will be possible for them to make decisions in other matters—like my case. Is it appropriate to entrust people like this with determining truth and righteousness? Isn't it odd that though they've been eating bread their whole lives, they can't agree about what it is, and yet these same good men can be so certain about my character?"

—TRADITIONAL SUFI TALE

CONTEMPLATION

The spiritual teachers, theologians, and religious leaders of our time, like that of Nasreddin's, generally hold a high reputation. But on what is this reputation based? They've published a book or books and been seen on television? Or they hold an esteemed position and are called guru or bishop or rabbi?

Such titles alone are insufficient to indicate whether such people merit their good reputation. Do they take risks and break from orthodox positions when necessary? Do they reveal their own miscues and times of doubt?

One's reputation must be founded on more than show.

LAND

Hear the word of the Lord, O people of Israel;
for the Lord has a controversy with the inhabitants of the land.
There is no faithfulness or kindness,
and no knowledge of God in the land;
there is swearing, lying, killing, stealing, and committing adultery;
they break all bounds and murder follows murder.
Therefore the land mourns,
and all who dwell in it languish,
and also the beasts of the field,
and the birds of the air,
and even the fish of the sea are taken away.

—BOOK OF HOSEA (HEBREW SCRIPTURES)

CONTEMPLATION

Thus Chief Seathl spoke:

Every part of this country is sacred to my people. Every hillside, every valley, every plain and grove, has been hallowed by some fond memory or some sad experience of my tribe.

Even the rocks that seem to lie dumb as they swelter in the sun along the silent seashore in solemn grandeur thrill with memories of past events connected with the fate of my people, and the very dust under your feet responds more lovingly to our footsteps than to yours, because it is the ashes of our ancestors, and our bare feet are conscious of the sympathetic touch, for the soil is rich with the life of our kindred. . . .

And when the last red man shall have perished from the earth and his memory among white men shall have become a myth, these shores shall swarm with the invisible dead of my tribe, and when your children's children shall think themselves alone in the field, the store, the shop, upon the highway, or in the silence of the woods, they will not be alone. . . . At night when the streets of your cities and villages shall be silent, and you think them deserted, they will throng with the returning hosts that once filled and still love this beautiful land.

To see and feel the land as beautiful, you must do beautiful acts there. If your ancestors have desecrated the land, then sanctify it again. Save the land, so that it will be beautiful for the generations to come.

CONFLICT

What have you done? The voice of your brother's blood cries out to me from the earth. Now then, you are cursed by the ground which has opened its mouth to take the blood of your brother from your hand. When you work the land, it will no longer give you its strength. You are to be a wanderer and a nomad on the earth.

—BOOK OF GENESIS (HEBREW SCRIPTURES)

◇

——————— ——————— ———————	*above*	*Ch'ien*	*The Creative, Heaven*
—— —— —— —— ———————	*below*	*K'an*	*The Abysmal, Water*

Heaven and water go their opposite ways.
The image of conflict.

The attribute of the creative is strength, that of the abysmal is danger, guile. Where cunning has force before it, there is conflict.

Conflict develops when one feels oneself to be in the right and runs into opposition.

If a man is entangled in a conflict, his only salvation lies in being so clear-headed and inwardly strong that he is always ready to come to terms by meeting the opponent halfway.

To carry on the conflict to the bitter end has evil effects even when one is in the right, because the enmity is then perpetuated.

—I CHING (CLASSICAL CHINESE TEXT)

CONTEMPLATION

This day is one of the world's newest holidays. It is Yom ha-Shoah, the Day of the Holocaust, in which Jews and many other peoples remember the terrors and destruction of that horrific conflict.

In the context of human-time, the Holocaust of more than fifty years ago is very recent, fresh, and raw. It was not the first (Cain and Abel), nor was it even the last one of our century.

One is spiritually naive, and therefore in a sense blasphemous and inhumane, in dismissing conflict as a reality. Remember, even Hitler thought he was right. So did (and still do) numerous leaders of religions.

The important thing, the I Ching concludes, is to avoid conflict—that is, to bring it to nothing. To do this we must make peace at the beginning and not let conflict get started. Remember: make peace this day.

FORM

As rivers flowing into the ocean find their final peace and their name and form disappear, even so the wise become free from name and form and enter into the radiance of the Supreme Spirit who is greater than all greatness.

In truth, who knows Brahman becomes Brahman.

—UPANISHADS (HINDU SACRED TEXT)

A branch of blossoms does not look like seed.
A man does not resemble semen. Jesus came from Gabriel's breath,
    but he is not in that form.
The grape doesn't look like the vine.
Loving actions are the seed of something completely different, a
    living-place.
No origin is like where it leads to.
We can't know where our pain is from.
We don't know all that we've done.
Perhaps it's best that we don't.
Nevertheless we suffer for it.

—WRITINGS OF RUMI (SUFI MYSTIC AND POET)

CONTEMPLATION

In the fields around your home, a multiplicity of flower-forms bloom. If God does not favor poppies over, say, roses, why then should you exclude certain teachers on the basis of their physical appearance, clothing, or language?

Sufis tell of a group of foreigners stranded in the desert. Terribly hungry and thirsty, at nightfall they each in turn cry out for the one food they yearn for most. Arguments immediately ensue. "No, that's not it," each protests. Then in their own language, each proclaims, "It's . . . !" A free-for-all of fighting breaks out among the whole group when a caravan of camels laden with grapes approaches. Grapes! Grapes!

It was exactly what they had all prayed for. Grapes!

BODY

◇

Would it not be a sign of great ignorance, my daughters, if a person were asked who he was, and could not say, and had no idea who his father or his mother was, or from what country he came? Though that is great stupidity, our own is incomparably greater if we make no attempt to discover what we are, and only know that we are living in these bodies, and have a vague idea, because we have heard it and because our Faith tells us so, that we possess souls. As to what good qualities there may be in our souls, or Who dwells within them, or how precious they are—those are things which we seldom consider and so we trouble little about carefully preserving the soul's beauty. All our interest is centered in the rough setting of the diamond, and in the outer wall of the castle—that is to say, in these bodies of ours.

—WRITINGS OF TERESA OF ÁVILA (CHRISTIAN MYSTIC)

◇

Behold this beautiful body, a mass of sores, a heaped-up lump, diseased, much thought of, in which nothing lasts, nothing persists.

Thoroughly worn out is this body, a nest of diseases, perishable. This putrid mass breaks up. Truly, life ends in death. Like gourds cast away in autumn are these dove-hued bones. What pleasure is there in looking at them?

Of bones is this house made, plastered with flesh and blood. Herein are stored decay, death, conceit, and hypocrisy.

Even ornamented royal chariots wear out. So, too, the body reaches old age. But the Dhamma of the Good grows not old. Thus do the Good reveal it among the Good.

—DHAMMAPADA (BUDDHIST SACRED TEXT)

CONTEMPLATION

On a day like today the wind may be blowing across one's face and the warm sun reaching into one's very bones. Sometimes, it just feels so good to have a body!

The temptation, especially in these times of good feeling, is to believe that we are this body and that without its sensitivity and response, we have no presence or meaning in this life. We are a "nobody."

A child told me once at a memorial service that he wished his friend's body was in an open casket, instead of having been cremated. He explained: "That way I could see it, and I'd know he was gone."

Bodies can be one place, even while alive, and we, our attention, mind, and souls in another.

MAY 7

ENLIGHTENMENT

Then I sought solitude, and here I soon became very melancholy. I would sometimes fall to weeping, and feel unhappy without knowing why. Then for no reason, all would suddenly be changed, and I felt a great, inexplicable joy, a joy so powerful that I could not restrain it, but had to break into song, a mighty song, with only room for the one word: joy, joy! And I had to use the full strength of my voice. And then in the midst of such a fit of mysterious and overwhelming delight, I became a shaman. I could see and hear in a totally different way. I had gained my *quameneq,* my enlightenment, the shaman-light of brain and body, and this in such a manner that it was not only I who could see through the darkness of life, but the same light also shone out from me, imperceptible to human beings, but visible to all the spirits of earth and sky and sea, and these now came to me and became my helping spirits.

—ACCOUNT OF IGLUIK SHAMAN

For now we see through a glass, darkly. But then face to face.

—PAUL'S FIRST EPISTLE TO THE CORINTHIANS
(CHRISTIAN NEW TESTAMENT)

CONTEMPLATION

If enlightenment can be described, it must be not as a state but as a process, not as light, but as a transformation to light.

Seen in this way, it is not only a select few high and holy personalities (you can fill in the blank with the one or ones you so revere) but all of us who are experiencing some form or degree of enlightening.

Did you understand today a passage in a book that previously was hidden from understanding?

Did you speak more gently to a child where in the past you may have shouted in anger?

Did you negotiate a new agreement with someone you had been darkly disputing?

That's enlightenment!

PATH TO FREEDOM

◇

For freedom Christ has set us free; stand fast therefore and do not submit again to a yoke of slavery. . . . For you were called to freedom; only do not use your freedom as a fleshly opportunity but through love be servants of one another.

—PAUL'S EPISTLE TO THE GALATIANS
(CHRISTIAN NEW TESTAMENT)

◇

Open yourself, create free space;
release the bound ones from their bonds!
Like a newborn child, freed from the womb,
Be free to move on every path.

—ATHARVA VEDA (HINDU SACRED TEXT)

CONTEMPLATION

His Holiness, the Dalai Lama, has taken this vow: "With the wish to free all beings, I shall always go for refuge to the Buddha, Dharma, and Sangha until I've reached full enlightenment."

The heart of Buddhist teaching is to achieve, through the eightfold path, liberation not only for oneself but for all.

The Dalai Lama acknowledges that the Jewish people have a secret of spiritual survival. "They," he says, ". . . even in very difficult times, . . . remember their liberation from slavery to freedom."

Can one be free when another is not?

MOTIVATION

◆

One Rosh Hashanah the Berdichever Rebbe searched for someone to blow the shofar. He asked each one who came forward, "What are your mystic thoughts when you blow the shofar?"

None of the answers he heard pleased him.

Finally one man came to him who confessed that he was unlearned and had no mystic thoughts.

"Then what do you think about when you blow the shofar?" the Berdichever asked him.

"I think of my four unmarried daughters who need husbands," the man replied. "I say to God, 'I am doing my duty to You by blowing the shofar. Now You do Yours for me.'"

And the Berdichever chose him to blow the shofar that year.

—TRADITIONAL CHASSIDIC JEWISH STORY

CONTEMPLATION

So you think you've got it tough. You've been working on something—a farm, a project, raising a child—for quite a while now, and there's still so much more to do.

Look at yourself. Do you still have the original spark of motivation and are just a little worn out by the effort, or has something radically changed in you?

Other people and divine forces will be motivated to add to your efforts when your motivation is strong. Are you expecting otherwise?

OPEN

◆

On a Sabbath, Jesus was teaching in one of the synagogues, and a woman was there who had been crippled by a spirit for eighteen years. She was bent over and could not straighten up at all. When Jesus saw her, he called her forward and said to her, "Woman, you are set free from your infirmity." Then he put his hands on her, and immediately she straightened up and praised God.

Indignant because Jesus had healed on the Sabbath, the synagogue ruler said to the people, "There are six days for work. So come and be healed on those days, not on the Sabbath."

The Lord answered him, "You hypocrites! Doesn't each of you on the Sabbath untie his ox or donkey from the stall and lead it out to give it water? Then should not this woman, a daughter of Abraham, whom Satan has kept bound for eighteen long years, be set free on the Sabbath day from what bound her?"

When he said this, all his opponents were humiliated, but the people were delighted with all the wonderful things he was doing.

Then Jesus went through the towns and villages, teaching as he made his way to Jerusalem. Someone asked him, "Lord, are only a few people going to be saved?"

He said to them, "Make every effort to enter through the narrow door, because many, I tell you, will try to enter and will not be able to. Once the owner of the house gets up and closes the door, you will stand outside knocking and pleading, 'Sir, open the door for us.'

"But he will answer, 'I don't know you or where you come from.'

"Then you will say, 'We ate and drank with you, and you taught in our streets.'

"But he will reply, 'I don't know you or where you come from. Away from me, all you evildoers!'"

—GOSPEL OF LUKE (CHRISTIAN NEW TESTAMENT)

CONTEMPLATION

Just as in the world of commerce, in the world of spirit there are openings.

Jesus came and offered healing and hope; very few were open to him and accepted. In fact, many condemned him and tried to close him off from the faithful.

When you get an opening, take it and consider yourself blessed. Given the chance, wouldn't you have wanted to be on a Galilean roadway when Jesus marched by?

MOTHER

◆

There was something formless yet complete
That existed before heaven and earth;
Without sound, without substance,
Dependent on nothing, unchanging,
All pervading, unfailing.
One may think of it as the Mother of all things under heaven.
Its true name we do not know.

—TAO TE CHING (CLASSICAL TAOIST TEXT)

◆

As a mother, even at the risk of her own life, protects and loves her child, her only child, so let a man cultivate love without measure toward the whole world, above, below, and around, unstinted, unmixed with any feeling of differing or opposing interests. . . . This state of mind is the best in the world.

—TEACHING OF THE BUDDHA

◆

Paradise is found at the feet of the mothers.

—TEACHING OF MUHAMMAD (PROPHET OF ISLAM)

CONTEMPLATION

As children, most of us would go to our mothers and be assured of a loving reception. With fathers, generally speaking, this was (and is) more problematic. We went to our mothers when we wanted to know love. The saintly Sri Ramakrishna asked:

Who can ever know God? I don't even try. I only call on Him as Mother. Let Mother do whatever She likes. I shall know Her if it is Her will: but I shall be happy to remain ignorant if She wills otherwise. . . . The young child wants only his mother. He doesn't know how wealthy his mother is, and he doesn't even want to know. He knows only "I have a mother, why should I worry?"

So, in a sense we can thank God for mothers and thank mothers for God. Say a blessing of gratitude to and for the mother or mothers in your life.

BELONGING

◇

Grant me the ability to be alone;
May it be my custom to go outdoors each day
among the trees and grasses,
among all growing things
and there may I be alone,
and enter into prayer
to talk with the one
that I belong to

—TEACHINGS OF NACHMAN OF BRATZLAV
(CHASSIDIC JEWISH RABBI)

◇

I commend to you our sister Phoebe, a servant of the church in Cenchrea. I ask you to receive her in the Lord in a way worthy of the saints and to give her any help she may need from you, for she has been a great help to many people, including me.

Greet Priscilla and Aquila, my fellow workers in Jesus Christ. They risked their lives for me. Not only I but all the churches of the Gentiles are grateful to them.

Greet also the church that meets at their house.

Greet my dear friend Epenetus, who was the first convert to Christ in the province of Asia.

Greet Mary, who worked very hard for you.

Greet Andronicus and Junias, my relatives who have been in prison with me. They are outstanding among the apostles, and they were in Christ before I was.

Greet Ampliatus, whom I love in the Lord.

Greet Urbanus, our fellow worker in Christ, and my dear friend Stachys.

Greet Apelles, tested and approved in Christ.

Greet those who belong to the household of Aristobolus.

Greet Herodion, my relative.

Greet those in the household of Narcissus who are in the Lord.

Greet Tryphena and Tryphosa, those women who work hard in the Lord.

Greet my dear friend Persis, another woman who has worked very hard in the Lord.

Greet Rufus, chosen in the Lord, and his mother, who has been a mother to me, too.

Greet Asyncritus, Phlegon, Hermes, Patrobas, Hermas, and the brothers with them.

Greet Philologus, Julia, Nereus and his sister, and Olympas and all the saints with them.

Greet one another with a holy kiss.

All the churches of Christ send greetings.

—PAUL'S EPISTLE TO THE ROMANS
(CHRISTIAN NEW TESTAMENT)

CONTEMPLATION

Two beautiful pictures of belonging—to God alone and ultimately, in Rabbi Nachman's case, and to a community of friends and fellow believers, in Paul's.

To belong, one must, like the good rabbi, be in a longing state of heart, praying for communion with the beloved. And you must also, like Saint Paul, be long in your relations and commitment.

IMITATION

Nasreddin, being very, very thirsty but alas very, very poor as well, looked for a way to pilfer some juicy fruit from the fruit seller's stall. The fruit seller, however, maintained a fox to watch out for such fellows as Nasreddin.

"Crafty fox," the merchant loudly addressed the guardian of his precious fruit, "every man may be a thief." Nasreddin listened intently from across the street. "Watch everyone," the fruit seller gave his parting instructions. "Notice whenever anyone does anything, and think if this activity has any bearing on the safety of your charge." With that, he left.

The first man the fox spied was Nasreddin, who instantly lay down as if asleep. The fox went to investigate, then concluded, "He's sleeping; he's not doing anything."

Soon the watchful fox could not help but fall asleep himself. Then Nasreddin awoke and helped himself to all the fruit he desired.

—TRADITIONAL SUFI TALE

CONTEMPLATION

Imitation is fraught with challenges and devoid of benefits.

Should you eventually succeed in speaking like, or looking like, or acting like someone else, even someone very admirable, what will you have achieved? The fox found this fruitless; so will you.

INTIMACY

◆

A great crowd followed [Jesus] and thronged about him. And there was a woman who had had a flow of blood for twelve years, and who had suffered much under many physicians, and had spent all that she had, and was no better but rather grew worse. She had heard the reports about Jesus, and came up behind him in the crowd and touched his garment. For she said, "If I touch even his garments, I shall be made well." And immediately the hemorrhage ceased; and she felt in her body that she was healed of her disease. And Jesus, perceiving in himself that power had gone forth from him, immediately turned about in the crowd, and said, "Who touched my garments?" And his disciples said to him, "You see the crowd pressing around you, and yet you say, 'Who touched me?'" And he looked around to see who had done it. But the woman, knowing what had been done to her, came in fear and trembling and fell down before him, and told him the whole truth. And he said to her, "Daughter, your faith has made you well; go in peace, and be healed of your disease."

—GOSPEL OF MARK (CHRISTIAN NEW TESTAMENT)

◆

The Lord is near to all who call upon Him, to all who call upon Him in truth.

—PSALM 145 (HEBREW SCRIPTURES)

CONTEMPLATION

How did Jesus know? Somehow even at a distance, Jesus and the yet-to-be-healed woman had established a real intimacy, not just a closeness but a bond of faith.

Muhammad is said to have claimed that Allah is closer to us than our jugular vein. This may be true. If we desire our most intimate partner to be continually close, we must, at least on occasion, call the beloved's name. This call is prayer.

FAMILY

◇

In a moonlit night on a spring day,
The croak of a frog
Pierces through the whole cosmos and turns it into a single family!

—WRITINGS OF CHANG CHIU-CHI'EN
(CLASSICAL ZEN BUDDHIST POET)

◇

We are part of the earth and it is part of us. . . . The perfume flowers are our sisters; the deer, the horse, these are our brothers; the rocky crest, the juices in the meadow, the body heat of the pony and men all belong to the same family.

—SAYING OF SEATHL (NATIVE AMERICAN CHIEF)

CONTEMPLATION

It's over a hundred years since Charles Darwin put forth the theories of natural selection and evolutionary change, linking humans to all living (and some extinct) creatures. He proposed: "If we choose to let conjecture run wild, then animals, our fellow brethren in pain, disease, suffering and famine—our slaves in the most laborious works, our companions in our amusements—they may partake of our origin in one common ancestor—We may be all netted together."

Netted together as family. This requires a new thinking, like Jesus' when he asked, "Who is my mother; who are my brothers and sisters?"

Well, who are?

PERFUME

Six days before the Passover, Jesus arrived at Bethany, where Lazarus lived, whom Jesus had raised from the dead. Here a dinner was given in Jesus' honor. Martha served, while Lazarus was among those reclining at the table with him. Then Mary took about a pint of pure nard, an expensive perfume; she poured it on Jesus' feet and wiped his feet with her hair. And the house was filled with the fragrance of the perfume.

But one of his disciples, Judas Iscariot, who was later to betray him, objected, "Why wasn't this perfume sold and the money given to the poor? It was worth a year's wages." He did not say this because he cared about the poor but because he was a thief; as keeper of the money bag, he used to help himself to what was put into it.

"Leave her alone," Jesus replied. "It was intended that she should save this perfume for the day of my burial. You will always have the poor among you, but you will not always have me."

Meanwhile a large crowd of Jews found out that Jesus was there and came, not only because of him but also to see Lazarus, whom he had raised from the dead.

—GOSPEL OF JOHN (CHRISTIAN NEW TESTAMENT)

Ointment and perfume rejoice the heart: so doth the sweetness of a man's friend that cometh of hearty counsel.

—BOOK OF PROVERBS (HEBREW SCRIPTURES)

CONTEMPLATION

When Lazarus came out of his tomb, renewed to life, he stank to high heaven! The sweet perfume of his burial ointments and of his dear friend Jesus' love were not enough to prevent this.

Yet this is the most we can do for each other in this life—to offer perfume. We tend to see this, like Judas, as wasteful and unimportant. It's not. Go to your friend, your beloved; bring the balm of your love.

DOVETAILING

◇

Once there were two brothers who shared a field. All the grain the farm produced, they shared evenly.

One of the brothers lived alone; the other had a wife and children. One day the single brother thought, "It's not right that I get half of everything. After all, my brother has a family to feed." So every night he secretly took part of his share and put it in his brother's storehouse.

The married brother, too, was thinking about their situation. "My brother has no one, no wife and children to love him and to take care of him when he's old." He decided to secretly bring a good portion of his grain to his brother's granary each night.

So, to both brothers' surprise, their stockpiles were continually replenished and remained evenly shared. Finally, one night, each carrying a sack of grain to deposit, halfway between their houses, the two brothers met. They immediately realized what was going on, and in great love, embraced.

God witnessed their coming together and proclaimed: "This is a holy place—a place of love—and here it is my temple shall be built."

—TRADITIONAL JEWISH TALE

◇

When two people are at one
in their inmost hearts
They shatter even the strength of iron
or of bronze
And when two people understand each other
in their inmost hearts
Their words are sweet and strong
like the fragrance of orchids.

—I CHING (CLASSICAL CHINESE TEXT)

CONTEMPLATION

Native Americans often begin and conclude prayers by saying Mitakuye Oyasin—all my relations—having been taught that the four-leggeds, the winged ones, plants, rocks, water, everything is related.

It is one thing to hold this thought in one's mind, quite another to experience this communion and communication with the spirit of another. When you find yourself in such a relationship (even with some newly discovered aspect of yourself), ride with it. This is a special horse!

VALUE

◆

A dervish named Aman made his way to see the great Caliph Haroun Ar-Rashid. The simple saint asked the Caliph, "If you were dying of thirst and stranded in the desert, what would you offer for a cup of water?"

Without hesitation, Haroun Ar-Rashid bellowed, "Half my kingdom!"

"And," Aman inquired, "what if this water you drank so bloated your bladder it endangered your life? What would you give then for the tablets that would remedy the condition and save your life?"

"The other half of my kingdom, certainly," proclaimed the wise Caliph.

"Why is it, then," Aman asked, "that you put such high value on your kingdom when by your own admission it is worth only a cup of water and a handful of medicinal tablets?"

—TRADITIONAL SUFI TALE

◆

Because we have heard and because faith tells us so, we know we have souls. But we seldom consider the precious things that can be found in this soul, or who dwells within it, or its highest value.

—WRITINGS OF TERESA OF ÁVILA (CHRISTIAN MYSTIC)

CONTEMPLATION

Modern societies ask that we do what the pious Haroun ar-Rashid, when he became aware of the situation, was unwilling to continue doing. Today's commercial machine demands that we sacrifice everything—our interests, our time, and even our health—for the sake of profit.

And where does the value of all this labor and enterprise go? Mostly into the hands of a very, very few.

What value are we obtaining from this system, when poll after poll indicate that the rich are no happier today than they were decades ago, nor are the poor?

If you value your life, place some of your energy and resources into spiritual labor and enterprise. You are worth it.

AWE

◇

The gods enter your being, some calling out and greeting you in fear. Great saints sing your glory, praying, "May all be well!"

The multitudes of gods, demigods, and demons are all overwhelmed by the sight of you. O mighty Lord, at the sight of your myriad eyes and mouths, arms and legs, stomachs and fearful teeth, I and the entire universe shake in terror.

O Vishnu, I can see your eyes shining; with open mouth, you glitter in an array of colors, and your body touches the sky. I look at you and my heart trembles; I have lost all courage and all peace of mind.

When I see your mouths with their fearful teeth, mouths burning like the fires at the end of time, I forget where I am, and I have no place to go. O Lord, you are the support of the universe; have mercy on me!

—BHAGAVAD GITA (HINDU SACRED TEXT)

◇

When the soul looks upon this Divine Sun, the brightness dazzles it. . . . And very often it remains completely blind, absorbed, amazed, and dazzled by all the wonders it sees.

—WRITINGS OF TERESA OF ÁVILA
(CHRISTIAN MYSTIC)

CONTEMPLATION

When Jacob beheld a vision of heaven and heard God speak a beautiful promise, he awoke from his dream not in delight but in terror. "How dreadful is this place!" he shouted.

It seems that we can only take so much of the Divine. With some experience of it, we feel awe; too much, and we feel awful. Absorb what you can now; when you're ready, you'll receive more awareness.

PERSONAL

◆

Now those that sealed were Nehemiah, the Tirshatha, the son of Hachaliah, and Zidkijah, Seraiah, Azariah, Jeremiah, Pashur, Amariah, Malchijah, Hattush, Shebaniah, Malluch, Harim, Meremoth, Obadiah, Daniel, Ginnethon, Baruch, Meshullam, Abijah, Mijamin, Maaziah, Bilgai, Shemaiah: these were the priests.

And the Levites: both Jeshua the son of Azaniah, Binnui of the sons of Henadad, Kadmiel;

And their brethren, Shebaniah, Hodijah, Kelita, Pelaiah, Hanan, Micha, Rehob, Hashabiah, Zaccur, Sherebiah, Shebaniah, Hodijah, Bani, Beninu. The chief of the people; Parosh, Pahathmoab, Elam, Zatthu, Bani, Bunni, Azgad, Bebai, Adonijah, Bigvai, Adin, Ater, Hizkijah, Azzur, Hodijah, Hashum, Bezai, Hariph, Anathoth, Nebai, Magpiash, Meshullam, Hezir, Meshezabeel, Zadok, Jaddua, Pelatiah, Hannan, Anaiah, Hoshea, Hananiah, Hashub, Hallohesh, Pileha, Shobek, Rehum, Hashabnah, Maaseiah, and Ahijah, Hanan, Anan, Malluch, Marim, Baanah.

—BOOK OF NEHEMIAH (HEBREW SCRIPTURES)

CONTEMPLATION

Why the long lists of who begat whom? Why the detailed genealogy of Jesus? Why did Nehemiah include each name of those who affixed their seal to a new covenant?

Because spirituality is a personal thing—the most personal dimension of one's life.

No one else can have insights for you, as yours are very personal and unique. No other person is authorized to make a commitment to practice or faith except you.

Each of the persons Nehemiah named, from Zidkijah to Baanah, sealed not with a single communal seal but with their own personal one. So did Nehemiah.

MAY 21
ENERGY

◆

"May I ask what this 'floodlike ch'i' is?"

"It is difficult to explain. This is a ch'i which is, in the highest degree, vast and unyielding. Nourish it with integrity and place no obstacle in its path, and it will fill the space between heaven and earth. It is a ch'i that unites righteousness and the Way. Deprive it of these, and it will collapse. It is born of accumulated rightness and cannot be appropriated by anyone through a sporadic show of rightness. Whenever one acts in a way that falls below the standard set in one's heart, it will collapse. . . . You must work at it and never let it out of your mind. At the same time, while you must never let it out of your mind, you must not forcibly help it grow either."

—WRITINGS OF MENCIUS
(CLASSICAL CHINESE TEACHER)

◆

As water descending on mountain crags wastes its energies among the gullies, so he who views things as separate wastes his energies in their pursuit.

—YAJUR VEDA (HINDU SACRED TEXT)

CONTEMPLATION

Today great energy (ch'i) and life force may be available to you. How are you going to use it?

If you assume your newfound energy allows you to overpower people and events and force them to your bidding, guess again. Attempting this will only backfire, and soon even your normal level of energy will be gone.

Today apply your energy where it is most needed, and it will be magnified. How will you know what to do? Be humble and ask.

DESIRE

◇

Gluscabi loved duck so much that whenever he could, he went out in the lake hunting for them. One fine day a great wind came up, so great that it blew Gluscabi's canoe right back to the shore. He paddled out again, and the wind blew even stronger, pushing him back once more. Four times he tried, and every time he got blown back.

Frustrated, for he so loved duck, he went to see his wise grandmother and asked, "Grandmother, what makes the wind blow?" She said, "Gluscabi, why do you want to know?" (for she knew he didn't really care about the source of the wind but had some selfish motive for asking). He replied, very simply, "Oh, just because." Grandmother said to herself, "I know he's up to something, but I will tell him anyway."

Grandmother spoke: "The wind comes from the Great Eagle, way up on top of the highest mountain. He flaps his wings, and that's what makes the wind blow." "Ah-ha," thought Gluscabi to himself.

So Gluscabi decided to climb the highest mountain to meet the Great Eagle. As he got closer and closer to the mountaintop, the wind blew stronger and stronger—so strongly that it blew off all of Gluscabi's clothes and even all his hair. Eventually, with great effort, Gluscabi succeeded in reaching the mountaintop and meeting the Great Eagle.

The Great Eagle trusted Gluscabi, for no human had ever reached the lofty peak before. But Gluscabi took advantage of the Great Eagle when he wasn't looking, pinned the Great Eagle's wings, and put him under a rock. He felt happy as he walked back down the mountain. Now that the Great Eagle was powerless, there would be no more wind, and Gluscabi could go duck hunting to his heart's content.

By the time he got back, the air was very still and hot—Gluscabi could hardly breathe. When he took his canoe back to the lake, he found the water so stagnant, foul, and mucky, he could barely paddle. So much to his dismay, he could not go duck hunting after all. Because Gluscabi stopped the wind, all this happened.

Gluscabi returned to see Grandmother, where he always went after he'd gotten into trouble. She asked, "What have you done? Tell me." Gluscabi confessed, and Grandmother said, "Well, it seems that you'd best go see the Great Eagle again." Gluscabi obeyed his grandmother's wishes. He untied the Great Eagle, released him from underneath the rock, and the wind began to blow again. The breath of life returned to the land.

—TRADITIONAL ABENAKI TRIBAL TALE
(NATIVE AMERICAN)

CONTEMPLATION

No permissible pleasure, the Talmud says, is to be denied to us. Jewish teaching goes even further—to not enjoy the earthly pleasures of food, sexual intimacy, celebration of song and dance—this was really a sin.

Where and when do we miss the target (the literal meaning of the Greek word typically translated as "sin") in aiming for our desires? Where and when are we true archers? Not only our individual balance and well-being but that of the world at large is affected by our cumulative accuracy. It is imperative to give much attention to the details of our desires and the playing-out of them.

JUSTICE

◆

When the Báb was imprisoned, a devoted disciple came to him. He brought a gift of honey to sweeten the Báb's days of servitude, and humbly offered it to his Master.

The Báb inspected the gift and instantly determined the honey to be of inferior quality. He asked the devoted follower how much he had paid for it. The poor fellow named the price. The Báb told him it was too much to pay and commanded that he return it at once to the seller.

The humble servant prepared to leave, in his mind wondering at the unexpected behavior of the Báb in refusing his gift. Once again the Báb ordered him to return the honey.

The Báb then explained to the disciple that the dishonest merchant had dishonored both the disciple and himself by this unjust transaction. Returning the honey would give the merchant an opportunity to see the error in what he had done and to set things right.

—TRADITIONAL BAHÁ'Í TALE

◆

Correct me, O YHVH, only in justice, not in Your wrath, lest You reduce me to nothing.

—BOOK OF JEREMIAH (HEBREW SCRIPTURES)

CONTEMPLATION

As the Báb adjured, no gift, no matter how sweet in appearance, can be truly offered if injustice, like a swarm of bees, is hovering angrily around it. He knew very well of injustice. He and his community of followers were severely persecuted, and tens of thousands were massacred by the rulers of Persia in the mid-1800s.

On this day in 1844 he publicly and formally declared himself as the Báb, the "Gate" to a new spiritual understanding. This was the origin of the Bahá'í faith, which was founded on concerns for justice, especially for women, at a time when such concerns were viewed as virtually blasphemous, not only in the upper echelons of the Islamic world but even in the supposedly democratic West. Today the highest authority in the Bahá'í faith is actually called the Universal House of Justice.

Though reduced in numbers to nearly nothing, the Báb's adherents, even after his execution, never retaliated in anger.

Perhaps the Báb had left them the sweetest honey of a gift—the knowledge that justice must be demanded of oneself first and that justice lived out will prevail.

FOLLOWING

◆

Once there lived a monk who was not too learned. His sermons were very boring to listen to, and there came a time when no one offered him alms food. So he migrated to another village, but benefiting from his previous experience, he did not go to the village monastery but resided in a makeshift monastery of bamboo and thatch on the edge of a small forest. As forest-dwelling monks were believed to be taking advanced meditative exercises, they were never expected to give any sermon, and the villagers flocked to the forest monastery, bringing offerings of alms food and robes.

After some weeks some of the villagers begged the monk not to expose himself any further to the ferocious animals of the forest, but to come and dwell in the village monastery. But the monk prudently remained in the forest. The fame of the forest-dwelling monk spread to the neighboring villages, and more and more people visited him and begged of him to come and dwell in their village monasteries. Then the monk thought to himself, "I must please my followers in some way or other. I must either go and reside in their monastery, or agree with them that there are wild animals in the forest, although I have come across none." So when some villagers again came and insisted that he should no longer expose himself to the ferocious animals of the jungle, he replied, "Yes, yes, laymen, only last night I saw a tiger under yonder tree, but I will risk my life to complete my meditative exercises." This remark made the monk even more popular, and he received more and more alms food and robes.

There was a mischievous fellow among the villagers and he, after a time, guessed that the monk was using his imagination. So one day he came alone and extended to the monk the usual invitation to the village monastery, referring as usual to the ferocious animals of the forest. "Yes, yes, layman," replied the monk as before. "Only last night I saw a tiger under yonder tree." "How big was it, my lord?" asked the mischievous villager, looking innocent. "It must have been between seven and nine cubits in length," replied the monk. The mischievous villager burst out laughing and said, "My lord, my lord, obviously you have never seen a tiger. No tiger can be bigger than the breadth of my lord's palm. So, sir, be careful next time when you are describing the tiger." The monk thanked the mischievous villager and promised to be more careful in the future.

A few days afterward a group of villagers arrived, and they again invited the monk to their monastery in the village, mentioning the danger from wild animals. "Yes, yes, laymen," replied the monk. "Only last night I saw a tiger under yonder tree, and it was as big as my palm." The villagers looked at him in silence and shook their heads. "What is the matter, laymen?" the monk asked feebly. "What is wrong with my tiger?" "My lord," the villagers replied, "the average length of a tiger is from seven to nine cubits." "My tiger was all right, my tiger was all right," wailed the monk, "but that mischievous villager dwindled it."

—TRADITIONAL BURMESE BUDDHIST TALE

CONTEMPLATION

Is your favorite spiritual teacher a real hero or a small paper tiger? Buddha, who always downplayed his own wisdom and encouraged his followers to discover their own, said: "One should follow the wise, the intelligent, the learned, the much enduring, the dutiful, the noble; one should follow a good and wise man, as the moon follows the path of the stars."

CHILDREN

◇

Is there any person among you who, being asked by his son for bread, would give him a stone; or being asked for a fish, would give a snake?

—GOSPEL OF MATTHEW (CHRISTIAN NEW TESTAMENT)

◇

O, our mother the earth, O our father the sky,
Your children are we, and with tired backs
We bring you gifts that you love
Then weave for us a garment of brightness
May the border be the standing rainbow
That we may walk fittingly where grass is green,
O our mother the earth, O our father the sky.

—TRADITIONAL TEWA TRIBAL PRAYER
(NATIVE AMERICAN)

CONTEMPLATION

There used to be a public service announcement that asked: "Do you know where your children are?" How is it possible to forget the children, for we too are children, and by doing so we fail to recognize and remember ourselves!

Children are a gift to and from God. They keep the whole thing going. We must, at the very least, hold them in safety and provide for them. Jesus knew this when he embraced them. The Japanese make this whole month Children's Month.

Here's what a Japanese poet, Shuntaro Tanikawa, wrote:

There are birds and so there is sky
There is sky and so there are balloons
There are balloons so children are running
Children are running so there is laughter
There is laughter so there is sadness
So there is prayer and ground for kneeling
There is ground so water is flowing
And there's today and tomorrow there is a yellow bird
So with all the colors, forms, and movement, there is the world.

MISTAKES

◇

Mullah Nasreddin was from a small village, and so finding himself amid a huge crowd in Baghdad he was understandably confused.

"I wonder," he said to himself, "how people here remember who they are and where they're going. I must pay attention, or I just might lose myself."

With that, Nasreddin went to the tent grounds with the idea of getting a little respite from the turmoil. "But how," he thought, "will I be certain to find myself again when I wake up from my nap?"

He decided to ask his newfound neighbor for help, not knowing that the man was a prankster.

"Here's what you do," the man said. "Take this inflated bladder and tie it to your leg. When you awake, look for the bladder. The man it's tied to will be you."

"Thanks so much," said Nasreddin.

A few hours later, Nasreddin arose from slumber. He immediately looked for the bladder and spotted it—on the leg of his new friend. "That must be me," he concluded.

Then, panicking, he beat on the man, crying, "Wake up, wake up—something's gone awfully wrong!"

The joker opened his eyes and asked innocently, "Whatever is the matter, friend?"

Nasreddin gestured to the bladder and shouted, "The bladder is there, so you must be me, but if you are me, who in God's good world am I?!"

—TRADITIONAL SUFI TALE

CONTEMPLATION

Of all the mistakes to make, this is the most serious: to think—no, to believe—that you are someone else so powerfully that you forget who you really are.

We are particularly susceptible to make this mistake with leaders, spiritual and worldly, therapists, and teachers—people whom we admire and who, in a powerful and most natural way, we wish to be.

Good trusted friends can be of great help here. They'll pop your balloon for you.

DOMINION

◆

Now at the beginning the twin spirits have declared their nature, the better and the evil, in thought and word and deed. And between the two the wise ones choose well; not so the foolish.

And when these two spirits came together, in the beginning they established life and nonlife, and that at the last the worst experience should be for the wicked, but for the righteous one the Best Mind.

Of these two spirits, the evil one chose to do the worst things; but the most Holy Spirit, clothed in the most steadfast heavens, joined himself unto Righteousness; and thus did all those who delight to please the Wise Lord by honest deeds.

Between the two, the false gods also did not choose rightly, for while they pondered they were beset by error, so that they chose the Worst Mind. Then did they hasten to join themselves unto Fury, that they might by it deprave the existence of man.

And to him came Devotion, together with Dominion, Good Mind, and Righteousness; she gave perpetuity of body and the breath of life, that he might be thine apart from them, as the first by the retributions through the metal.

And when their punishment shall come to these sinners, then, O Wise One, shall thy Dominion, with the Good Mind, be granted to those who have delivered Evil into the hands of Righteousness, O Lord!

—GATHAS (ZOROASTRIAN SACRED TEXT)

CONTEMPLATION

A joke that tickled us at Seminary goes as follows: a poor man scraped together just enough money to buy an old run-down farm. The very next day he began to make improvements on the neglected property. After two years of hard work and good management, the farm began to prosper. Having caught wind of the farmer's good fortune, the village priest showed up. "Well, neighbor," he declared, "God be praised, for He has done wonders with your farm." "Pardon me, Father," retorted the man, "but you should have seen the farm when it was in God's hands."

Dominion is not a given. When you have reclaimed and/or added to a "field"—then you hold dominion in it.

FAME

◆

A young disciple of Naftali of Ropshitz once came to him and asked, "Holy Master, why do you always wear white trousers?"

"I cannot tell you," replied the rabbi. "It's a secret."

The rabbi's answer only served to pique the young man's curiosity. Again and again he came to Naftali and begged to know the secret of his white trousers.

Finally Naftali said to him, "Very well, I will tell you. But first you must fast for six days."

So the young man fasted for six days. Then he came to the rabbi and said, "I have done what you requested. Now, holy master, tell me the secret."

"First swear to me that you will tell no one as long as you live."

And the young man swore.

Naftali led him into a room, then a second room, and finally a third, locking all the doors behind him as they passed from one room into the next. All the while the young man held his breath, certain that the rabbi was about to unveil one of the holiest mysteries.

After checking the locks one last time, the rabbi beckoned to the young man to come close and then bent down to whisper into his ear, "The reason I wear white trousers is that they are the cheapest."

"For this I had to fast for six days!" the young man cried. "Why make such a secret of something so trivial?"

The rabbi smiled. "Because if people found out, they would all want to wear white trousers, and then the price would go up. Now don't forget your promise—don't tell anyone as long as you live!"

—TRADITIONAL CHASSIDIC JEWISH TALE

CONTEMPLATION

Jesus knew there was a price to pay for fame.

No wonder he told the leper; no wonder he told the blind; no wonder he told the crippled: "Tell no one." Jesus foresaw that people would celebrate him rather than God and revere the message bearer rather than the message. Fame does have certain rewards, but true understanding is rarely one of them.

ROSE

◇

The wilderness and the solitary place shall be glad for them: and the desert shall rejoice and blossom as the rose. It shall blossom abundantly and rejoice even with joy and singing: The glory of Lebanon shall be given unto it, the excellency of Carmel and Sharon, they shall see the glory of the Lord and the excellency of our God.

—BOOK OF ISAIAH (HEBREW SCRIPTURES)

◇

O, Friend! In the garden of thy heart plant naught but the rose of love.

—WRITINGS OF BAHÁ'U'LLÁH (BAHÁ'Í FAITH)

◇

This I know. That the only way to live is like the rose which lives without a why.

—WRITINGS OF MEISTER ECKHART
(CHRISTIAN MYSTIC AND POET)

CONTEMPLATION

Glorious! The rose is a promise of glorious confidence. A rose tells us that life can be—is—beautiful. A rose arises from the earth, is blessed by the sun, and through its thorny existence speaks to us of dying, too. Christian philosopher George Meredith sweetly inquires, "In the hand that made the rose, shall I with trembling fall?" We may only respond as we view and smell a splendid rose: "Ah!"

REVELATION

◇

Wert thou to cleanse the mirror of thy heart from the dust of malice, thou wouldst apprehend the meaning of the symbolic terms revealed by the all-embracing Word of God made manifest in every dispensation, and wouldst discover the mysteries of divine knowledge. Not, however, until thou consumeth with the flame of utter detachment those veils of idle learning, that are current among men, canst thou behold the resplendent morn of true knowledge.

—WRITINGS OF BAHÁ'U'LLÁH (BAHÁ'Í FAITH)

◇

"I" and "you" are the veil
Between heaven and earth;
Lift this veil and you will see
No longer the bond of sects and creeds.

When "I" and "you" do not exist,
What is mosque, what is synagogue?
What is the Temple of Fire?

—WRITINGS OF MAHMUD SHABISTARI
(SUFI MYSTIC AND POET)

CONTEMPLATION

Draw back the veil of your own soul today.
   What will you see? The Holy of Holies or a cloud of prejudice?
   When you look in this mirror strongly (and it will take great strength), eventually you will be revealed to yourself.
   It is not yet one face but many. When it is one, know it will be beautiful!

WORRY

◇

Life was wonderful
when you stood at your fishing-hole
on the ice.
But was I happy waiting at my fishing hole?

No, I was always worried
for my little hook,
in case it never got a bite.
Yes, I worried constantly.

Life was wonderful
when you danced in the feasting-house.
But did this make me any happier?
No, I always worried
I'd forget my song.
Yes, I worried constantly.

Life was wonderful . . .
And I still feel joy
each time the daybreak
whitens the dark sky
each time the sun
climbs over the roof of the sky.

—TRADITIONAL INUIT TRIBAL SONG (NATIVE AMERICAN)

CONTEMPLATION

*Are you a worrier rather than a warrior? So what? Our Inuit relatives know
that worry is part of life, nothing to be ashamed of, nothing to suppress.*

If the joy came unbidden and unconnected to worry, would it be as wonderful?

JUNE

CERTAINTY

◆

And thus did We show Ibrahim the kingdom of the heavens and the earth and that he might be of those who are sure.

So when the night overshadowed him, he saw a star; said he: Is this my Lord? So when it set, he said: I do not love the setting ones.

Then when he saw the moon rising, he said: Is this my Lord? So when it set, he said: If my Lord had not guided me, I should certainly be of the erring people.

Then when he saw the sun rising, he said: Is this my Lord? Is this the greatest? So when it set, he said: O my people! surely I am clear of what you set up (with Allah).

Surely I have turned myself, being upright, wholly to Him Who originated the heavens and the earth, and I am not of the polytheists.

And his people disputed with him. He said: Do you dispute with me respecting Allah? And He has guided me indeed; and I do not fear in any way those that you set up with Him, unless my Lord pleases; my Lord comprehends all things in His knowledge; will you not then mind?

And how should I fear what you have set up (with Him), while you do not fear that you have set up with Allah that for which He has not sent down to you any authority; which then of the two parties is surer of security, if you know?

Those who believe and do not mix up their faith with iniquity, those are they who shall have the security and they are those who go aright.

—QUR'AN (HOLY BOOK OF ISLAM)

CONTEMPLATION

An anonymous Japanese poet wrote:

> *I have always known*
> *That at last I would*
> *Take this road,*
> *but yesterday*
> *I did not know*
> *it would be today.*

A nuclear physicist couldn't have expressed the troubling principle of un-certainty better: If you can determine space (location) of atomic particles, you cannot determine time-frame (speed) and vice versa. No wonder we're even more confused and shaky in our faith (in either science or religion) than old Ibrahim. Look to the God-core in you for certainty.

ASSUMPTION

The Mullah Nasreddin's donkey was carrying a load of salt to market when they came to a stream. Commanded to go across, the donkey did, and all the salt dissolved. Nasreddin was infuriated, the donkey delighted to be unburdened.

The next time they came to the stream, the donkey was carrying wool. Going through the water, the wool became sodden and increased by many, many times its original weight. The donkey sagged under the load.

"Ha!" Nasreddin gloated to the donkey. "You must have thought that passing through a stream you always get off lightly!"

—TRADITIONAL SUFI TALE

The race was open to everyone, so Nasreddin brought his only available mount—a huge ox. The other racers laughed. Oxen cannot run, and this one was obviously slow indeed. "But," Nasreddin explained, "when it was just a calf, it ran friskily, just as fast as a young horse. Now that it's so much bigger, should it not be so much faster?"

—TRADITIONAL SUFI TALE

The poor Mullah Nasreddin saved enough money to purchase a donkey. He was told that all donkeys, including his, needed a certain quantity of food each day. "That sounds like a lot," he said to himself, and decided to see if his donkey could get by on less. To accustom his donkey to this, every day Nasreddin reduced the amount he fed the animal.

Finally, the day's rations were reduced to bits of grain. The donkey keeled over and died.

"Too bad," Nasreddin concluded. "With just a little more time, I could have gotten the donkey used to eating nothing at all."

—TRADITIONAL SUFI TALE

CONTEMPLATION

Assumptions about burdens, growth, charity. The poor mullah's list could go on and on as ours does.

One of the most common of assumptions is that everyone else (well, at least your friends) has the same assumptive conclusions that you do.

Dare to find out.

WILL

◇

The pious in Nasreddin's village intoned constantly the phrase: "May the will of Allah be done."

"This is always so," Nasreddin commented one day.

"What do you mean, Mullah?" they asked. "Can you illustrate this assertion?"

"Yes, it's obvious," Nasreddin replied. "If God's will wasn't in every instance being done, then surely, at least once, there'd be a chance for *my* will to be done, don't you see?"

—TRADITIONAL SUFI TALE

◇

Nevertheless, not as I will, but as thou wilt.

—GOSPEL OF MATTHEW (CHRISTIAN NEW TESTAMENT)

CONTEMPLATION

Why did Jesus' erstwhile disciples try to keep the young children from him? Possibly because the master's helpers thought that this particular bunch were like most kids—willful pests.

This was assuredly a projection on the disciples' part, for it was they who incessantly bothered Jesus with disputes about who would sit at his right hand in the kingdom of heaven. They assumed that power to impose their wills would then be theirs.

A traditional Kikuyu tribal chant adopts a much more appropriate and beneficial attitude: "O great Elder, ruler of all things, earthly and heavenly: I am your warrior, ready to act in accordance with your will."

AIR

I am he from whom none can hide, in any act which he may do, or be about to do, or have done in the past, be he god or man. Air is my name, but one might also call me Zeus. I, as a god should be, am everywhere— here in Athens, in Patrae, in Sicily, in all cities, in every home, in every one of you. There is no place where is not Air. And he who is present everywhere, because he is everywhere of necessity knows everything.

—WRITINGS OF PHILEMON
(GREEK PHILOSOPHER AND POET)

Mankind and the other animals live on air, by breathing; and it is to them both soul and mind.

The soul of all animals is the same, namely air which is warmer than the air outside, in which we live, though much colder than that near the sun.

In my opinion that which has intelligence is what men call air, and by it everything is directed, and it has power over all things; for it is just this substance which I hold to be God.

—WRITINGS OF DIOGENES
(GREEK PHILOSOPHER AND POET)

CONTEMPLATION

If the ancient Greeks are right, and atmos *or air is the very essence of God, then what happens when we foul the atmosphere?*

Do we lose our pneuma, *our holy spirit, our soul?*

Here's a great spiritual irony: The city of Athens's air has become so polluted and acidic that most holy sites have been tarnished or in some cases damaged beyond reclamation.

In the Book of Ezekiel, the prophet himself invokes God's aid in restoring the old dried bones of slain warriors to life:

God sent the winds, and they lived and stood upon their feet. . . .

Each one of us must be an Ezekiel now.

SIMPLICITY

When I was a youth I remained aloof from worldly affairs,
Devoting myself to my books and my lyre,
Wearing ragged clothes I was happy
And content with this complete poverty.
But there came a time of change,
Of holding a horse's reins and wandering on the roadways.
I tossed aside my scrolls, prepared my baggage,
To be for a while separated from my garden and field.
In the far distance the solitary boat vanishes.
My thoughts for home spin out like a thread.
Have I not journeyed far and wide,
Rising and descending over a thousand li?
My heart keeps with my home near the lakes and hills.
Looking at clouds I am chagrined by the high-flying birds,
Seeing fish swim I stand ashamed near the water.
The perfect ideal is locked in my heart,
No outward circumstances will ever corrupt it.
I shall follow the natural course
And at last return to a hermit's abode.

—WRITINGS OF TAO YUAN-MING
(CLASSICAL CHINESE CLASSICAL POET)

CONTEMPLATION

One of my favorite prayers is from The Course in Miracles, *which brings the teachings of Jesus to us in a new light. It is simply, "I need do nothing."*

Now, of "course" (a little humor here), this prayer doesn't mean to do absolutely nothing and just wait for heaven to reward you. It means to remove the "I" from the doing, so that you're not just doing things for yourself.

It means simply going about the business at hand. Like Saint Francis building stone by stone his community's first rustic monasteries. Like Mahatma Gandhi quietly walking to the sea to obtain, for all Indians, salt free from taxation. Like Gautama leaving the ascetic forest life and seating himself under a fig tree until he awakened as the Buddha.

When you come to it, really, it's as simple as that.

BEGINNINGS, MIDDLES, ENDINGS

◆

The disciples said to Jesus, "Tell us how our end will be." Jesus said, "Have you discovered then the beginning that you look for the end? For where the beginning is, there will the end be. Blessed is he who will take his place in the beginning; he will know the end and will not experience death."

—GOSPEL OF THOMAS
(APOCRYPHAL CHRISTIAN TEACHING)

◆

The great God Shiva and his wife, the Goddess Parvati, disguised as a holy man and disciple, came to this world to offer salvation.

This new saint would not only tell a person's past, he prophesied the future, too. Very soon, flocks of people came, including a group of devotees.

One, who appeared to be their leader, inquired, "Guru Maharaj, will you tell me when I will obtain salvation? In winter I meditate sitting in cold water up to my neck; in summer I meditate encircled by fire. For years I have eaten each day only a single meal of fruit and milk."

"You are indeed a very good yogi, practicing such hard austerities," the guru said. The man, hearing this praise, became excited. The saint continued, "If you keep doing your *sadhana* with such devotion, you can have salvation after three births." Shocked and disappointed, the devotee returned to his friends muttering, "Still three births!"

One after another then told of their good work and received an answer—seven, ten, even twenty or thirty births for some. Finally, the last man, thin and ugly, came forward from his hiding place. "O, Holy One," he timidly confessed, "I don't do any practice at all, but I love God's creation. I try not in any way to harm anyone. Can I receive salvation?"

Shiva scratched his head, paused, then said, "Well, if you go on loving God in this way, maybe after a thousand births, you too may find salvation."

The man, hearing this, shouted in joy, "I can get salvation! I can get salvation!" As he danced in ecstasy, his body became a flame, as did Shiva's and Parvati's. The three flames joined as one and ascended instantly to Mount Kailasha, the heavenly realm.

—TRADITIONAL HINDU TALE

CONTEMPLATION

It is not for us to know with definition what stage, level, or position we are at on the spiritual plane. Interestingly, even the Goddess Parvati was confused and perplexed by the events of the sojourn to the earthly realm. In an add-on to the story, Shiva explains that the last man, unencumbered by pride and ego, was at a pure state of innocence, faith, and true surrender. This is the "beginner's mind" of Zen. This is the "becoming as a child" of which Jesus spoke so highly. This is, in a spiritual sense, the only way to be.

SPEED

◇

Three young men went out to their fields to harvest millet. It began to rain. One of the men carried a basket of millet on his head. The earth was wet from the rain, and the man slipped. His foot skidded from the city of Bamako to the town of Kati. The basket of millet on his head began to fall. The man reached into a house as he slid by and picked up a knife. He cut the tall reed grass that grew along the path, wove a mat out of it, and laid it on the ground beneath him. Spilling from the falling basket, the millet fell upon the mat. The man arose, shook the millet from the mat back into the basket, and said, "If I had not had the presence of mind to make a mat and put it beneath me, I would have lost my grain."

The second young man had forty chickens in fifteen baskets, and on the way to his millet field he took the chickens from the baskets to let them feed. Suddenly a hawk swooped down, its talons ready to seize one of the chickens. The man ran swiftly among his chickens, picked them up, put each one in its proper basket, covered the baskets, and caught the swooping hawk by its talons. He said, "What do you think you are doing—trying to steal my chickens?"

The third young man and the first young man went hunting together. The first man shot an arrow at an antelope. The other man leaped forward at the same instant, caught the antelope, killed it, skinned it, cut up the meat, stretched the skin out to dry, and placed the meat in his knapsack. Then he reached out his hand and caught the first man's arrow as it arrived. He said, "What do you think you are doing—trying to shoot holes in my knapsack?"

—TRADITIONAL MENDE TRIBAL TALE (WEST AFRICA)

CONTEMPLATION

Acting with speed, when necessary, can be a wonderful thing.

But speed in spiritual matters rarely brings good results. Try to accelerate your meditation practice. You won't get enlightened—only crazier thoughts and perhaps a headache.

Much as we may begrudge it, the transmission of spiritual-oriented ideas takes a good while to settle in and develop, for both individuals and societies.

Mahatma Gandhi ought to know. He nurtured the Indian independence movement for nearly fifty years. He said, "There is more to life than increasing its speed."

MYSTERY

◇

The Tao that can be told
is not the eternal Tao.
The name that can be named
is not the eternal Name.

The unnamable is the eternally real.
Naming is the origin
of all particular things.

Free from desire, you realize the mystery.
Caught in desire, you see only the manifestations.

Yet mystery and manifestations
arise from the same source.
This source is called darkness.

Darkness within darkness.
The gateway to all understanding.

—TAO TE CHING (CLASSICAL TAOIST TEXT)

CONTEMPLATION

All of us are assuredly like the poor fellow walking on the riverbank, in the tra-
ditional Indian anecdote. He watches helplessly as the swift waters carry a
beautiful walking stick downstream. "How precious this stick is," the man
thinks, but despite repeated dives into the river, he comes up empty-handed. He
just can't get a grasp on this stick, no matter what.

Religions attempt to explain the mystery; true prophets and sages do not,
recognizing in humility their inadequacy to do so. Like the Buddha, they re-
frain from grasping and rather simply point a finger to the moon.

Everyone, consciously or unconsciously, eventually comes up with a cosmol-
ogy, description, or philosophical belief about the "way it is." That's all right—
but understand that it's just a stick, more or less waterlogged, that you're now
holding in your hands. The mystery remains.

CROSSING

Then the Lord said to Moses, "Why are you crying out to me? Tell the Israelites to move on. Raise your staff and stretch out your hand over the sea to divide the water so that the Israelites can go through the sea on dry ground. And I will gain glory through Pharaoh and all his army, through his chariots and his horsemen."

Then the angel of God, who had been traveling in front of Israel's army, withdrew and went behind them. The pillar of cloud also moved from in front and stood behind them, coming between the armies of Egypt and Israel. Throughout the night the cloud brought darkness to the one side and light to the other side; so neither went near the other all night long.

Then Moses stretched out his hand over the sea, and all that night the Lord drove the sea back with a strong east wind and turned it into dry land. The waters were divided, and the Israelites went through the sea on dry ground, with a wall of water on their right and on their left.

The Egyptians pursued them, and all Pharaoh's horses and chariots and horsemen followed them into the sea. During the last watch of the night the Lord looked down from the pillar of fire and cloud at the Egyptian army and threw it into confusion.

He made the wheels of their chariots come off so that they had difficulty driving. And the Egyptians said, "Let's get away from the Israelites! The Lord is fighting for them against Egypt."

But the Israelites went through the sea on dry ground, with a wall of water on their right and on their left. That day the Lord saved Israel from the hands of the Egyptians, and Israel saw the Egyptians lying dead on the shore. And when the Israelites saw the great power the Lord displayed against the Egyptians, the people feared the Lord and put their trust in him and in Moses his servant.

—BOOK OF EXODUS (HEBREW SCRIPTURES)

If you long to know what is hard to know and can resist the temptations of the world, you will cross the river of life.

—DHAMMAPADA (BUDDHIST SACRED TEXT)

CONTEMPLATION

Before crossing the sea, stillness. After crossing the sea, exaltation. Another before, another sea or river to cross, another after . . . to the promised land . . . another crossing. . . .

JUNE 10

TALK

◇

A hunter goes into the bush. He finds an old human skull. The hunter says: "What brought you here?" The skull answers: "Talking brought me here." The hunter runs off. He runs to the king. He tells the king: "I found a dry human skull in the bush. It asks you how its father and mother are."

The king says: "Never since my mother bore me have I heard that a dead skull can speak." The king summons the Alkali, the Saba, and the Degi and asks them if they have ever heard the like. None of the wise men has heard the like, and they decide to send a guard out with the hunter into the bush to find out if his story is true and, if so, to learn the reason for it. The guard accompanies the hunter into the bush with the order to kill him on the spot should he have lied.

The guard and the hunter come to the skull. The hunter addresses the skull: "Skull, speak." The skull is silent. The hunter asks as before: "What brought you here?" The skull does not answer. The whole day long the hunter begs the skull to speak, but it does not answer. In the evening the guard tells the hunter to make the skull speak and, when he cannot, kills him in accordance with the king's command. When the guard is gone, the skull opens its jaws and asks the dead hunter's head: "What brought you here?" The dead hunter's head replies: "Talking brought me here!"

—TRADITIONAL NUPE TRIBAL TALE (WEST AFRICA)

CONTEMPLATION

When you talk, is it to share wisdom? Is your talk of beauty, of encouragement, of God?

Moses spoke these words of God in the wilderness:

Hear, O Israel,
the Lord Our God, the Lord is One.
And these words which I command to you this day
shall be upon your heart.
And you shall teach them to your children
and shall talk of them when you sit in your house,
and when you walk by the way,
and when you lie down,
and when you rise.

FATHER

◇

Do you thus requite the Lord,
you foolish and senseless people?
Is not he your father, who created you,
who made you and established you?

He found [Israel] in a desert land,
in the howling waste of the wilderness;
he encircled him, he cared for him,
he kept him as the apple of his eye.
Like an eagle that stirs up its nest,
that flutters over its young,
spreading out its wings, catching them,
bearing them on its pinions,
the Lord alone did lead him,
and there was no foreign god with him.

—BOOK OF DEUTERONOMY (HEBREW SCRIPTURES)

◇

I tell you, Shariputra,
You men
Are all my children,
And I am your Father.
For age upon age, you
Have been scorched by multitudinous woes,
And I have saved you all.

—LOTUS SUTRA (BUDDHIST SACRED TEXT)

CONTEMPLATION

*Honor your father today. You only have one, and if he's no longer living, honor
his memory and spirit.*

*Tell stories. Leave nothing out. Did he hurt you? Tell it. Did he lift you up
in playfulness or to help you avoid injury? Tell that, too.*

How else can you know other earthly and heavenly fathers?

RIPE

◇

Through the ripening of the fruits of his actions, he does not attain any rest, like a worm caught within a whirlpool. The desire for liberation arises in human beings at the end of many births, through the ripening of their past virtuous conduct.

—YAJUR VEDA (HINDU SACRED TEXT)

◇

And the next day as they came out of Bethany, he got hungry. And spotting a leafy fig tree from a distance, he came to see if in fact he could find anything on it, but when he got to it, he found nothing but leaves, because it wasn't fig season. And in response he said to it, "Never again shall anyone eat your fruit," and his students were listening to him. And in the morning, traveling along they saw the fig tree withered to its roots. And Peter, remembering, says to him, "Master, look, the fig tree you cursed has withered away."

—GOSPEL OF MARK (CHRISTIAN NEW TESTAMENT)

CONTEMPLATION

However it is you got here, through past lives or only this one, when you've become a true fruit of spirit, it is your obligation to ripen. Others may have the excuse of ignorance; you don't.

Passover for Jews and Easter for Christians provide a blast of spiritual light meant to quicken spiritual growth. Seven weeks hence the grain should be ripening. To now. To this day.

These movements to ripening must reach maturity. Don't fight it, or you may wither miserably. Allow the sun of hope and gladness to touch you every day.

JUNE 13
PRACTICALITY

◆

Journeying in India, the Mullah Nasreddin, a self-proclaimed philosopher of the highest degree, came across a yogi living in a hut. "Certainly," he said to himself, "a pious thinker such as this and I have much to share," and with that Nasreddin entered the hermit's abode.

The yogi informed Nasreddin that yes, indeed, he had devoted his life in service to all beings, the birds and fish and all animals.

"I beseech you to allow me to join you," Nasreddin said. "I, too, hold to this outlook. In fact, a fish once saved my life."

"Wonderful!" the yogi said. "I'd be pleased to have your company. Through all my years of devotion, I have yet, like you have, sir, to reach such a dear relationship with my animal friends.

"Just imagine," the yogi went on, "to be on such intimate terms with a fish that it came to save your life!"

So Nasreddin meditated and lived with the yogi for a good while, learning the yogi's ways. Nasreddin contemplated on his belly and learned complex and twisted postures.

At last, the yogi asked, "Please, good sir, if you would be kind, tell me how it is you achieved such communion with a fish. I would be most honored to hear the story of how a fish saved your life."

"I'm not certain," Nasreddin hesitated, "now that I know so much about your philosophy of things, that telling you would be such a good idea."

Undaunted, the yogi pleaded with Nasreddin. "Such a profound experience and with one of God's creatures—a fish. Please, good master," he persisted, bowing tearfully before Nasreddin.

"All right," Nasreddin said, "though you may not, considering your philosophy, really understand the nature of what I now reveal to you. The fish truly did save my life. I was about to die of starvation when I caught it. I ate it and lived."

—TRADITIONAL SUFI TALE

CONTEMPLATION

When it comes to paying the bills or finding a job, we do whatever it takes. But somehow when it comes to the development of character and conscience, we believe nature will take its course.

Don't wait until your soul is starving. Be practical now. Cast your line.

POSSIBILITY

◇

A bat, a bramblebush, and a gull decided to form a business partnership. The bat borrowed money to finance the enterprise, the bramblebush invested in cloth, and the gull contributed a quantity of copper ingots. They then set out by ship to sell their wares abroad. En route their ship ran into a violent storm and capsized; and though the three partners managed to escape with their lives, all their goods were lost. Ever since, the gull has hovered around the seacoast, hoping that some of his copper will be washed ashore by the waves; the bat, fearful of his creditors, has kept well hidden during the day, venturing out only at dusk; and the bramblebush plucks at the garments of passersby, to see if any of the cloth really is his.

—FABLE OF AESOP (CLASSICAL GREEK)

◇

I assure you, if you have a mustard seed's worth of faith, you'll tell this mountain to move from here to there and it will move; nothing will be impossible for you.

—GOSPEL OF MATTHEW (CHRISTIAN NEW TESTAMENT)

CONTEMPLATION

In the beginning, at the time of the world's and humans' creation, the possibilities of evolution, of new creation were virtually limitless. So it is with us as children, when we have faith in ourselves as powers on the earth.

This is natural. But it is also understandable that—like the bat, bramblebush, and gull beset by failure and criticism—we would pull back to a safer, more limited position.

In spiritual practice, thankfully, there is no such thing as failure. You can't fail at meditation or prayer. You'll always get something and build something from the experience.

So go ahead. Explore the possibilities again.

HABIT

◇

A thief was obsessed with only one thought: to have vast quantities of gold. Early one morning he dressed in his normal attire and went to the marketplace. He entered the shop of the moneychanger and proceeded to rob him of all the gold in the shop. It was not difficult for the police to track down the thief and arrest him, but they were perplexed as to why he had committed the crime in broad daylight.

"When I was taking the gold," the thief replied, "I saw no one at all; all that I saw was the gold, nothing but the gold."

—TRADITIONAL WORLD STORY

◇

What are the six channels for dissipating wealth? Taking intoxicants; loitering in the streets at unseemly hours; constantly visiting shows and fairs; addiction to gambling; association with evil companions; the habit of idleness. . . .

Gambling and women, drink and dance and song,
Sleeping by day and prowling around by night,
Friendship with wicked men, hardness of heart,
These causes six bring ruin to a man.

Gambling and drinking, chasing after those
Women as dear as life to other men,
Following the fools, not the enlightened ones,
He wanes as the darker half of the moon.

The drunkard always poor and destitute;
Even while drinking, thirsty; haunting bars;
Sinks into debt as into water stone,
Soon robs his family of their good name.

One who habitually sleeps by day
And looks upon the night as time to rise
Licentious and a drunkard all the time,
He does not merit the rank of householder.

—SIGALOVADA SUTTA (BUDDHIST SACRED TEXT)

CONTEMPLATION

There are bad habits and good habits. Both are largely out of our control, at least at times, because, like the unfortunate thief, we have unconscious patterns of attitude and perception that override our conscious desire and sometimes even our common sense. You've got to go beyond your habitual self. This is why prayer with the Higher Power and sharing the habit of prayer are so powerfully effective.

SHE AND HE

◇

When you make the two one,
and when you make the inner as the outer
and the outer as the inner
and the above as the below,
and when you make the male and female
into a single one,
so that the male will not be male
and the female not be female . . .
then shall you enter the Kingdom.

—GOSPEL OF THOMAS (APOCRYPHAL CHRISTIAN TEACHING)

◇

All life, all pulsation in creation throbs with the mighty declaration of the biune truth of Shiva-Shakti, the eternal He and the eternal She at play in manifestation.

—KULARNAVA TANTRA (HINDU SACRED TEXT)

◇

I am Atum, the creator of the Eldest Gods,
I am he who gave birth to Shu,
I am that great He-She,
I am he who did what seemed good to him,
I took my space in the place of my will,
Mine is the space of those who move along
like those two serpentine circles.

—TRADITIONAL EGYPTIAN RITUAL

CONTEMPLATION

It is said among many peoples that females and males lived exclusively in the company of their own kind, sometimes for ages.

What brought them together?

A legend of the indigenous people of Australia claims that men desired the exquisitely made weapons that only women fashioned. In some Native American tellings, it was the skins and pelts men could provide that, in part at least, moti-

vated the women to accept interactions with them. Then also, there was the phys-
ical (and later emotional) pleasure from their coming together, female and male.

When we allow this convergence to take place in our souls, dropping the at-
tachment to rigid formulas of how it's supposed to be, then the spiritual pleas-
ure and creative potency obtained can be immense. We approach divinity.

MARRIAGE

◇

The twain in one are joined today. May their right hands be tied by the bond of love in lasting union. May the mind of one blend with the mind of the other and the heart be in tune with the heart. May the twin spirits be a composite spirit in joy and sorrow, success and failure, prosperity and adversity. May the two come nearer to each other in Good Thoughts, Good Words, and Good Deeds from day unto day.

May each transmit something good of each to the others. May each take the best that is in the other, and give something better than the best. May each give of one's goodness what the other lacks and give mutual completion to each other in life.

Locked in the embrace of wedded love, may they live for each other, may they share each other's feelings, may they lighten each other's load in life, and may they live in the loving fellowship of minds and hearts. May each elevate and embellish what nature has bestowed on the other. With hearts knitted together, may the two be the whole world to each other. May each one be life for the other. May he be hers and she be his wholly for all the days of their lives. May each cleave faithfully unto each in body and mind and spirit as the vine that twines its tendrils around the tall tree. May better than the best come unto them. May it be so even as we pray, *Ahura Mazda*.

—TRADITIONAL ZOROASTRIAN MARRIAGE PRAYER

◇

Marriage is half the tradition.

—TEACHING OF MUHAMMAD (PROPHET OF ISLAM)

◇

Each soul and spirit, prior to its entering into this world, consists of a male and female united into one being. When it descends on this earth, the two parts separate and animate two different bodies. At the time of marriage, the Holy One, blessed be He, who knows all souls and spirits, unites them again as they were before, and they again constitute one body and one soul, forming as it were the right and left of one individual.

—ZOHAR (CLASSICAL JEWISH KABBALISTIC TEXT)

Marriages, of any kind, bring tremendous spiritual upheaval. The nuclear blast of marriage can be (and typically is) both extraordinarily uplifting and challenging.

There is a story told of Mother Teresa of Calcutta. After praising her extraordinary work, an interviewer for the BBC remarked that in some ways service might be a bit easier for Mother Teresa than for us ordinary householders. After all, she had no possessions, no car, no insurance, and no husband. "This is not true," she replied at once. "I am married, too." She held up the ring that nuns in her order wear to symbolize their wedding to Christ. Then she added, "And he can be very difficult sometimes!"

JUNE 18

PROGRESS

On this path effort never goes to waste, and there is no failure.

—BHAGAVAD GITA (HINDU SACRED TEXT)

At that time, He will first open for them a tiny aperture of light, then another somewhat larger, and so on until He will throw open for them the supernal gates which face on all the four quarters of the world. . . . For we know that when a man has been long shut up in darkness, it is necessary, on bringing him into the light, first to make for him an opening as small as the eye of a needle, and then one a little larger, and so on gradually, until he can endure the full light. . . . So, too, a sick man who is recovering cannot be given a full diet all at once, but only gradually.

—ZOHAR (CLASSICAL KABBALISTIC JEWISH TEXT)

CONTEMPLATION

When one is sick and anxious, whether physically or spiritually (and aren't they directly related anyway?), it may be difficult to see that any progress has been made at all.

Want confidence? See how the rosebush grows. As old leaves are eaten and fall, new ones are coming in, vital and green. As sweet-smelling roses widen to fullness and decay, small buds (look—2, 3, 5, 8 . . . petals, and more) are popping up beside them.

Progress is paradoxical and mysterious. But as you are living and making effort, know you are progressing.

DIFFICULTY

A poisonous snake bit a farmer's child, and the child died. The farmer, overcome by grief and rage, took his ax and set up a vigil outside the snake's hole, ready to strike the creature down as soon as it emerged. Eventually the snake put his head out of the hole, and the farmer struck; but the blow missed its mark, splitting in two the rock that stood at the entrance to the snake's home. The farmer now thought it prudent to revise his plan and sought to make peace with the snake. But the snake said: "We can never be friends with such reminders of our enmity always before our eyes—for me, the split rock; for you, your child's tombstone."

—FABLE OF AESOP (CLASSICAL GREEK)

So a man who is learning to use his eyes should begin by seeing a cart-load of firewood; a man who is learning to use his ears should begin by hearing the clang of bells. Whenever there is ease within there are no difficulties outside.

—BOOK OF LIEH-TZU (CLASSICAL TAOIST TEXT)

Easy for all to offer in worship a green leaf to the Lord. Easy for all to give a mouthful to the cow. Easy for all to give a handful when sitting down to eat. Easy for all to speak pleasant words to others.

—TIRUMANTIRAM (HINDU SACRED TEXT)

CONTEMPLATION

Sometimes things get out of hand, like with our friends the snake and the farmer, and we're caught between a rock and a hard place. Ouch! That's difficult to rectify.

Much better to learn skills of spiritual vision and listening; then such difficulties may never come into being.

Find ease within. The world's full of ease.

ARROGANCE

◆

Do not keep talking so proudly or let your mouth speak such arrogance, for the Lord is a God who knows, and by him deeds are weighed.

—FIRST BOOK OF SAMUEL (HEBREW SCRIPTURES)

◆

When Indra had grown arrogant after killing Vrtra and Visvarupa, he ordered Visvakarman to construct a magnificent palace for him. After this a Brahmin boy appeared before him and said, "My friend, I know Kasyapa the progenitor and the ascetic hermit Marici, who are both your friends. And I have praised Brahma, the lord creator who sprang from Vishnu's navel, and the supreme protector Vishnu, endowed with the quality of sattva, and also the vast single ocean of the dissolution, devoid of creatures and most horrifying. And now I ask you, Sakra, how manifold is creation? How manifold indeed is the Eon? How many are the eggs of Brahma; how many are the Indras? Who can attain them? If motes of dust and drops of rain can be numbered, O overlord of the gods, still there shall be no number to the Indras, as the wise know well. Just as the eggs of Brahma are innumerable, as are the drops of the sweat of existence, so are the eggs of Brahma as countless as his hairs. How many gods are there in one egg of Brahma? And how many of the likes of you?"

Meanwhile the Supreme Person saw a swarm of ants moving in a file a hundred bow-lengths long. He said nothing but remained there silent like the deep ocean. When he saw the Brahmin boy's mirth and heard his song, Indra asked him in utter astonishment, his throat dry, "Why are you laughing, great Brahmin? Tell me why at once? Who are you, ocean of virtues hidden behind illusion, bearing the shape of a child?"

In reply, Krishna, who bore the shape of the young Brahmin, began to expound the wisdom that even great yogins find most difficult to attain: "That swarm of ants that I observed, each one following the one ahead, have every one been Indras in the world of the gods by virtue of their own past action. And now, by virtue of their deeds done in the past, they have gradually fallen to the state of ants."

—TRADITIONAL HINDU TALE

CONTEMPLATION

On a day like today, with the sun nearing its strongest showing, it's tempting to boast of our grand power and arrogantly strut our stuff.

But if even the Gods must acknowledge their conventionality . . . Arrogance then is a poor spiritual strategy; try service and friendship instead.

SUN

◇

Upon the riverbank they stand
To watch the Boat of Ra go forth
Golden in the sun
Their eyes are dazzled
And they fall to the earth.

—TRADITIONAL EGYPTIAN PRAYER

◇

"O Wakan Tanka, be merciful to me! I am doing this that the people may live!" The sun dancers stood at the foot of the sacred tree . . . and blew upon eagle-bone whistles. The dancers all moved around to the east . . . the south . . . the west . . . the north, all the time blowing upon their skull eagle-bone whistles. Then the dancers all began to cry. . . .

—DESCRIPTION OF LAKOTA SUN DANCE
(NATIVE AMERICAN)

◇

As the sun lights up the world,
the Self dwelling in the field is the source
of all light in the field.

—BHAGAVAD GITA (HINDU SACRED TEXT)

CONTEMPLATION

On the summer solstice, Wiccans and other earth-centered worshippers celebrate the holy day of Litha, the Feast of the Sun on High. At the peak of his power, the Solar Hero sacrifices his energy in service to the Goddess and the well-being of the people.

Solstice literally means "a pause in position of the sun." *As the sun does, so may we be stilled today; resolve to be of brilliant service.*

DIRECTION

O our Father, the Sky, hear us and make us strong.

O our Mother the Earth, hear us and give us support.

O Spirit of the East, send us your Wisdom.

O Spirit of the South, may we tread your path of life.

O Spirit of the West, may we always be ready for the long journey.

O Spirit of the North, purify us with your cleansing winds.

—TRADITIONAL LAKOTA TRIBAL PRAYER
(NATIVE AMERICAN)

In all the ten directions of the universe,

There is only one truth.

—WRITINGS OF RYOKAN (CLASSICAL JAPANESE
BUDDHIST TEACHER)

CONTEMPLATION

In the Garden of Eden, God asks Adam, "Where are you?" after Adam and Eve have eaten of the fruit. God's real question (for obviously God knew where Adam was) is the question for every person: "Where are you . . . going? Toward what goal? What direction are you taking?"

Are you taking the direction toward Shalom—peace and wholeness—in your life? Check your own spiritual map. On course, great! Off course, pull over now. Ask for directions.

ENVY

◇

Morning and Evening were brothers.

But their father Mahu (God) did not treat them equally. To Morning, his firstborn, he gave innumerable subjects and great riches, while the younger brother, Evening, received only a calabash with two types of beads—nana and azamun—the only two things Mahu had not given to Morning.

One day Morning fell ill. The doctor said he could cure him, but he needed a nana and an azamun bead. So Morning's subjects went out to look for the beads, but none had them except Evening.

"How much money will you give me for these pearls?" Evening asked.

"One hundred cowries for each bead," they replied.

So Evening gave them two beads, and Morning was cured.

Left alone, Evening began to think. He began to wish that Morning would fall ill many times, so that he could get many cowries. Then he remembered that whenever Morning approached, the leaves of the calabash rolled up and shut themselves. So he arranged for entirely open calabash leaves to fall under Morning's feet—and Morning fell ill immediately. Thus he made his brother fall ill as many times as he liked, and gradually he gained possession of all his brother's cowries.

Morning's subjects began to desert him, and they gathered round Evening and made him their king.

—TRADITIONAL FON TRIBAL STORY (WEST AFRICA)

CONTEMPLATION

You already have everything you need. When Evening became king, you can be assured he acquired all the tribulations of royalty, including potential harm arising from the envy of those around him.

Does the peahen envy the peacock or enjoy his brilliance? After all, she's the one he wants.

MEDITATION

◇

"Do you enjoy your work?" asked the yogin. "Do I look happy?" asked
the smith. "The fire, sparks, and heat all torment me. I must suffer just to
make a living."

The yogin then asked for food, and as he ate, the smith and his wife
said to him, "We offered you alms, and it is amazing that you take food
from the hands of low-caste people. We are most happy at this." The yogin then asked them, "Don't you practice the Dharma?" "We are of such
low caste—who would instruct us?" they replied. "If you have faith in the
Dharma," said the yogin, "and are able to practice, I will give you instructions." They were elated. They pleased the yogin with their venera-
tion and many offerings, and then asked for the instructions. The yogin,
having given the initiation that transfers spiritual power, also gave them
instructions on the visualizations of the three mystic veins in this way:

"Meditate within yourself that you see the bellows, fuel, fire, and the
hammering of iron, just as you do in the external world. Make the two
veins, *lalana* and *rasana,* the bellows. Consider the central vein, the *avad-
huti,* as the anvil. Let the consciousness be the smith. Ignite the fire of
knowledge, and make conceptualizations the coal; then hammer the iron
of the three poisons. When the great joy and the nondual Dharma-body
ripen as a result, there will be light."

—TRADITIONAL TIBETAN BUDDHIST TALE

CONTEMPLATION

Meditation, for most people, is the highlight of their day.

*Why? Somewhat because meditation brings new and strong light to the
spirit; somewhat because their workaday lives are so dreary and oppressive.*

*What if, like the ardent smith and his wife, you brought your work skills and
powers to meditation and your meditative calmness and clarity to affairs of
business? Try it: it works!*

IMPARTIALITY

◆

The Supreme Reality stands revealed in the consciousness of those who have conquered themselves. They live in peace, alike in cold and heat, pleasure and pain, praise and blame. They are completely filled by spiritual wisdom and have realized the Self. Having conquered their senses, they have climbed to the summit of human consciousness. To such people a clod of dirt, a stone, and gold are the same. They are equally disposed to family, enemies, and friends, to those who support them and those who are hostile, to the good and the evil alike. Because they are impartial, they rise to great heights.

—BHAGAVAD GITA (HINDU SACRED TEXT)

◆

But to wear out your brain trying to make things into one without realizing that they are all the same—this is called "three in the morning." What do I mean by "three in the morning"? When the monkey trainer was handing out acorns, he said, "You get three in the morning and four at night." This made all the monkeys furious. "Well, then," he said, "you get four in the morning and three at night." The monkeys were all delighted. There was no change in the reality behind the words, and yet the monkeys responded with joy and anger. Let them, if they want to. So the sage harmonizes with both right and wrong and rests in Heaven the Equalizer. This is called walking two roads.

—WRITINGS OF CHUANG-TZU
(CLASSICAL TAOIST TEACHER)

◆

"Are you not like the Ethiopians to me,
O people of Israel?" says the Lord.
"Did I not bring up Israel from the land of Egypt,
and the Philistines from Caphtor and the Syrians from Kir?"

—BOOK OF AMOS (HEBREW SCRIPTURES)

CONTEMPLATION

If, as the Bible says, God is not a respecter of persons and has not chosen any group or nation either for special favor or censure, how in God's name can we? Have feelings of prejudice or racism? Fight them. This is one area that must be dealt with seriously and urgently.

ASSENT

◇

Now when Balaam saw that it pleased the Lord to bless Israel, he did not resort to sorcery as at other times, but turned his face toward the desert. When Balaam looked out and saw Israel encamped tribe by tribe, the Spirit of God came upon him and he uttered his oracle.

"The oracle of Balaam son of Beor,
the oracle of one whose eye sees clearly,
the oracle of one who hears the words of God,
who sees a vision from the Almighty,
who falls prostrate, and whose eyes are opened:

"How beautiful are your tents, O Jacob,
your dwelling places, O Israel!
Like a lion they crouch and lie down,
like a lioness—who dares to rouse them?

"May those who bless you be blessed
and those who curse you be cursed!"

Then Balak's anger burned against Balaam. He struck his hands together and said to him, "I summoned you to curse my enemies, but you have blessed them these three times. Now leave at once and go home! I said I would reward you handsomely, but the Lord has kept you from being rewarded."

Balaam answered Balak, "Did I not tell the messengers you sent me, 'Even if Balak gave me his palace filled with silver and gold, I could not do anything of my own accord, good or bad, to go beyond the command of the Lord—and I must say only what the Lord says'?"

—BOOK OF NUMBERS (HEBREW SCRIPTURES)

CONTEMPLATION

It's one thing to say "Okay, fine," when things are going your way. It's a leap of consciousness to give your assent, your amen or blessing, to people or circumstances that trouble you.

The prophet Habakkuk faced the imminent devastation of his people by invading barbarians. He not only assented to God's will, he proclaimed:

Though the fig tree does not blossom,
nor the fruit be on the vines,
the produce of the olive fail,
and the fields yield no food,
and the flock be cut off from the fold,
and there be no herd in the stalls,
yet I will rejoice in the Lord,
I will exult in the God of my salvation.

GREAT AND SMALL

◇

Prince Jen made an enormous fishhook with a huge line, baited it with fifty bullocks, settled himself on top of Mount K'uai-chi, and cast with his pole into the eastern sea. Morning after morning he dropped the hook, but for a whole year he got nothing. At last a huge fish swallowed the bait and dived down, dragging the enormous hook. It plunged to the bottom in a fierce charge, rose up, and shook its dorsal fins until the white waves were like mountains and the sea waters lashed and churned. The noise was like that of gods and demons, and it spread terror for a thousand li. When Prince Jen had landed his fish, he cut it up and dried it, and from Chih-ho east, from Ts'ang-wu north, there was no one who did not get his fill. Since then the men of later generations who have piddling talents and a penchant for odd stories all astound each other by repeating the tale.

Now if you shoulder your pole and line, march to the ditches and gullies, and watch for minnows and perch, then you'll have a hard time ever landing a big fish. If you parade your little theories and fish for the post of district magistrate, you will be far from the Great Understanding. So if a man has never heard of the style of Prince Jen, he's a long way from being able to join with the men who run the world.

—WRITINGS OF CHUANG-TZU
(CLASSICAL TAOIST TEACHER)

◇

He is self-luminous and more subtle than the smallest; but in him rest all the worlds and their beings.

—MUNDAKA UPANISHAD (HINDU SACRED TEXT)

CONTEMPLATION

What a magnificent creature a human is!

We stand next to the angels shoulder to shoulder, yet the Leviathans tower over us and make us feel puny (we assume) even in the eyes of God. Author and teacher Marianne Williamson addressed this issue: "Our deepest fear," she wrote, "is not that we are inadequate. Our deepest fear is that we are powerful beyond measure. It is our light, not our darkness, that most frightens us. We ask ourselves, who am I to be brilliant, gorgeous, talented, and fabulous? Actually, who are you not to be? You are a child of God. Your playing small doesn't serve the world. There's nothing enlightened about shrinking so that other people won't feel insecure around you. We were born to make manifest the glory of God that is within us."

COMPLETION

A man of Ch'u in charge of sacrifices to the gods gave his assistants a goblet of wine. One apprentice said to the others, "This isn't enough for all of us. Let's each draw a snake in the dirt, and the one who finishes first can drink the wine." They agreed and began drawing. The first to finish his snake reached for the goblet and was about to drink. But as he held the wine in his left hand, his right hand kept on drawing. "I can make feet for it," he said. Before he was done, another man finished drawing and snatched the goblet, saying, "No snake has feet." And he drank up the wine.

—WRITINGS OF CHAN KUO-TS'E
(CLASSICAL CHINESE TEACHER)

A horse once met a frog. The horse said: "Take this message to a snake for me, and you can have all the flies swarming around me."

The frog answered: "I like the reward, but I can't promise that I can complete the work."

—TRADITIONAL SUFI ANECDOTE

CONTEMPLATION

You've got to know when you're complete. You've got to know when you're not yet complete.

Imagine, as the Pagans who created the Runic symbols did, this 8-pointed symbol of completion:

Now consider some work or life project you're doing. Are you complete?

FULFILLMENT

◆

Once there was a poor man who wished for a fortune. One day he noticed a small purse lying on the floor of his house. When he picked it up, a heavenly voice declared, "Inside this purse you will find one coin. When you remove it, another will appear in its place. You may take from it as many coins as you wish, but you may not spend even one of them until you throw the purse into the river, where it will turn into a fish."

The poor man opened the purse and found a single coin inside. When he took it out, he found another coin where the first had been. All that day and all that night, he drew coins from the wonderful purse, until he had filled a large sack with gold coins.

The next morning he discovered that he was hungry, but there was no food in the house. Yet he was unwilling to spend any of his gold coins for food, so he went out to the streets to beg. He spent the few coins that he received to buy bread, then returned home and filled up another sack of gold from the purse.

The next day he was hungry again, so he took the purse down to the river to throw it in. But he could not bring himself to throw away the source of his good fortune. So again he went to beg on the streets.

So it went day after day. Often he went down to the river to throw the purse in, but he could never bring himself to do it. When he died many years later, they found his house full of gold, but not a crust of bread anywhere.

—TRADITIONAL JEWISH TALE

CONTEMPLATION

The following is a true story.

Once there was a man who, due to poverty, had immigrated to a new country, far from his native land. Oh, how he longed to return, but because he was still poor (and was a bit of a drunkard to boot), he did not have the means to do so.

Finally he got a city job as a street cleaner. The pay was decent, but although he could afford them, he bought no new clothes at all and wore his ratty, raggy outfit both while on the job and off duty. He bought and ate only old potatoes and soon-to-be-discarded produce.

For forty years or so he went on in this manner. Then he vanished. "Have you seen Mr. So-and-so?" the people in the neighborhood asked each other anxiously. Six months and not a sign of him.

Then one day he was back—picking up garbage on the streets again in his awful clothes—as if he had never gone. But there was something oddly new about him—a Mona Lisa–like smile of sweet satisfaction. He didn't say a word about it, but we knew. He'd been six heavenly months back in the old country!

WASTEFUL

◇

Miriam-Hannah, the wife of Reb Nissen the scribe, once sent her husband to market to buy a milch cow.

When Miriam-Hannah saw the cow at her door, she grabbed a pail and ran out to milk her cow, but it wasn't long before she returned to the house, blazing with fury, her pail empty.

"May the devil take both you and the cow—you old goat!" she shrilled.

"What's the matter?" mumbled Reb Nissen, turning pale as a sheet.

"You ask yet? Your precious cow doesn't want to give me one drop of milk!"

"Maybe you don't know how. Let me try!"

So Reb Nissen took up the pail and went outside to woo the cow.

It didn't take long before he returned with empty pail in hand.

"You ought to be ashamed of yourself, Miriam-Hannah," he rebuked her sternly. "How could you say the cow doesn't want to give any milk? Believe me—to give she wants, but, poor thing, she can't!"

—TRADITIONAL CHASSIDIC JEWISH TALE

◇

Useless is a great yield of milk
From a cow that kicks the pail over.

—WRITINGS OF HADRAT MUINUDIN CHISHTI
(SUFI MASTER)

CONTEMPLATION

The cow won't give milk. What a waste!

The cow will give milk, but some of it is lost. What a waste!

Will we ever stop this wasteful complaining? Today Zoroastrians celebrate Ghambar Maidyoshem, the holy time of sowing a summer crop and harvesting the grain of winter. Some seed will be planted and eaten by rodents. Some grain will rot in storage and feed mold organisms.

It's a beautiful system. What a waste not to enjoy it.

JULY

WEEDS

◇

Mullah Nasreddin decided to start a flower garden. He prepared the soil and planted the seeds of many beautiful flowers. But when they came up, his garden was not just filled with his chosen flowers but was overrun by dandelions. He sought out advice from gardeners all over and tried every method known to get rid of them, but to no avail. Finally he walked all the way to the capital to speak to the royal gardener at the sheikh's palace. The wise old man had counseled many gardeners before and suggested a variety of remedies to expel the dandelions, but mullah had tried them all. They sat together in silence for some time, and finally the gardener looked at Nasreddin and said, "Well, then I suggest you learn to love them."

—TRADITIONAL SUFI TALE

◇

Jesus said, "The Kingdom of the Father is like a man who had [good] seed. His enemy came by night and sowed weeds among the good seed. The man did not allow them to pull up the seeds; he said to them, 'I am afraid that you will go intending to pull up the weeds and pull up the wheat along with them.' For on the day of the harvest the weeds will be plainly visible, and they will be pulled up and burned."

—GOSPEL OF THOMAS
(APOCRYPHAL CHRISTIAN TEACHING)

CONTEMPLATION

The weeds of our lives—our neuroses, hatreds, and spite—are with us daily. Fertilized by provocative enemies and (unknowing) friends, these weeds can grow wildly if you let them. It's good to make efforts like meditation or self-awareness practices to try to cut them off.

But remember, your soul is a fertile field. Bees need more than one kind of flower from which to sip ambrosia. So do you. Your weeds provide diversity, nourishment and, ultimately, character and spiritual strength.

TWINS

◇

After a time the Sky Woman gave birth to twins. One, who became the Good Spirit, was born first. The other, the Evil Spirit, while being born, caused her mother so much pain that she died during his birth.

The Good Spirit immediately took his mother's head and hung it in the sky. It became the sun. From his mother's body he fashioned the moon and stars and placed them in the sky. The rest of his mother's body he buried under the earth. That is why living things find nourishment in the soil. They spring from Mother Earth.

The Evil Spirit put darkness in the western sky to drive the sun before it.

The Good Spirit created many things that he placed upon the earth. The Evil Spirit tried to undo the work of his brother by creating evil. The Good Spirit made tall and beautiful trees such as the pine and hemlock. The Evil Spirit stunted some trees. He covered some with thorns and placed poison fruit on them. The Good Spirit made animals such as the deer and the bear. The Evil Spirit made poisonous animals, lizards and serpents to destroy the animals of the Good Spirit's creation. The Good Spirit made springs and streams of good, pure water. The Evil Spirit breathed poison into many of the springs.

After mankind and the other creatures of the world were created, the Good Spirit bestowed a protecting spirit upon each of his creations. He then called the Evil Spirit and told him that he must cease making trouble upon the earth. This the Evil Spirit refused to do. The Good Spirit became very angry with his wicked brother and challenged him to combat, the victor to become ruler of the earth. They fought for many days; finally the Evil Spirit was overcome. The Good Spirit now became ruler over the earth. He banished his wicked brother to a dark cave under the earth. There he must always remain.

But the Evil Spirit has wicked servants who roam the earth.

—TRADITIONAL MOHAWK TRIBAL TALE
(NATIVE AMERICAN)

CONTEMPLATION

Zoroastrians provide an almost identical tale, revealed in the mountains of ancient Persia, of the Wise Lord, Ahura Mazda, and his great antagonist, Ahriman. At this time, when the year divides in two, people celebrate both the sowing of new green and the harvest.

This seems to our dualistic minds to be not only a contradiction, but an impossibility. Such is our nature—to be of twin spirits, complex and divergent, confused and lucidly aware—and capable of celebrating this very condition, too!

TROUBLE

◇

But man is born unto trouble, as sure as the sparks fly upward. I would seek unto God, and unto God would I commit my cause.

—BOOK OF JOB (HEBREW SCRIPTURES)

◇

Once Teltza, the beautiful only daughter of Shmuel the Shingle-Maker and Dvarshe the Midwife, was sweeping the floor of their poor house when she began to imagine her future.

"Here I am," she thought, "fifteen years old and beloved of everybody. I'm young and pretty and happy as a lark. In a year or two Papa will find me a fine young scholar, and we'll be married with song, dance, and a delicious feast to which the whole town will be invited. A year later I'll give birth to a fine, healthy son, and what a grand party we'll have at his *bris*! And then will come his bar mitzvah—but oh, no! What if he cries: 'My head, my head!' and dies like the son of the Shunnamite in the Bible?"

In a short time word spread throughout Chelm that a great disaster had befallen Teltza and her family. Soon all the people of the town came running to express their sympathy, and they began crying together with the grieving family. Along came the rabbi and asked them why they were all crying.

"There is only one thing to do," declared the rabbi. "We must all chant Psalms to avert the disaster."

Then along came the miller, the only person in town who had not been born in Chelm, and asked them why they were crying.

With a voice choked with sobs, Teltza told him her sad tale.

The miller threw back his head and laughed. "What a silly girl you are! Your sorrow is based on four great 'ifs'—if you marry, and if you have a son, and if he gets sick on his bar mitzvah, and if he dies. But none of these things has happened!"

Instantly Teltza stopped crying and smiled. When the others saw this, they too stopped their tears and broke into smiles. Soon everyone was laughing and slapping each other on the back.

"You see, my fellow Jews," beamed the rabbi, "nothing helps in a time of trouble like chanting Psalms. It never fails!"

—TRADITIONAL JEWISH TALE

Trouble itself they send away troubled who do not trouble themselves at the sight of it.

—TIRUKURAL (HINDU SACRED TEXT)

CONTEMPLATION

Have we got trouble? Oy! But think right now about some terrible trouble you had yesterday or last week. Can you even remember what exactly the matter was? What about a year ago today? Or ten years ago on July third?

Don't let the past or the future trouble you. Jesus told his disciples: "Peace I leave with you. Do not let your hearts be troubled, and do not let them be afraid."

SYMBOL

◇

In the Village of the Straw Hat, formerly known as Kasa, is a temple called Ryufuku, which was burned terribly during the wars. The roof was destroyed, so the statue of its deity stood subject to the rays of the sun and the wetness of the dew.

A maiden of much loveliness dwelled in the nearby town. Her father, once wealthy and highly esteemed, had fallen into the meanest of poverty and therefore had not a single *ryo* to provide for her marriage and only a few to keep the rice-pot full.

Before the Ryufuku temple had been burned, the good-hearted young lady had made her prayers there, petitioning for relief of her dire circumstances and for a good husband. After the temple burned, the priests and the worshippers abandoned it; still the young lady returned every day to pray to the Goddess Kannon amidst the ruins of the temple.

One day, as she was so worshipping, a downpour of rain fell from the heavens. "It is not right and proper," she said to herself, "that my head should be protected, while the Holy One's is not." So she removed her straw hat and placed it reverentially on the deity's head and bowed again in worship.

As fortune would have it, a nobleman from the Royal City, journeying with his entourage to Kyoto, beheld this most poignant scene—the Goddess Kannon, with a straw hat perched beautifully on her head, and a hatless, drenched young lady prostrate at her feet.

The nobleman bade his deputy to stay behind and, after questioning the girl, to rejoin the troop and report her answer.

When the girl arose, the deputy inquired, "Oh my dear lady, how is it that you bestow your hat on this statue made of insensitive stone, that knows no difference between sun and rain?"

She replied, "If that is what it is, how does it hear my prayers, then?" and went on her way.

When the nobleman heard of the young lady's sayings, he clasped his hands together in joy and admiration. "Surely," he proclaimed, "this is wisdom of the highest order. For in truth it is not to the image but what it symbolizes that we pray. The lady's straw hat itself is a symbol—of her love and devotions to the Gods! Where," he reflected, "could I find a better marriage for my son than this wise young lady?"

And so it came to be that she married the nobleman's son, who, after his father's death, rebuilt the temple, became its patron, and established it as the family shrine for all time.

The image of the deity to this day wears a hat of straw, and the symbol of a straw hat is displayed on all the sacred temple furnishings. The temple itself is known throughout the land as the Temple of the Straw Hat and the village as the Village of the Straw Hat.

—TRADITIONAL JAPANESE BUDDHIST TALE

CONTEMPLATION

A straw hat is not a temple. A temple is not worship.

Buddha pointed to the moon. Did you think the moon was real or the finger pointing to it?

When flags wave in the wind, we see first one side, then the other. Which is the true symbol?

HAPPINESS

◆

At an inn, Nasreddin met a man who was completely disconsolate. "What's the matter?" he asked.

The man answered, "Nothing in life interests me anymore. I've got enough money so that I don't have to work, enough to take a trip like this to new places, but so far I've found nothing new, even here, that is exciting or even interesting."

Nasreddin immediately snatched the wayfarer's bag and ran off down the road.

The man chased after him, and although Nasreddin was burdened by the heavy bag, he was familiar with the pathways and shortcuts and soon outdistanced the man he had robbed.

Nasreddin placed the man's bag on the roadside and hid himself, awaiting the arrival of the traveler.

Soon the poor man trudged up, even more unhappy than previously, because of the loss of his belongings. When he saw his bag, he ran to it, now exultant and very, very happy.

—TRADITIONAL SUFI TALE

CONTEMPLATION

There are two roads to happiness—the via negativa, wherein the restitution of loss produces a newfound happiness of sorts, and the via positiva, where you carry happiness with you and offer it to others. The latter is a far surer and smoother road.

Ma Yoga Shakti Saraswati, a renowned yoga and dharma teacher of more than thirty years and now a renunciate at age seventy, says: "The place to be happy is here. The time to be happy is now. The way to be happy is to make others so."

LONELINESS

◇

Then Elijah said to them, "I am the only one of the Lord's prophets left, but Baal has four hundred and fifty prophets. Get two bulls for us. Let them choose one for themselves, and let them cut it into pieces and put it on the wood but not set fire to it. I will prepare the other bull and put it on the wood but not set fire to it. Then you call on the name of your god, and I will call on the name of the Lord. The god who answers by fire—he is God."

Then all the people said, "What you say is good."

Elijah said to the prophets of Baal, "Choose one of the bulls and prepare it first, since there are so many of you. Call on the name of your god, but do not light the fire." So they took the bull given them and prepared it.

Then they called on the name of Baal from morning till noon. "O Baal, answer us!" they shouted. But there was no response; no one answered. And they danced around the altar they had made.

At noon Elijah began to taunt them. "Shout louder!" he said. "Surely he is a god! Perhaps he is deep in thought, or busy, or traveling. Maybe he is sleeping and must be awakened."

—FIRST BOOK OF KINGS (HEBREW SCRIPTURES)

◇

The Great Way has no gate;
there are a thousand different paths;
once you pass through the barrier,
you walk the universe alone.

—WRITINGS OF WU-MEN
(CLASSICAL ZEN BUDDHIST TEACHER AND POET)

CONTEMPLATION

There he was, Elijah, the one and only prophet of the God of the Israelites, facing an angry King Ahab and Queen Jezebel and a somber but potentially violent mob. What a lonely position!

Yet Elijah, who taunted the group of Baal's prophets about the inattention and distance of their god, was sure God was with him.

Today the earth is at its greatest distance from the sun. Perhaps you feel lonely this day, and uncertain of blessing and love in your life. There's a depth of connection that can be discovered only through such loneliness.

BUSINESS

When your merchandise went out on the seas, you satisfied many nations; with your great wealth and your wares, you enriched the kings of the earth.

Now you are shattered by the sea in the depths of the waters; your wares and all your company have gone down with you.

All who live in the coastlands are appalled at you; their kings shudder with horror and their faces are distorted with fear.

The merchants among the nations hiss at you; you have come to a horrible end and will be no more.

—BOOK OF EZEKIEL (HEBREW SCRIPTURES)

In five ways does a noble master minister to his servants and employees as the nazir: by assigning them work according to their strength, by supplying them with food and wages, by tending them in sickness, by sharing with them unusual delicacies, by granting them leave at times.

In five ways, thus ministered to by their master, do servants and employees love him: They rise before him, they lie down to rest after him, they are content with their wages, they do their work well, and they carry about his praise and good fame.

—SIGALOVADA SUTTA (BUDDHIST SACRED TEXT)

CONTEMPLATION

There's bad business and good business; bad businesspeople, like the Tyreans whom Ezekiel cursed, and good businesspeople, like Lydia of Philippi. A seller of highly prized purple dyes and garments, Lydia had a sizable enterprise and a community of fellow workers who evidently trusted her. When Paul came preaching the gospel, Lydia embraced it, and soon her circle had as well. Thus was the first Christian church-group founded in Europe. Imitating Jesus without knowing it, Lydia was "doing her Father's business"—very profitable indeed!

PRECARIOUS

◇

And so they arrived. Yaa WoRa told Ngeesi to look at the fruits out there in the middle of the Hot Water, saying that he was really worn out from hunger and that Ngeesi should climb and get him some to eat. This was his trick to kill Ngeesi. Ngeesi heard what his elder brother said, and since his brother was hungry, what could he do? He said his big brother should sit down while he climbed for the fruit. He climbed way up, way up above the big island over there in the middle of the Hot Water. When one looked at the way the water boiled and churned, no, it wasn't something for people to go into. So Ngeesi picked the fruit and threw it to the shore; his brother took it. He picked more and threw to the shore; his brother took it. He ate fruit until he was satisfied.

Then Ngeesi picked some and threw down, telling his elder brother to gather them so that when he got down, he could eat his share to get strength and go home. He picked his and threw them to the edge of the grass, and his big brother gathered them all on the ground. Then Ngeesi swung his foot down to grasp the vine and climb down to his brother to eat his fruit and go home, but his elder brother pulled out a big machete, aimed at the vine, and cut it *ndung*. The vine swung out and hung over the middle of the water *ngileng*. The vine swung out and hung over the middle of the water *ngileng*, leaving the brother up in the tree in the middle of the water *weq*!

—TRADITIONAL GBAYA TRIBAL STORY (WEST AFRICA)

◇

A man should not breed a savage dog, nor place a shaking ladder in his house.

—TRADITIONAL JEWISH SAYING

CONTEMPLATION

Life is precarious enough without allowing others or ourselves to make it more so. Don't push it.

But if you do find yourself out on a limb, in your daily life or in your spiritual practice, pray about it. In truth, the word prayer *comes from the Latin* precarius. *Prayer is always of benefit to the prayerful. Sometimes it's all you can do. And it's enough.*

TOO LITTLE, TOO MUCH

◇

Once there was a terrible drought in the land of Israel. It was already the month of Adar, which usually marks the end of the rainy season and the beginning of spring, but no rains had fallen all winter long.

So the people sent for Honi the Circle-Maker.

He prayed, but still no rains came. Then he drew a circle in the dust and stood in the middle of it. Raising his hands to heaven, he vowed, "God, I will not move from this circle until You send rain!"

Immediately a few drops fell, hissing as they struck the hot white stones.

But the people complained to Honi, "This is but a poor excuse for rain, only enough to release you from your vow."

So Honi turned back to heaven and cried, "Not for this trifling drizzle did I ask, but for enough rain to fill wells, cisterns, and ditches!"

Then the heavens opened up and poured down rain in buckets, each drop big enough to fill a soup ladle. The wells and the cisterns overflowed, and the wadis flooded the desert. The people of Jerusalem ran for safety to the Temple Mount.

"Honi!" they cried. "Save us! Or we will all be destroyed like the generation of the Flood! Stop the rains!"

Honi said to them, "I was glad to ask God to end your misery, but how can I ask for an end to your blessing?"

The people pleaded with him, and he finally agreed to pray for the rain to stop. "Bring me an offering of thanksgiving," he told them, and they did.

Then Honi said to God, "This people that You brought out of Egypt can take neither too much evil nor too much good. Please give them what they ask so that they may be happy."

So God sent a strong wind that blew away the fierce rains, and the people gathered mushrooms and truffles on the Temple Mount.

—TRADITIONAL JEWISH TALE

CONTEMPLATION

Too little prayer, and you forget God. Too much meditation, and you may forget your family.

Want to be just right? Forget about either/or thinking. Concentrate on your daily spiritual work. It's not this, not that. Just is.

WORSHIP

◇

A great saint was on a pilgrimage when he approached Mecca. Tired from his journey, he lay down on the earth and after a few hours was briskly awakened by an irate Muslim. "It is the time when everyone bows their head toward Mecca and you have your feet pointing to the Lord."

The saint half opened his eyes and told the man to adjust his feet in a direction where they would not point to the Lord.

—TRADITIONAL SUFI TALE

◇

Even the incompetent, indeed, should worship, ending with the offering of sacrificial food, ending with light. He who daily does this shall obtain progress toward the Auspicious.

—KARANA AGAMA (HINDU SACRED TEXT)

CONTEMPLATION

Who should worship? Everyone. How is worship to be done? If you are saintly in your devotions, the very pointing of your toes is worship.

Don't worry about the form. Whatever works for you works for God also.

PAYMENT

A king once said to his slave: "Go to market and buy me a fish!"

The slave went and bought a fish, but the fish stank.

"I swear by your life," cried the king, "that I will not forgive you for your stupidity, unless you accept one of three punishments: either you eat the fish yourself, or you pay back what it cost, or you let me give you a hundred lashes!"

"I will eat the fish," said the slave.

But he had no sooner begun to eat than he felt nauseated.

"Better give me the hundred lashes!" he begged the king.

So they began to count the lashes one by one. When they had counted fifty, the slave felt that he was near death.

"Better let me pay for the fish!" he cried.

What did the slave profit from it all? He ate the rotten fish, he got fifty lashes, and in the end he paid!

—TRADITIONAL JEWISH TALE

CONTEMPLATION

Like the ingenious slave, we hope, we wish, we pray we're going to get away with our mismanagement and stupidity.

Today is World Population Day, and many environmentalists and, strangely enough, economists believe that the earth and those of us living on it are already beginning to pay for excessive population.

What about the spiritual costs? It is difficult, Mahatma Gandhi said, to speak of God to one who has no bread. This is also true of one who has no space or no wilderness or no relief from intrusive noise.

Only a few religious leaders are willing to look at these issues for fear of offending or losing their own populations of the faithful. We must no longer be enslaved to this cowardice. We must be honest.

CHARACTER

◇

The laundryman's donkey carried heavy loads of wash all day long and eventually its energy became depleted. The laundryman was both compassionate and wise, so he placed a panther skin for warmth on the donkey and let him out in a neighboring pasture to graze. He hoped that in this way the donkey would recuperate.

Believing he was a panther, everyone, man and beast alike, left the donkey to eat at his leisure. One man, dressed in a grayish cloak, became so frightened at the sight of a panther in the field he started to run away.

The donkey, believing he saw a lovely female donkey moving in the distance, decided to give chase. The man only ran faster, and the donkey let out a loud braying love-call, for it was possible, he thought, that the female, too, had mistaken him for a panther.

When the man heard the braying sound, he knew this was no panther, but only a donkey. He stopped, drew out his bow, and killed the donkey then and there.

—TRADITIONAL TALE OF INDIA

CONTEMPLATION

As with both the donkey and the hunter, our true character is revealed most obviously in times of great difficulty or crisis. The doubting donkey brays; the hunter, in response, slays.

Can we be of greater character than they who merely act out of fear and habit?

The wise Chassid Rabbi Enoch believed so. In his commentary on the verse of the psalm, "The heavens are the heavens of the Lord, but the earth hath He given to the children of men," he said:

"The heavens are the heavens of the Lord"—you see, they are already of a heavenly character. "But the earth hath He given to the children of men"—so that they might make of it something heavenly.

TRICKSTER
◇

Kareya was the god who in the very beginning created the world. First he made the fishes in the ocean; then he made the animals on land; and last of all he made a man. He had, however, given all the animals the same amount of rank and power.

So he went to the man he had created and said, "Make as many bows and arrows as there are animals. I am going to call all the animals together, and you are to give the longest bow and arrow to the one that should have the most power, and the shortest to the one that should have the least."

So the man set to work making bows and arrows, and at the end of nine days he had turned out enough for all the animals created by Kareya. Then Kareya called them all together and told them that the man would come to them the next day with the bows, and the one to whom he gave the longest would have the most power.

Each animal wanted to be the one to get the longest bow. Coyote schemed to outwit the others by staying awake all night. He thought that if he was the first to meet the man in the morning, he could get the longest bow for himself. So when the animals went to sleep, Coyote lay down and only pretended to sleep. About midnight, however, he began to feel genuinely sleepy. He got up and walked around, scratching his eyes to keep them open. As time passed, he grew sleepier. He resorted to skipping and jumping to keep awake, but the noise woke some of the other animals, so he had to stop.

About the time the morning star came up, Coyote was so sleepy that he couldn't keep his eyes open any longer. So he took two little sticks and sharpened them at the ends, and with these he propped his eyelids open. Then he felt it was safe to sleep, since his eyes could watch the morning star rising. He planned to get up before the star was completely up, for by then all the other animals would be stirring. In a few minutes, however, Coyote was fast asleep. The sharp sticks pierced right through his eyelids, and instead of keeping them open, they pinned them shut. When the rest of the animals got up, Coyote lay in a deep sleep.

The animals went to meet the man and receive their bows. Cougar was given the longest, Bear the next longest, and so on until the next-to-last bow was given to Frog.

The shortest bow was still left, however.

"What animal have I missed?" the man cried.

The animals began to look about, and they soon spied Coyote lying fast asleep. They all laughed heartily and danced around him. Then they led him to the man, for Coyote's eyes were pinned together by the sticks and he could not see. The man pulled the sticks out of Coyote's eyes and gave him the shortest bow. The animals laughed so hard that the man began to pity Coyote, who would be the weakest of them all. So he prayed to Kareya about Coyote, and Kareya responded by giving Coyote more cunning than any other animal. And that's how Coyote got his cunning.

—TRADITIONAL ARRA-ARRA/KAROK TRIBAL TALE
(NATIVE AMERICAN)

CONTEMPLATION

When you think about it, we humans are the weakest of the animals. We possess no tearing teeth, no wings to fly and escape our attackers, no great bulk or terrible speed of foot. We are perhaps weaker and more pathetic than our brother Coyote.

So we have to be clever, too. George Gurdjieff, the odd master teacher of esoteric Christianity and Sufism, repeatedly urged his early-twentieth-century students to be clever. So did Jesus when sending his disciples on their initial missions. "Be as innocent as doves," he instructed them, and, he added, "wise as serpents."

To evolve spiritually it is essential to be clever. Otherwise, you'll find, like Coyote, that your habitual thoughts and ways somehow keep you from awakening.

Coyote acted on his own. The cleverest thing we can do is join with others. Then they can watch out for us, too.

WASHING

Knowing that his Father had given everything into his hands and that he had come from God and was going back to God, he got up from the table and put his clothes on and took a linen towel and tied it around his waist. Then he poured water into the basin and started washing his students' feet and drying them with the towel around his waist. So he comes to Simon Peter, who says to him, "Lord, are *you* going to wash *my* feet?"

Answered Jesus, "For now you don't know what I'm doing, later you will know."

—GOSPEL OF JOHN (CHRISTIAN NEW TESTAMENT)

That happiness that belongs to a mind that by deep meditation has been washed clear of all impurity and has entered within the Self, cannot be described by words; it can be felt by the inward power only.

—MAITRANYANA BRAHMANA UPANISHAD
(HINDU SACRED TEXT)

CONTEMPLATION

Said Peter to Jesus' offering of washing: "Never in the world are you going to wash my feet." The whole idea of being washed (as anyone who has been baptized in a cold body of water will testify) is shocking.

It is only later (Jesus said, and it's true) that the effects and understanding come. In truth many early Christians felt that a real baptism had taken place only when a person showed a subsequent change in behavior.

Spiritual washing must be, then, like its physical counterpart: a regular procedure. You can't just wash your hands once—look what happened to Pontius Pilate.

POWER

If people have no faith, I don't know what they are good for. Can a vehicle travel without a link to a source of power?

—ANALECTS (CLASSICAL CONFUCIANIST TEXT)

Arriving at the marketplace, a poor priest, dressed in rags, begged for a pear from a rich farmer. Instead, the busy farmer cursed the priest for pestering him. The market guard, seeing the large crowd getting upset at the farmer's refusal, bought a single pear himself and gave it to the priest. The humble priest thanked the guard, turned to the crowd, and announced, "Please allow me to offer some fragrant pears to all of you."

"But you have only one yourself," they said, "and no money to buy more."

"I need only one," he replied, proceeded to gobble up the precious pear, and removed a single seed from its core. The priest took this seed, quickly dug a small hole, and planted it. He asked for a large bucket of hot water and poured it over the pear seed.

Behold! A tiny seedling appeared. In what seemed like just a brief moment, it became a full-grown tree laden with masses of ripe, golden pears. The priest calmly picked the luscious fruits, presented them to the people, and his promise fulfilled, walked on.

—TRADITIONAL TAOIST TALE

All power is given unto me in heaven and in earth.

—GOSPEL OF MATTHEW
(CHRISTIAN NEW TESTAMENT)

CONTEMPLATION

Power is available to us. Even Jesus, considered by his disciples to be the most powerful healer and manifestor, conceded that his comrades could do as much or more. Greater things shall you do than I did, he told them with complete confidence and faith. Connected to the Source, you can command turbulent waters to be peaceful as Jesus is said to have done, or bring down heavenly rains to parched South Dakota lands, like Lakota Medicine people of our generation. The world asks this of you: Claim and proclaim your power today.

A precious child, Sasha Grace, at the age of three, put it this way: "When you give yourself to God, God gives you back to yourself, and then you have to use the power."

YOU

◆

When Hayyim of Zanz was a young man, he set about trying to reform his country from its evil ways. But when he reached the age of thirty, he looked around and saw that evil remained in the world. So he said, "Perhaps I was too ambitious. I will begin with my province." But at the age of forty his province, too, remained mired in evil. So he said, "I was still too ambitious. From now on I will only try to lift up my community." But at fifty he saw that his community had still not changed. So he decided only to reform his own family. But when he looked around, he saw that his family had grown and moved away, and that he now remained alone.

"Now I understand that I needed to begin with myself."

So he spent the rest of his life perfecting his own soul.

—TRADITIONAL JEWISH TALE

CONTEMPLATION

When God commanded Moses and his brother Aaron, they didn't answer, "Who, me?"

On the other hand, neither did they (nor should you) put themselves forward presumptuously as candidates for God's work.

The story is told of the renowned Rabbi Aaron, the first High Priest's namesake, and his beloved childhood friend. The boys studied together in the cheder, *the beginner's school, and as very young men left the village together to learn Torah and wisdom from a great master. There they stayed for many years, devoted to their training, until Aaron was given blessing and went home.*

Soon thereafter, the friend thought: "Aaron and I have been together all this time; if he was ready to return, I must be also." And with that, without a word, he took off for their native village.

He arrived in the middle of the night, bedraggled and tired from the journey, but even so he headed straight for his friend Aaron's house.

He knocked. He could hear Aaron's voice: "Who is it?"

"It's me."

No response. He called again, certain that Aaron recognized him: "It's me! It's me!"

"I don't know anyone who is a me. Go back and study."

MERIT

◆

Suppose a bodhisattva sees that a vicious robber intends to kill many people for the sake of wealth; or intends to harm virtuous shravakas, pratyekabuddhas, or bodhisattvas; or intends to do other things that will cause him to fall into the Uninterrupted hell. When seeing this, the bodhisattva will think, "If I kill that person, I will fall into the hells; if I do not kill him, he will commit crimes which will lead him to the Uninterrupted hell, where he will suffer greatly. I would rather kill him and fall to the hells myself than let him undergo great suffering in the Uninterrupted hell."

Then, deeply regretting the necessity for this action, and with a heart full of compassion, he will kill that person. In doing this, he does not violate the bodhisattva precepts; instead, he generates many merits.

—YOGACHARA BHUMI SHASTRA
(BUDDHIST SACRED TEXT)

CONTEMPLATION

The robber with murder in his eyes was killed by the Bodhisattva not because he merited death, but because he merited compassion.

Look more closely at each person and situation in your life. Don't just accept what society or your religion thinks is right and merited. Think for yourself.

DANCING

We always make offerings to the sun
And to the mountains
And to the stars.
That is why we live here . . .
We are the Elder Brothers.
We have not forgotten the old ways.
How could I say that I do not know how to dance?
We still know how to dance.
We have forgotten nothing.
We know how to call the rain.
If it rains too hard we know how to stop it.
We call the summer.
We know how to bless the world and make it flourish.

—TRADITIONAL KOGI TRIBAL SONG (NATIVE AMERICAN)

When the Creator dances, the worlds He created dance.

—TIRUMANTIRAM (HINDU SACRED TEXT)

CONTEMPLATION

The Kogi people continue to live in what was, until very recently, unintruded rain forests of South America. They danced and blessed their already blessed world.

Then oil was found. A delegation came to America, to Los Angeles, to meet with oil company executives. In a high-rise office building, the Kogi attempted to explain what was happening to the spirit of the land and the people as a consequence of drilling and extraction. With their words, they could not reach the executives. Then . . . they danced!

A good agreement followed.

HOLINESS

◇

What are the eighteen special dharmas of a Buddha? From the night when the Tathagata knows full enlightenment, to the day when he becomes extinct in Nirvana, during all this time:

1. He does not stumble.
2. He is not rash or noisy in his speech.
3. He is never deprived of his mindfulness.
4. He has no perception of difference.
5. His thought is never unconcentrated.
6. His evenmindedness is not due to lack of consideration.
7. His zeal never fails.
8. His vigor never fails.
9. His mindfulness never fails.
10. His concentration never fails.
11. His wisdom never fails.
12. His deliverance never fails.
13. All the deeds of his body are preceded by cognition, and continue to conform to cognition.
14. All the deeds of his voice are preceded by cognition, and continue to conform to cognition.
15. All the deeds of his mind are preceded by cognition, and continue to conform to cognition.
16. His cognition and vision regarding the past period of time proceed unobstructed and freely.
17. His cognition and vision regarding the future period of time proceed unobstructed and freely.
18. His cognition and vision regarding the present period of time proceed unobstructed and freely.

—SATASAHASRIKA PRAJNARAMITA
(BUDDHIST SACRED TEXT)

CONTEMPLATION

In Eastern traditions, generally speaking, holiness is achieved through abstention and withdrawal.

In Western traditions, generally speaking, holiness is achieved through sacrifice and belief.

You are your own tradition. Whatever is wholly you is holiness for you.

STUMBLING

◆

And David went up, and all Israel, to Baalah, that is, to Kirjath-jearim, which belonged to Judah, to bring up thence the ark of God the Lord, that dwelleth between the cherubim, whose name is called on it. And they carried the ark of God in a new cart out of the house of Abinadab: and Uzza and Ahio drove the cart. And David and all Israel played before God with all their might, and with singing, and with harps, and with psalteries, and with timbrels, and with cymbals, and with trumpets.

And when they came unto the threshing-floor of Chidon, Uzza put forth his hand to hold the ark, for the oxen stumbled. And the anger of the Lord was kindled against Uzza, and he smote him, because he put his hand to the ark: and there he died before God.

And David was displeased, because the Lord had broken forth upon Uzza: wherefore that place is called Perez-uzza to this day. And David was afraid of God that day, saying, How shall I bring the ark of God home to me?

—FIRST BOOK OF CHRONICLES (HEBREW SCRIPTURES)

CONTEMPLATION

Retreat. In many lands, primarily in Asia, Buddhist nuns and monks begin now a special three-month period, withdrawing from the great rains and into their inner selves. The world is a place where much is out of balance. Our mission is to make it right. We must, however, make ourselves right. Meditation is one methodology.

When the rains stop, these same nuns and monks will often join villagers in the work of repair and building. Though the earth has dried, it is still easy to stumble carrying heavy loads of wood and brick up mountain pathways. It's amazing how little is spilled!

MOON

◇

Then Rabbi Simeon said:

The secret of Solomon's wisdom was in the name of the moon when blessed from every side.

In his days the moon was magnified and reached her fullness.

A thousand mountains rose before her, and she blew them away with a puff.

A thousand mighty rivers flowed before her, and she swallowed them at a draught.

Her nails reached out in a thousand and seventy directions, and her hands in twenty-four thousand, so that nothing could escape her.

From between her legs a youth emerged who stretched from one end of the world to the other with sixty clubs of fire.

And his name was Enoch son of Jered.

Under him are stationed many Living Creatures, and the moon's hair is fastened under them and called "the scepter's knobs."

Her hands and feet take hold of it; she's like a lion clinging to his prey.

Her nails are those who call to mind the sins of men, inscribing them with rigor and exactness.

The parings of her nails are those who do not cleave to the King's Body and suck from the side of uncleanness when the moon begins to wane.

So Solomon, after he had inherited the moon in its fullness, also desired to inherit it in its defective state, to gain the knowledge of the spirits and the demons, inheriting the moon on every side.

—ZOHAR (CLASSICAL KABBALISTIC JEWISH TEXT)

CONTEMPLATION

The moon has many phases and turnings; so do our minds.

From the invisible, meditative "no mind" to full-blown revelatory lunacy, all is possible as we draw on the moon and she draws on us.

The esoteric teacher George Gurdjieff repeatedly told his students of the inherent tension between us and the cosmic spiritual forces of the moon. He warned of becoming "food for the moon." To be blessed rather than consumed in your spiritual work, like Solomon, address all the sides, angles, and phases of your practice.

FRUITFUL

◇

Rajah Koranya had a king banyan tree called Steadfast, and the shade of its widespread branches was cool and lovely. Its shelter broadened to twelve leagues. . . . None guarded its fruit, and none hurt another for its fruit. Now there came a man who ate his fill of fruit, broke down a branch, and went his way. Thought the spirit dwelling in that tree, "How amazing, how astonishing it is, that a man should be so evil as to break off a branch of the tree, after eating his fill. Suppose the tree were to bear no more fruit." And the tree bore no more fruit.

—ANGUTTARA NIKAYA (BUDDHIST SACRED TEXT)

◇

The fruit of the spirit is love, joy, peace, patience, kindness, generosity, faithfulness, gentleness, and self-control.

—PAUL'S EPISTLE TO THE GALATIANS
(CHRISTIAN NEW TESTAMENT)

CONTEMPLATION

No matter how fruitful you are, unintending or malevolent people can hurt you. You must guard yourself, your inner self carefully. Be aware that your fruits of the spirit, your calmness and strength, are looked upon enviously and greedily by some. You pick the time and place to offer your fruits.

HUMILITY

◆

One summer day, Chao-chou was sitting with his disciple Wen-yüan when a comical, yet brilliant idea came to him. "Wen-yüan," he proposed, "let's have a contest. Whoever of us can identify ourselves with the lowest of the low will 'win' and pay the 'loser' a cake." Wen-yüan accepted and the contest was on.

The master Chao-chou went first. "I am an ass," he said. Wen-yüan responded: "I am the buttocks of the ass." Chao-chou's turn: "I am the ass's defecation." Wen-yüan retorted: "I am a worm on the defecation of the ass." Chao-chou broke and could not go on. "And what," he asked, "are you doing there?" Without missing a beat, Wen-yüan said, "I am taking my summer holiday."

Chao-chou conceded. "You win," he declared. "Now give over the cake!"

—TRADITIONAL ZEN BUDDHIST TALE

◆

Humility is the Queen without whom none can checkmate the divine King.

—WRITINGS OF TERESA OF ÁVILA (CHRISTIAN MYSTIC)

CONTEMPLATION

Such an odd thing—humility leads to honor. If the last shall be first and the first last, then we all should be racing to get to places of honor last and, like the two good monks, to places of humility first. Get ready, go!

CAPACITY

◇

A young man who had a bitter disappointment in life went to a remote monastery and said to the abbot: "I am disillusioned with life and wish to attain enlightenment to be freed from these sufferings. But I have no capacity for sticking long at anything. I could never do long years of meditation and study and austerity; I should relapse and be drawn back to the world again, painful though I know it to be. Is there any short way for people like me?"

"There is," said the abbot, "if you are really determined. Tell me, what have you studied? What have you concentrated on most in your life?"

"Why, nothing really. We were rich, and I did not have to work. I suppose the thing I was really interested in was chess. I spent most of my time at that."

The abbot thought for a moment, and then said to his attendant: "Call such and such a monk, and tell him to bring a chessboard and men." The monk came with the board, and the abbot set up the men. He sent for a sword and showed it to the two. "Oh, monk," he said, "you have vowed obedience to me as your abbot, and now I require it of you. You will play a game of chess with this youth, and if you lose, I shall cut off the head of this man. Chess is the only thing he has ever tried hard at, and if he loses, he deserves to lose his head also." They looked at the abbot's face and saw that he meant it.

They began to play. With the opening moves the youth felt the sweat trickling down to his heels as he played for his life. The chessboard became the whole world; he was entirely concentrated on it. At first he had somewhat the worst of it, but then the other made an inferior move, and he seized his chance to launch a strong attack. As his opponent's position crumbled, he looked covertly at him. He saw a face of intelligence and sincerity, worn with years of austerity and effort. He thought of his own worthless life and a wave of compassion came over him. He deliberately made a blunder and then another blunder, ruining his position and leaving himself defenseless.

The abbot suddenly leaned forward and upset the board. The two contestants sat stupefied. "There is no winner and no loser," said the abbot slowly; "there is no head to fall here. Only two things are required"—and he turned to the young man—"complete concentration, and compassion.

You have today learned them both. You were completely concentrated on the game, but then in that concentration you could feel compassion and sacrifice your life for it. Now stay here a few months and pursue our training in this spirit, and your enlightenment is sure."

He did so and got it.

—TRADITIONAL ZEN BUDDHIST TALE

The baboon is a climber, but he does not forget that he could fall.

—TRADITIONAL ISWANA TRIBAL PROVERB
(SOUTHERN AFRICA)

CONTEMPLATION

Often you don't know your own capacity, until life and/or a good teacher sends you a challenge. Don't worry; you'll be up for it. Just don't overestimate your capacity to climb. Some trees are particularly shaky and very, very high!

SHARING

◇

Once a princess raised a starling and taught him to speak. She locked him in a golden cage and brought him to her room. But because he was not free to come and go, his heart was filled with sadness.

One day a knight came to the king and queen and asked them to guard his house and lands while he went traveling. On his way out of the palace, he passed the princess's room. From his gilded cage, the starling addressed him.

"My soul is weary from my barred prison," said the starling. "Although I have done no wrong, I was stolen from my family and shut up here among humankind. I ask that you remember me in your travels, kind sir, and if ever you see a bird like me, tell him of my plight and bring me back his reply."

The knight promised to do as the starling asked.

Near the sea the knight saw a starling and told him of his fellow's plight. Suddenly the bird fell down and lay lifeless upon the ground. The knight threw water upon him, wrapped him in his cloak, and tried to revive him, but it was no use. The bird was dead.

The knight then went on his journey, and when he returned, he told the princess's starling what had happened. The bird thanked him, and the knight returned to his home.

The next morning the princess found her bird lying dead at the bottom of his golden cage. She threw water upon him, held him in her hands, and tried all she could to revive him, but all life seemed gone from him. She wept and cast him aside upon the ground. As soon as she left the room, the starling spread his wings and flew away.

—TRADITIONAL JEWISH TALE

CONTEMPLATION

You have wisdom to share. If you're an elder, don't just sit back and assume, because younger people appear uninterested (or even disrespectful at times), that they—and you—could not benefit from exchanges of experience. If you're a younger person, be bold. Speak out. Things are changing so fast, you may be the first to discover some new way of dealing with a technological difficulty. Or a moral one.

Share. As Jewish mothers have been saying for millennia: "It couldn't hurt!"

TRAVEL

Before this Lieh-tzu liked travel. Hu-tzu asked him:

"What is it you like so much about travel?"

"The joy of travel is that the things which amuse you never remain the same. Other men travel to contemplate the sights, I travel to contemplate the way things change. There is travel and travel, and I have still to meet someone who can tell the difference!"

—BOOK OF LIEH-TZU (CLASSICAL TAOIST TEXT)

Three friends were curious about the size and shape of the earth. They were so curious that they decided to go exploring. They had traveled for three days and two nights when they came to an enormous ice-house. "Let's go in," one of the friends said. And so they went into the house, which seemed to be without end. They followed the halls in order not to get lost. Where was the passage through which they'd entered? They walked for days, for months, for years. At last they grew very weary. It was all they could do to crawl now. Then two of the friends could no longer crawl, and they sat down and died. The third friend managed to find the exit-passage. His kayak was exactly where he'd left it. He came back to his people as a very old man. And he told them, "The earth is simply a very big ice-house."

Then he died, too.

—TRADITIONAL INUIT TRIBAL TALE (NATIVE AMERICAN)

Not by any traveling is the world's end reached. Verily I declare to you that within this fathom-long body with its perceptions and its mind lies the world, its arising and its ceasing, and the Way that leads to its cessation.

—SAMYUTTA NIKAYA (BUDDHIST SACRED TEXT)

CONTEMPLATION

Travel plans are an oxymoron. If you are so sure of what you're going to see that you can plan the excursion, why bother to go? When you travel, be open to finding people better than you—and the better aspects of yourself as well.

You want to return from travel in the world or inside yourself a changed person—in a different and hopefully more enlightened place.

JULY 27
SAFETY

There is none like unto the God of Jeshurun, who rideth upon the heaven in thy help, and in his excellency on the skies. The eternal God is thy refuge, and underneath are the everlasting arms: and he shall thrust out the enemy from before thee; and shall say, Destroy them. Israel then shall dwell in safety alone.

—BOOK OF DEUTERONOMY (HEBREW SCRIPTURES)

The Lord dwells in the hearts of all creatures and whirls them around upon the wheel of maya. Run to him for refuge with all your strength, and peace profound will be yours through his grace.

—BHAGAVAD GITA (HINDU SACRED TEXT)

CONTEMPLATION

Sometimes it feels like we're spinning, that a whirlwind of disturbances has descended on us.

Today marks the beginning of hurricane season in the Caribbean; on Hurricane Supplication Day, prayer and ritual requests for safety from these terribly destructive storms are most fervent.

It is wise to look for refuge now. Find the person(s), the practice, the community, and place where your spiritual safety is assured.

You may stand upright there.

SILLINESS
◇

One day the citizens of Chelm, a town renowned for its wisdom, decided that they needed a Chief Sage. So they met in council and chose one among them for the position. But when this man walked through the streets of the town, no one treated him as different from any other citizen.

"Is this why you elected me?" he protested. "To remain unrecognized and unacclaimed?"

So they decided to buy him a pair of golden shoes to distinguish him from ordinary Chelmites. But on the next rainy day, the mud in the streets blackened the golden shoes, and no one knew that he was the Chief Sage, and thus no one paid any attention to him.

Enraged, he stormed into the council room.

"If I do not get more respect immediately, I'll resign as Chief Sage!" he cried.

"You're right!" agreed the council members. "We must protect the dignity of our Chief Sage."

So they ordered for him a pair of fine leather shoes to protect his golden shoes from the mud. The new shoes did keep the mud out, but they also kept the gold in, so that nobody could see that he was wearing special shoes befitting a Chief Sage. And so still no one paid attention to him.

Then they ordered the shoemaker to make new shoes for the Chief Sage, this time cutting holes in the leather.

"This way the leather will keep the mud out, but the holes will reveal the golden shoes underneath," they reasoned. "Now nobody will fail to recognize the Chief Sage!"

But when the Chief Sage walked through the streets, the mud oozed in through the holes and covered up the gold. So they stuffed straw into the holes to keep out the mud, but now the gold was covered up again.

"This is an outrage!" cried the Chief Sage. "A scandal! A disgrace! I demand that you do something!"

So the council members consulted all that day and long into the night, until at last they discovered a solution. They called the Chief Sage and said to him, "From now on, you will wear ordinary leather shoes when you walk in the street, but you will wear a pair of golden shoes on your hands. That way everyone will know that you are the Chief Sage of Chelm!"

—TRADITIONAL JEWISH TALE

CONTEMPLATION

When all wrapped up in protecting our sense of dignity, we can be just so silly. The truly blessed are those who are free from such concerns of pride.

A friend has an autistic child. He regularly broke or spilled things or put objects in new (and hard-to-trace) places. Exasperated, at times the mother would cajole her son and tell him how important it was to take his actions seriously. His response: "Silly." God only knows if he meant her, him, or just the whole darn world. She'd just have to laugh.

"Silly."

ENTRYWAY

◇

There are many roads leading to the Tao, but essentially they can be subsumed under two categories. The one is "entrance by way of reason" and the other "entrance by way of conduct."

By "entrance by way of reason" we mean the understanding of the fundamental doctrines through the study of the scriptures, the realization, upon the basis of a deep-rooted faith, that all sentient beings have in common the one True Nature, which does not manifest itself clearly in all cases only because it is overwrapped by external objects and false thoughts. If a man abandons the false and returns to the true, resting single-heartedly and undistractedly in pure contemplation (*pi-kuan*), he will realize that there is neither self nor other, that the holy and profane are of one essence. If he holds on firmly to this belief and never swerves from it, he will never again be a slave to the letter of the scriptures, being in secret communion with reason itself and altogether emancipated from conceptual discrimination. In this way he will enjoy perfect serenity and spontaneity. This is called "entrance by way of reason."

"Entrance by way of conduct" refers to the four rules of conduct under which all other rules can be subsumed. They are (1) the rule of nonrequital of hatred, (2) the rule of adaptation to variable conditions and circumstances of life, (3) the rule of nonattachment, and (4) the rule of acting in accord with the Dharma.

—WRITINGS OF BODHIDHARMA
(CLASSICAL ZEN BUDDHIST TEACHER)

CONTEMPLATION

Entering into a committed spiritual life should give one pause. It's a serious step. The entryway or door, as Jesus says, will be opened.

Once inside . . .

PURIFICATION

◇

Blessed are the pure in heart
for they shall see God.

—GOSPEL OF MATTHEW (CHRISTIAN NEW TESTAMENT)

◇

A newly accepted monk came to Master Joshu, and said, "I have just entered this monastery. Please give me instructions."
Joshu answered, "Have you had your breakfast?"
"Yes," replied the monk.
"Then," said Joshu, "wash your bowls."
The monk understood.

—TRADITIONAL ZEN BUDDHIST ANECDOTE

◇

The body is cleansed by water,
the internal is purified by truthfulness,
the individual soul by sacred learning,
the intellect by true knowledge.

—LAWS OF MANU (HINDU SACRED TEXT)

CONTEMPLATION

Oh-harai-taisai (Grand Purification Ceremony) takes place this day at Shinto shrines throughout Japan and the world. Traditionally, a large ring of woven grasses and reeds is placed at each shrine's entryway, and those who desire to complete shubatsu (purification) must first pass through the ring. In ancestral times Izanagi purified himself by diving to the river bottom. In this way, he became not only purified but also deified. From Izanagi came forth into the world the primordial Goddess of the Sun and God of Storms.

To love, you must be willing to undergo purification; to purify, you must be willing to love.

WITHDRAWAL

	above	Ch'ien	The Creative, Heaven
	below	Ken	Keeping Still, Mountain

The power of the dark is ascending. The light retreats to security, so that the dark cannot encroach upon it. This retreat is a matter not of man's will but of natural law. Therefore in this case withdrawal is proper; it is the correct way to behave in order not to exhaust one's forces.

In the calendar this hexagram is linked with the sixth month (July–August), in which the forces of winter are already showing their influence.

THE JUDGMENT

Retreat. Success.
In what is small, perseverance furthers.

—I CHING (CLASSICAL CHINESE TEXT)

Find a quiet retreat for the practice of yoga, sheltered from the wind, level and clean, free from rubbish, smoldering fires and ugliness, and where the sound of waters and the beauty of the place help thought and contemplation.

—YAJUR VEDA (HINDU SACRED TEXT)

CONTEMPLATION

It is at the peak of your powers that it is most important to withdraw from the world for contemplation and refreshment.

In this time of potency, people will be flocking to you, asking and demanding much of you. It happened to Jesus, and his response was to do his "yoga" out on a boat or up in the hills. Away.

Get away from the world for a while and into yourself.

AUGUST

WORK

◇

The harvest is ample but the workers are few.

—GOSPEL OF MATTHEW (CHRISTIAN NEW TESTAMENT)

◇

For each we have appointed a divine law and a traced-out way. Had God willed, He could have made you one community. But that He may try you, He made you as you are. So vie one with another in good works.

—QUR'AN (HOLY BOOK OF ISLAM)

◇

These offerings are born of work, and each guides humankind along a path to Brahman. Understanding this, you will attain liberation. The offering of wisdom is better than any material offering, Arjuna; for the goal of all work is spiritual wisdom.

—BHAGAVAD GITA (HINDU SACRED TEXT)

CONTEMPLATION

Here's what Thich Nhat Hanh, Vietnamese Buddhist spiritual teacher and peacemaker, says: "For some people, working is unpleasant, and they suffer when they have to work. I do many kinds of work, and if you forbid me from binding books, from gardening, from writing poetry, from practicing walking meditation, from teaching children, I will be very unhappy. To me work is pleasant."

We know he's right; we agree that work, by and large, is a great benefit for us. It provides money and a measure of security for us and our families and binds societies together in common practice and common cause. Thich Nhat Hanh's conclusion: "On the wooden board outside of the meditation hall in Zen monasteries, there is a four-line inscription. The last line is, 'Don't waste your life.'"

TEACHERS

◇

The whole world seeks to attain the transcendent state. Except through meeting the preceptor, the transcendent state may not arise.

—ADI GRANTH (SIKH SACRED TEXT)

◇

One day a large assembly of the Buddha's students gathered, awaiting his address. He said nothing, only smiled and gently held a flower in his fingers silently before them. Only one monk, Kashapa, smiled as well. The Buddha then spoke, "I have the Dharma-Eye, which is not expressed in words but transmitted mind to mind. This teaching I have given to the great Kashapa."

—TRADITIONAL BUDDHIST ANECDOTE

◇

It is no problem for me to discern silently, to study tirelessly, and to teach indefatigably. I can do nothing for those who do not ask themselves what to do.

Good people consistently practice virtue and learn how to teach.

—ANALECTS (CLASSICAL CONFUCIANIST TEXT)

◇

Ascend to me, up the mountain, and be there. To you I will give the stone tablets, the Law and the commandments which I have written to teach them.

—BOOK OF EXODUS (HEBREW SCRIPTURES)

◇

The world is full of half-enlightened masters. . . . They bestow their grandiose teachings upon the unwary.

The true master understands that enlightenment is not the end but the means.

She shares her divine energy with her students, encouraging them, creating trials to strengthen them, scolding them to awaken them, directing the streams of their lives toward the infinite ocean of the Tao.

The highest truth cannot be put into words. Therefore the greatest teacher has nothing to say. She simply gives herself in service, and never worries.

—HUA HU CHING (TAOIST SACRED TEXT)

◇

And now Abinadi said unto them: "Are you priests and pretend to teach this people . . . ?"

—BOOK OF MORMON

◇

I asked for one kiss, you gave me six.
Who was teacher is now student.
Things good and generous take form in me and the air is clear.

—WRITINGS OF RUMI (SUFI MYSTIC AND POET)

CONTEMPLATION

Teachers often do shocking things. If you have had good teachers in the past, consider yourself lucky. If you want a teacher, pray. If you have a true spiritual teacher, you are blessed.

Bless them in return, all those who have been your teachers on the way. Send kisses.

MUSIC

◇

Music expresses the harmony of the universe, while rituals express the order of the universe. Through harmony all things are influenced, and through order all things have a proper place. Music rises to heaven, while rituals are patterned on the earth. . . . Therefore the Sage creates music to correlate with Heaven and creates rituals to correlate with the Earth. When rituals and music are well established, we have Heaven and Earth functioning in perfect order.

—BOOK OF RITUAL (CLASSICAL CONFUCIANIST TEXT)

◇

Make a joyful noise unto the Lord, all ye lands.

—PSALM 100 (HEBREW SCRIPTURES)

◇

In the cosmic Void is He absorbed,
Where plays the unstruck mystic music—
Beyond expression is this miraculous wonder.

—ADI GRANTH (SIKH SACRED TEXT)

CONTEMPLATION

The world music phenomenon of today is unique only in its scope. As far back as we can trace, drum rhythms, chants, melodies, and songs have spread from one village to another and one culture to another far more easily than religious ritual or doctrine.

Music has two basic dimensions, the personal/communal and the sacred, and it has always been used to serve human and divine purposes.

David, before he became king of Israel, played soothing harp music to console the anxiety-ridden King Saul. According to legend, the same shepherd lad, David, composed many magnificent psalms, both the poetry and the accompanying music.

Certain woodland Native American tribes, in this late summer period, gathered for festivals of music. Not only were traditional sacred songs and melodies (the equivalent of Christian hymns) shared, but also awards were given to the creators of the best new popular songs of humor or love.

Whatever the music in your heart today, be it silly or soulful, sing it out!

DEATH

◇

Do not say, "They are dead!" about anyone who is killed for God's sake. Rather they are living, even though you do not notice it.

—QUR'AN (HOLY BOOK OF ISLAM)

◇

All the living must die, and dying, return to the ground; this is what is called kuei. The bones and flesh molder below and, hidden away, become the earth of the fields. But the spirit issues forth and is displayed on high in a condition of glorious brightness. The vapors and odors which produce a feeling of sadness are the subtle essences of all things, and also a manifestation of the shen nature.

—BOOK OF RITUAL (CLASSICAL CONFUCIANIST TEXT)

◇

If you desire to take wing as a bird,
Then leave to the vultures this carrion world.

—MAHMUD SHABISTARI (SUFI MYSTIC AND POET)

CONTEMPLATION

This story is told of the modern saint, Ramana Maharshi. When he was on his deathbed, his devotees grieved so uncontrollably, he heard them wailing in the far-off rooms. He asked one attendant, "Why do they despair so deeply?" "It is because you are leaving them." Ramana Maharshi responded with surprise. "But where," he inquired, "do they think I could go?"

Dr. Elisabeth Kübler-Ross, who has attended many, many deaths, found this to be true:

> Those who have the strength and love to sit with a dying patient in the *silence that goes beyond words* will know that this moment is neither frightening nor painful, but a peaceful cessation of the functioning of the body. Watching a peaceful death of a human being reminds us of a falling star; one of a million lights in a vast sky that flares up for a brief moment only to disappear into the endless night forever. To be a therapist to a dying patient makes us aware of the uniqueness of each individual in this vast sea of humanity.

Death can be a revelation. Attend to it now.

AWKWARD

◆

Coyote met Old Spider Woman, who was carrying a bundle. Coyote was very curious about what was inside, but even when Old Spider Woman started to take off the cover, Coyote still could not see. Carefully Old Spider Woman reached her hands inside and, one by one, she began placing the stars contained there into the sky, making designs of great beauty with them. The Pleiades, the Big Dipper, and many groups of stars did she make in this beautiful way.

Still there were many, many more stars left in the bundle, so Coyote cried out, "I want to place the stars in the sky, too. That way we'll be finished much faster." And with that, he grabbed the bundle and, not listening to Old Spider Woman's protest of caution, Coyote completely removed the cover. All the stars instantly sped skyward with no direction or pattern whatsoever. So Coyote was right; the task, through his awkward efforts, was done in no time at all.

Old Spider Woman sighed and reprimanded Coyote for spoiling her intention to make more beautiful constellations for all her relatives to see.

Coyote simply replied, "Oh, it's all right," and walked away as if he were not the one who had caused the stars to be arranged in such a disorganized way.

That is how Coyote made the stars to be where they are in the sky.

—TRADITIONAL HOPI TRIBAL TALE (NATIVE AMERICAN)

CONTEMPLATION

Things may be difficult enough in your life, and you may be awkward in dealing with them even when you have a clear intention. How much more awkward are you (and how much more problematic are the results) when, like Coyote, you have mixed motives?

The prophet Elijah adjured the Israelites to stop hopping as birds do from one tree limb to another in terms of their worship. Hint: You're bound to slip up sometimes.

DESTRUCTION

◇

And when ye shall see Jerusalem compassed with armies, then know that the desolation thereof is nigh. Then let them which are in Judea flee to the mountains; and let them which are in the midst of it depart out; and let not them that are in the countries enter thereinto. For these be the days of vengeance, that all things which are written may be fulfilled. But woe unto them that are with child, and to them that give suck, in those days! for there shall be great distress in the land, and wrath upon this people.

And there shall be signs in the sun, and in the moon, and in the stars; and upon the earth distress of nations, with perplexity; the sea and the waves roaring; Men's hearts failing them for fear, and for looking after those things which are coming on the earth: for the powers of heaven shall be shaken. And then shall they see the Son of man coming in a cloud with power and great glory.

—GOSPEL OF LUKE (CHRISTIAN NEW TESTAMENT)

CONTEMPLATION

Today, the heavens themselves were shaken with great power of destruction and from clouds woe befell all the nations.

The first atomic bomb was dropped, this day, not by God in some final act of covenant-breaking, but by human design. If one must unleash such powerful force today, let it explode in your heart, revealing and releasing your will to destroy.

DUTY

King Priyadarshi, the Beloved of the Gods, says: People perform various ceremonies. Among the occasions on which ceremonies are performed are sicknesses, marriages of sons or daughters, children's births, and departures or journeys. Women in particular have recourse to many diverse, trivial, and meaningless ceremonies.

It is right that ceremonies be performed. But this kind bears little fruit. The ceremony of Dharma (*Dharma-mangala*), on the contrary, is very fruitful. It consists in proper treatment of slaves and servants, reverence to teachers, restraint of violence toward living creatures, and liberality to priests and ascetics. These and like actions are called the ceremonies of Dharma.

Therefore, a father, son, brother, master, friend, acquaintance, or even a neighbor ought to say about such actions, "They are good; they should be performed until their purpose is achieved. I shall observe them."

Other ceremonies are of doubtful value. They may achieve their purpose, or they may not. Moreover, the purposes for which they are performed are limited to this world.

The ceremony of Dharma, on the other hand, is not limited to time. Even if it does not achieve its object in this world, it produces unlimited merit in the next world. But if it produces its object in this world, it achieves both effects; the purpose desired in this world and unlimited merit in the next.

It has also been said that liberality is commendable. But there is no greater liberality than the gift of Dharma or the benefit of Dharma. Therefore, a friend, well-wisher, relative, or companion should urge you when the occasion arises, saying, "You should do this; this is commendable. By doing this you may attain heaven." And what is more worth doing than attaining heaven?

—ROCK EDICT OF KING ASHOKA
(CLASSICAL BUDDHIST TEXT)

CONTEMPLATION

Are you going through the motions or really doing your duty / dharma? Are you showing up (and showing off) at worship services or sincerely worshiping? Are you studying just enough to get by or researching challenging material? Are you acting ceremoniously toward the homeless or volunteering at the food bank? My friend, doing your dharma is most commendable. Urge your friends, too.

AUGUST 8

TOLERANCE

The vile are ever prone to detect the faults of others, though they be as small as mustard seeds, and persistently shut their eyes against their own, though they be as large as Vilva fruit.

—GARUDA PURANA (HINDU SACRED TEXT)

The monk Hakuin lived the simple and pure life of the monastery, true to all his vows. When he was called to live in the town, he accepted this and maintained his pious ways.

One day a very young woman, obviously pregnant, together with her parents the village grocers, crossed the street to Master Hakuin's hut. She accused the monk of being the father of her child. In reply, Hakuin said only, "Is that so?"

Some months later the child was born, and again the family returned to see Hakuin. Holding him liable, they put the newborn into Hakuin's arms. In response, all the monk said was "Is that so?" and he took the baby into his care.

For over a year, Hakuin nurtured the infant with the kind of deep devotion he gave to his religious duties. Then once more the young woman returned, this time with a young man, the fish-seller's son, their neighbor. They confessed that shame had prevented them from telling the truth at the beginning. But having told their families, they now wished to have their child back. Master Hakuin simply said, "Is that so?" and gave the child to its mother and father.

—TRADITIONAL ZEN BUDDHIST ANECDOTE

Do not judge your comrade until you have stood in his place.

—MISHNAH (JEWISH SACRED TEXT)

CONTEMPLATION

Is there anything that an animal will not tolerate from its young? Some mothers will even nurse and raise persistent newborns of another species.

Thus, tolerance is kindness—the application of love to every being as one of your own kind. When you let yourself to be in the heart of this nonprejudiced, unmoving, ultimately human place, kindness comes as a natural consequence.

SERPENT

Listen to this, and hear the mystery inside:
A snake catcher went into the mountains to find a snake.
He wanted a friendly pet, and one that would amaze
audiences, but he was looking for a reptile, something
that has no knowledge of friendship.
It was winter.
In the deep snow he saw a frighteningly huge dead snake.
He was afraid to touch it, but he did.
In fact, he dragged the thing into Baghdad,
hoping people would pay to see it.
This is how foolish
we've become! A human being is a mountain range!
Snakes are fascinated by us! Yet we sell ourselves
to look at a dead snake.
We are like beautiful satin
used to patch burlap. "Come see the dragon I killed,
and hear the adventures!" That's what he announced,
and a large crowd came,
but the dragon was not dead,
just dormant! He set up his show at a crossroads.
The ring of gawking rubes got thicker, everybody
on tiptoe, men and women, noble and peasant, all
packed together unconscious of their differences.
It was like the Resurrection!
He began to unwind the thick ropes and remove
the cloth coverings he'd wrapped it so well in.
Some little movement.
The hot Iraqi sun had woken
the terrible life. The people nearest started screaming.
Panic! The dragon tore easily and hungrily
loose, killing many instantly.
The snake-catcher stood there,
frozen. "What have I brought out of the mountains?" The snake
braced against a post and crushed the man and consumed him.
The snake is your animal-soul. When you bring it

into the hot air of your wanting-energy, warmed
by that and by the prospect of power and wealth,
it does massive damage.

—WRITINGS OF RUMI (SUFI POET AND MYSTIC)

CONTEMPLATION

If you're going to dance with serpent energy (as the Hopi do at this time in their Snake Dance Festival), be prepared.

The subconscious is powerful. If you're good and ready to handle its serpentine medicine, great. Otherwise, you'd best find a medicine person to work with.

INTEGRITY

◆

One day while a group of animals were having a meeting, Land Turtle got up and told them that Leopard was his father's horse. When the meeting broke up, Gray Squirrel ran as fast as he could go to Leopard's house.

Said Squirrel, "The only thing is, Turtle said that you were his father's horse and he could prove it."

"What! Turtle called me a horse? He must be losing his mind. In fact, Squirrel, I have been thinking about roasting the fool with pepper and eating him with young cassavas," Leopard growled furiously. Leopard jumped up and put on his clothes and dashed off to Turtle's house. "Say, look here, Turtle, why did you tell all the animals that I was your father's horse?"

Turtle got up trembling. "Me, uncle? If it weren't for the malaria I have, I would surely go and disprove this lie," Turtle said.

"I am so furious, Turtle, I don't mind taking you on my back to get this lie straightened out." Leopard lifted Turtle and put him on his back. They had not gone quite a mile when Turtle slipped and fell to the ground. "What is the matter? Why did you fall?" Leopard inquired.

"Uncle, your back is too hard and the ride is very uncomfortable. If you can let me fix a seat to sit on, I think I can make it." Turtle went and made a fine seat and put it on Leopard's back and commenced riding again. In less than a mile, again Turtle fell to the ground. This time the excuse was that he had nothing to hold on to while riding. Turtle suggested that a rope passing through Leopard's mouth would be just the ideal thing he wanted. Leopard agreed to the rope, and Turtle passed it to his mouth and held on to it. They had not gone far when Turtle fell again, for the third time. Leopard was getting annoyed, but he had to live up to his side of the bargain. This time Turtle wanted ropes tied to the seat so he could rest his legs. As they got near their destination, Turtle again fell to the ground. This time he needed a long switch for the flies who were bothering him. Leopard said, "Oh, sure, get down and get yourself a switch." When they got to the village, Turtle began to beat Leopard on the behind as hard as he could. Leopard started galloping like a horse. All the animals came out and hollered, "Ho-o-o! Turtle was right when he said Leopard was his father's horse!" When Turtle got down this time, he ran home as fast as he could and went back into his hole.

—TRADITIONAL VAI TRIBAL TALE (WEST AFRICA)

CONTEMPLATION

Turtle better run! He counted on Leopard's integrity to do the right thing and follow through. What if Leopard returns to his original intention of roasting the fool? Don't fool around with your own or anyone else's integrity. Smell fire?!

STAGES

◆

Narada said: When the mendicants who had taught me what I knew had departed, I did the following in my childhood. I was my mother's only child. She was a naive woman, a servant. As I, her son, had no other recourse, she lavished her love on me. Being herself dependent, she was unable to provide for me, though she was eager to do so. People in the employ of a rich man are like wooden puppets. I lived with a Brahmin family to which I devoted my attentions, a little boy five years old, innocent of any knowledge of direction, place, or time.

One night my mother went out of the house to milk the cow, and on the way she stepped on a snake, which, urged by Time, bit the poor woman. Thinking it was a favor of the lord who wishes his devotees well, I at once set out in a northerly direction. I passed through prosperous countrysides, cities, villages, pastures, mining camps, hamlets, mountain settlements, plantations, woods, and parks, over mountains variegated with colorful minerals, where the tree limbs had been broken off by elephants, through pools with safe water, lotus ponds visited by the gods with warbling birds and whirring bees.

Then, still alone, I saw a large forest dense with reed, bamboo, and cane, fearful and dangerous, infested with snakes, owls, and jackals. Exhausted in body and soul, hungry and thirsty, I bathed, drank, and rinsed at a river pool, until I was rested. Then, sitting under a peepal tree in the deserted wilderness, I began to reflect on the Self which, as I had heard, dwells in oneself. While I was meditating on his lotus feet, my mind was overcome with emotion and my eyes filled with tears of yearning. Hari slowly became present in my heart. Filled with the fullness of love, my body thrilled. I was enraptured; merged in an inundation of bliss, I saw no more duality. But when this dear vision of the form of the blessed lord faded, and I to my sorrow no longer beheld him, I rose quickly, disturbed and distressed. Straining to see him again, I collected my mind in my heart; but though seeing, I was blinded, frustrated as one diseased.

While I was thus striving in the wilderness, he spoke to me, invisible, in a deep and gentle voice, as though to assuage my sorrow, "Child, you cannot see me in this life, for I am invisible to sham yogins whose taints have not been removed by maturity. I showed you this form to inspire your longing; for the good man who longs for me slowly relinquishes all desires. When by long attendance on good people your mind has become steadfastly fixed on me and you have abandoned this unspeakable world, you shall become mine. A mind that is fastened on me will never stray: even when creation comes to an end, he will by my grace remember me."

With this he ceased speaking, that great being, the lord who showed no other mark than sky; and with a sense of grace I bowed my head to him who is greater than the great.

—TRADITIONAL HINDU TALE

CONTEMPLATION

Childhood, independence, old age—these are the natural stages a person journeys through in life. For some they may be charming; for others fraught with difficulty. Life also affords a chance to develop spiritually. This transformation also occurs in stages, but here you are the director of the play. When you've completed a certain part, it's fine to take an intermission and savor the accomplishment.

But don't forget you're due back on stage for the next act. Your cue is coming up.

LEGACY

◇

And here is the account of a maiden, the daughter of a lord named Blood Gatherer. Blood Gatherer is the name of her father, and Blood Woman is the name of the maiden.

And when he heard the account of the fruit of the tree, her father retold it. And she was amazed at the account: "I'm not acquainted with that tree they talk about. 'Its fruit is truly sweet!' they say, I hear," she said.

Next, she went all alone and arrived where the tree stood. It stood at the Place of Ball Game Sacrifice: "What? Well! What's the fruit of this tree? Shouldn't this tree bear something sweet? They shouldn't die, they shouldn't be wasted. Should I pick one?" said the maiden.

And then the bone spoke; it was here in the fork of the tree: "Why do you want a mere bone, a round thing in the branches of a tree?" said the head of One Hunahpu when it spoke to the maiden. "You don't want it," she was told.

"I do want it," said the maiden.

"Very well. Stretch out your right hand here, so I can see it," said the bone.

"Yes," said the maiden. She stretched out her right hand, up there in front of the bone.

And then the bone spit out its saliva, which landed squarely in the hand of the maiden.

And then she looked in her hand, she inspected it right away, but the bone's saliva wasn't in her hand.

"It is just a sign I have given you, my saliva, my spittle. This, my head, has nothing on it—just bone, nothing of meat. It's just the same with the head of a great lord: it's just the flesh that makes his face look good. And when he dies, people get frightened by his bones. After that, his son is like his saliva, his spittle, in his being, whether it be the son of a lord or the son of a craftsman or an orator. The father does not disappear, but goes on being fulfilled. Neither dimmed nor destroyed is the face of a lord, a warrior, craftsman, orator. Rather, he will leave his daughters and sons. So it is that I have done likewise through you. Now go up there on the face of the earth; you will not die. Keep the word. So be it," said the head of One and Seven Hunahpu—they were of one mind when they did it.

This was the word Hurricane, Newborn Thunderbolt, Raw Thunder-bolt had given them. In the same way, by the time the maiden returned to her home, she had been given many instructions. Right away something was generated in her belly, from the saliva alone, and this was the generation of Hunahpu and Xbalanque.

—POPUL VUH (MAYAN SACRED TEXT)

CONTEMPLATION

What are you pregnant with? You cannot merely take of the fruits of spirit and this world-tree and say you have lived a righteous life. You must birth something to leave a legacy for the world.

DETERMINATION

◇

Long ago there was a giant who loved to kill humans, eat their flesh, and drink their blood. He was especially fond of human hearts. "Unless we can get rid of this giant," people said, "none of us will be left," and they called a council to discuss ways and means.

One man said, "I think I know how to kill the monster," and he went to the place where the giant had last been seen. There he lay down and pretended to be dead.

Soon the giant came along. "Ah, good," he said, "this one is still warm and fresh. What a tasty meal he'll make; I can't wait to roast his heart."

Carrying the man home, the giant dropped him in the middle of the floor right near the fireplace. Then he saw that there was no firewood and went to get some.

As soon as the monster had left, the man got up and grabbed the giant's huge skinning knife. Just then the giant's son came in, bending low to enter. He was still small as giants go, and the man held the big knife to his throat. "Quick, tell me, where's your father's heart? Tell me or I'll slit your throat!"

The giant's son was scared. He said, "My father's heart is in his left heel."

Just then the giant's left foot appeared in the entrance, and the man swiftly plunged the knife into the heel. The monster screamed and fell down dead.

Yet the giant still spoke: "Though I'm dead, though you killed me, I'm going to keep on eating you and all the other humans in the world forever!"

"That's what you think!" said the man. "I'm about to make sure that you never eat anyone again." He cut the giant's body into pieces and burned each one in the fire. Then he took the ashes and threw them into the air for the winds to scatter.

Instantly each of the particles turned into a mosquito. The cloud of ashes became a cloud of mosquitoes, and from the midst the man heard the giant's voice laughing, saying, "Yes, I'll eat you people until the end of time."

And as the monster spoke, the man felt a sting, and a mosquito started sucking his blood, and then many mosquitoes stung him, and he began to scratch himself.

—TRADITIONAL TLINGIT TRIBAL TALE

(NATIVE AMERICAN)

CONTEMPLATION

Who was more determined, the man or the giant? Both achieved a valuable end. Let the Tao be your determination. Classical Taoist teacher Liu I-ming writes: "The Tao is as deep as can be—who is willing to pursue it closely? If you don't go into the tiger's lair, how can you catch its cub? If you don't wash out the stone and sand, how can you pick out the gold? . . . carefully seek the heart of heaven and earth with firm determination. Suddenly you will see the original thing; everywhere you meet the source, all is a forest of jewels."

REST

◇

The more you strive to stop motion in order to attain rest,
The more your rest becomes restlessness.
As long as you are stuck in dualism,
How can you realize oneness?

The object is an object for the subject,
The subject is the subject for the object:
Know that the relativity of the two
Rests ultimately on one emptiness.

—WRITINGS OF SENG-TS'AN
(CLASSICAL ZEN BUDDHIST TEACHER)

◇

So she gleaned in the field until even, and beat out that she had
gleaned: and it was about an ephah of barley.

And she took it up, and went into the city: and her mother-in-law saw
what she had gleaned: and she brought forth, and gave to her that she had
reserved after she was sufficed.

And her mother-in-law said unto her, "Where hast thou gleaned today?
and where wroughtest thou? blessed be he that did take knowledge of
thee." And she shewed her mother-in-law with whom she had wrought,
and said, "The man's name with whom I wrought today is Boaz."

And Naomi said unto her daughter-in-law, "Blessed be he of the Lord,
who hath not left off his kindness to the living and to the dead." And
Naomi said unto her, "The man is near of kin unto us, one of our next
kinsmen."

And Ruth the Moabitess said, "He said unto me also, 'Thou shalt keep
fast by my young men, until they have ended all my harvest.'"

And Naomi said unto Ruth her daughter-in-law, "It is good, my daughter, that thou go out with his maidens, that they meet thee not in any
other field."

So she kept fast by the maidens of Boaz to glean unto the end of barley harvest and of wheat harvest; and dwelt with her mother-in-law.

Then Naomi her mother-in-law said unto her, "My daughter, shall I
not seek rest for thee, that it may be well with thee?"

—BOOK OF RUTH (HEBREW SCRIPTURES)

CONTEMPLATION

As the Bible tells it, even God rested after the six-day period of amazing creative effort.

We give ourselves little rest. We are chasing the best jobs, the best schools, the best vacations—constantly believing in the "if only I had this, then I could rest easy" theory. Stop.

Re-create your original notion of what a good life is. Take a Sabbath day regularly.

CLOTHING

◇

One day, three swindlers, pretending to be weavers of the greatest skill, told the King they could make a very special cloth. This cloth and the clothing made from it could be seen only by legitimate offspring, but to the illegitimately born the same clothing would be completely invisible.

The King thought this was marvelous. With the weavers' clothing, the King could easily determine who the rightful sons and heirs were, and who were false in their claims. So he provided the weavers with a mansion to dwell in and to use as a workshop. The King also gave the weavers all the jewels, gold, and silk they had informed the King were necessary to produce their unique cloth.

They put up their looms, and every day, all day long, the weavers feigned busyness at their prescribed task of fulfilling the King's order.

When it seemed the cloth would be ready, the King sent first his chamberlain to inspect it. The chamberlain visited the workshop and chatted with the weavers and saw nothing of the magical cloth. He was afraid, of course, to report such a thing to the King, so he told the King that he had indeed seen the most wonderful cloth.

The King was duly pleased, and he sent another deputy to the weavers' workshop. This deputy spoke just as the chamberlain had.

The King then felt it was high time he saw this magical cloth himself, and off he went.

For the King, the weavers gave the most eloquent and elegant description of the cloth. They described in detail the skillful processes they had used to make it, and spoke of their pride in meeting his request. The King listened and stared but he could see no cloth at all, much less the magnificent cloth the weavers claimed they had made. He began to feel queasy about himself. What if he was not the true son of the King, his father? Would he be forced to renounce his sovereignty?

The King hastened to praise the cloth mightily, and to all who inquired he repeated the tale the weavers had told him about the origin and design of the magical cloth.

Whoever the King sent to view the cloth returned, understandably, with glorious reports of its splendor.

The day of the great celebration was nigh, and the weavers brought the King's new clothes for him to wear on this occasion.

The crowds that day were very surprised to see the King dressed, or rather not dressed, as he was. But the word spread that only the illegitimate could not see the King's splendorous clothing, and soon, very soon indeed, all the people were quiet and self-reflective.

That is, all but one. A black fellow stepped forward and addressed the King thus: "Oh King, I am completely disinterested in my parentage. Therefore I may tell you, Sire, that you are parading around without a single stitch of clothing!"

—TRADITIONAL MOORISH/SPANISH TALE

CONTEMPLATION

In describing the woman of virtue, the Bible says, "Strength and honor are her clothing." Taoist master Lao-tzu concurs: "The sage," he says, wears clothes of coarse cloth but carries jewels in his bosom. Sufis, including those from the land of the Moors, wore such simple wool garments that many believe the appellation "Sufi" itself comes from the Arabic suf or wool.

A modern sage, Mahatma Gandhi, accepted an invitation from the King of England (and proclaimed Emperor of India), George V. Although subject to ridicule, Gandhi went in his traditional native attire, a simple robe and shawl. Asked afterward if he felt underdressed, he answered, "His Majesty had enough clothes on for the both of us."

SURGERY

◆

And when Phinehas, the son of Eleazar, the son of Aaron the priest, saw it, he rose up from among the congregation, and took a javelin in his hand; and he went after the man of Israel into the tent, and thrust both of them through, the man of Israel, and the woman through her belly. So the plague was stayed from the children of Israel. And those that died in the plague were twenty and four thousand.

—BOOK OF NUMBERS (HEBREW SCRIPTURES)

◆

Sh hab wa chu'i na'ana. They say it happened long ago. All was well with the O'odham, the People. All was in harmony. But then a great snake came from out of Earth. It came to the place where the people lived and began to devour them. It sucked the people into its mouth. Those people who escaped the great snake called to Itoi, Elder Brother.

"Help us!" they called.

Itoi came then from his home on Waw Giwulk. He came from his house in the center of the world.

"Give me an obsidian knife and four greasewood sticks," Elder Brother said.

Then Itoi took the knife and sticks and went to meet the great snake.

The snake sucked Elder Brother into its mouth, but he stuck the first greasewood stick into the snake's mouth and wedged it open. It sucked him down into its throat, but he stuck the second greasewood stick in the great snake's throat and wedged it open. It sucked him down into its esophagus, but he stuck the third greasewood stick in and held its esophagus open. It sucked him down into its belly, but he wedged in the fourth greasewood stick and held its belly open.

In the great snake's belly, Itoi listened. He listened for the sound of its heart. With his obsidian knife he slashed the heart and then ran out of the great snake, pulling free each greasewood stick as he ran. So Itoi killed the great snake.

Elder Brother went back to the O'odham and told them the danger was over. Then he went back to his home on Waw Giwulk. *Am o wa'i at hoabdag.* That is at the center of the basket.

—TRADITIONAL O'ODHAM TRIBAL TALE
(NATIVE AMERICAN)

CONTEMPLATION

Is some aspect of your being plaguing you? A habit? An attitude? A way of life that is really leading to death?

Don't wait. Scrub up. Grab your best surgical tools and excise it.

Surgery is not only recommended; in your case, it's the only action possible.

PURPOSE

One day David was in his garden, and he noticed a spider's web glistening with morning dew.

"How wise You are, O God, and how wonderful is the world You have created. But of what use is the spider who weaves garments that no one wears?"

God answered David, "The time will come when you will need this creature, and then you will understand why it was created."

Not long afterward Saul's evil spirit again visited him, and he pursued David in order to kill him. David fled to the wilderness and hid in a cave. Saul's men pursued him there and began to search the caves looking for him.

As David cowered at the back of his cave, he heard the footsteps of the soldiers nearing the mouth of the cave. And he gave himself up for lost.

But just then he noticed a spider overhead, and as he watched, it began spinning a web in front of him, stretching from the roof of the cave down to the floor.

Moments later, when Saul's men entered the cave, they saw the web and said, "Look, here is an unbroken spider's web. Surely no one has come in here for days!" And they left without searching the cave.

So David was saved from certain death. And never again did he question God's wisdom in creating the spider.

—TRADITIONAL JEWISH TALE

White-Buffalo-Cow-Woman-Appears, you have prayed to Wakan-Tanka, the Great Spirit, you will now go forth among your people in a holy manner, and you will be an example to them. You will cherish those things which are most sacred in the universe; you will be as Mother Earth—humble and fruitful. May your steps, and those of your children, be firm and sacred!

—TRADITIONAL LAKOTA TRIBAL WOMEN'S INITIATION RITUAL
(NATIVE AMERICAN)

CONTEMPLATION

Go forth among the people of your circle, your land, your world in a holy manner. This is your purpose. Are you a spider? Spin beautiful and strong webs of art. Do you sing? Sing to the Creator and to people's hearts. Are you a trader in goods? Make them wholesome and of high quality.

The ultimate purpose?

The Dalai Lama, addressing a crowd of thirty thousand, including many of the world's great religious figures, said: "The purpose of life"—he chuckled—"is . . . to be . . . happy!"

IDOLIZATION

◆

Once there reigned a king who was malevolent, ignorant, a worshipper of idols. The king promised that if his personal idol bestowed a boon on him, he would capture the next three passersby and compel them to commit themselves to idolatry.

The king's wish came to be, and so he ordered his soldiers to bring back the next three wayfarers. These were a scholar, a descendant of the Prophet Muhammad, and a prostitute. The king forced them before his idol and ordered them to bow in submission to it.

The scholar pontificated: "One is permitted, the learned ones say, to pretend conformity with the customs of a land, if compelled, without incurring any real legal or moral culpability." His speech concluded, he made obeisance to the idol.

The descendant of the Prophet Muhammad spoke next: "Since I carry the very blood of the Prophet himself, and therefore maintain the special privilege of protection, all my actions are thereby pure. I may do as this king commands." He, too, bowed in worship to the idol.

The prostitute then said: "I have no scholarly learning on these subjects, nor may I claim any special position, so I'm afraid that regardless of what you choose to do to me, I cannot go along and worship your idol, or even give the appearance of doing so."

The mad king's mind was instantly made whole on hearing the prostitute's declaration. He saw clearly the falseness of the two men who had bowed to the idol, and at once had them decapitated. The prostitute was set free.

—TRADITIONAL SUFI TALE

CONTEMPLATION

The Hindu festival Raksha Bandhan takes place at this time. Raksha Bandhan literally means "to tie protection on," and to protect their brothers from harm, Indian girls and women fix amulets on their arms.

If placing objects were all they did, this would be as silly as bowing before Gods and Goddesses made of metal or wood.

It's easy to succumb to idolization; the whole world's doing it. Your conscience is your only protection.

INITIATION

◆

About eight days after Jesus said this, he took Peter, John, and James with him and went up onto a mountain to pray. As he was praying, the appearance of his face changed, and his clothes became as bright as a flash of lightning. Two men, Moses and Elijah, appeared in glorious splendor, talking with Jesus. They spoke about his departure, which he was about to bring to fulfillment at Jerusalem. Peter and his companions were very sleepy, but when they became fully awake, they saw his glory and the two men standing with him. As the men were leaving Jesus, Peter said to him, "Master, it is good for us to be here. Let us put up three shelters— one for you, one for Moses, and one for Elijah." (He did not know what he was saying.)

While he was speaking, a cloud appeared and enveloped them, and they were afraid as they entered the cloud. A voice came from the cloud, saying, "This is my Son, whom I have chosen; listen to him." When the voice had spoken, they found that Jesus was alone. The disciples kept this to themselves and told no one at that time what they had seen.

—GOSPEL OF LUKE (CHRISTIAN NEW TESTAMENT)

CONTEMPLATION

Much as you might want to be initiated, you've got to be asked by a master or the master-in-you.

Initiation is a very serious business. Jesus selected his initiates carefully because of the risks involved to their souls and bodies inherent to the experience. In the Gospel of Thomas, Thomas relates that Jesus "took him and withdrew and told him three things." When Thomas returned to his companions, they asked him, "What did Jesus say to you?"

Thomas said to them: "If I tell you one of the things which he told me, you will pick up stones and throw them at me; a fire will come out of the stones and burn you up."

There is danger in initiation, and much required of the initiate. If and when you are ready, you will be offered it.

ALTAR

◇

Paul then stood up in the meeting of the Areopagus and said: "Men of Athens! I see that in every way you are very religious. For as I walked around and looked carefully at your objects of worship, I even found an altar with this inscription: TO AN UNKNOWN GOD. Now what you worship as something unknown I am going to proclaim to you.

"The God who made the world and everything in it is the Lord of heaven and earth and does not live in temples built by hands. And he is not served by human hands, as if he needed anything, because he himself gives all men life and breath and everything else. From one man he made every nation of men, that they should inhabit the whole earth; and he determined the times set for them and the exact places where they should live. God did this so that men would seek him and perhaps reach out for him and find him, though he is not far from each one of us."

—BOOK OF ACTS (CHRISTIAN NEW TESTAMENT)

CONTEMPLATION

Altars are places where people try to reach God. If you worship at an altar, you can, like Paul, appreciate the sanctity of an altar unlike your own and honor the people worshiping there for their religious spirit. While what you place on your altar is entirely up to you, you will gain much from others, too, if you have an understanding like the Sufi mystic Rumi. "I go," he said, "into the church, the synagogue, the mosque. . . . I see only one altar."

PROBLEM

When we are sad, we cry, and when we are joyful, we laugh.
Nose vertical, eyebrows horizontal.
Hunger, thirst, warmth, and cold, are natural.
Why create problems that don't exist?

—WRITINGS OF TRAN THAI TONG
(CLASSICAL VIETNAMESE BUDDHIST)

A fox fell into a well and could not get out. A thirsty goat peered over the edge and, on seeing the fox down there, asked whether the water was good to drink. The fox, hiding his distress, eloquently extolled the quality of the water and invited the goat to join him. The goat, at the risk of his neck, managed to clamber down and, after drinking his fill, consulted with the fox as to the best way of getting out again. "It is easy if we help each other," said the fox. "Just brace your forelegs against the side and raise your head up high. I will climb over you, and when I have gotten out, I will pull you up." The goat willingly agreed to the plan, and the fox, having used the goat's shoulder, head, and horns as a ladder, scrambled over the side of the well and promptly disappeared from sight. When the goat berated him for not keeping his side of the agreement, the departing fox called back: "Look here, friend, if your head was good for anything besides sprouting horns, you would have known better than to get into a well without having a way to get out."

—FABLE OF AESOP (CLASSICAL GREEK)

CONTEMPLATION

Baba Hari Dass, the silent guru, writes: "Everybody has problems." And especially in spiritual practice, this is so. Have you been doing yoga, sitting in meditation, or participating in a prayer circle for a while? Have you noticed that what seemed like insurmountable problems at the beginning (say, like just being able to sit quiet for a few minutes) now seem ridiculous? But other, new "problems" have surfaced.

This is natural and predictable. You'll get past these problems, too. Just don't get overly confident, and for God's sake don't get overly concerned either.

ANCESTORS

◇

Before Abraham was born, I was.

—GOSPEL OF JOHN (CHRISTIAN NEW TESTAMENT)

◇

The blessings of the
Gods of heaven and earth—
Without these,
How could we exist,
Even for a day, even for a night?

Forget not the grace
Of generations of ancestors;
From age to age, the ancestors
Are our own *ujigami,*
Gods of our families.

Father and mother
Are gods of the family;
Even so, honor them as gods with
Heartfelt service,
All you of human birth.

—NORINAGA MOTOORI (CLASSICAL SHINTO TEXT)

◇

Those who worship the devas will go to the realm of the devas; those who worship their ancestors will be united with them after death; those who worship phantoms will become phantoms; but my devotees will come to Me.

—BHAGAVAD GITA (HINDU SACRED TEXT)

CONTEMPLATION

In telling Moses his holy name, God declared (and thereby reassured Moses) that he was the God of Abraham, the God of Isaac, and the God of Jacob, the three revered ancestral patriarchs. Why did he not just say—God of Abraham, Isaac, and Jacob?

Because although our ancestors can bestow knowledge of many things on us, a personal relationship with the Divine cannot be handed down from one generation to the next. It is up to us to recreate this.

Our responsibility is to the next seven generations, Native Americans say. Preserve wisdom; take care of the earth and each other; honor the elders and the children, both born and yet to be born.

NEEDS

You create women's seed, men's semen.
You comfort and nurse the child in its mother's womb;
you soothe even its inner weeping.
When the time comes for it to descend,
to breathe and face the outer world,
you open the infant's mouth wide to
receive what it needs from you.
When the chick rouses and speaks within the egg,
you give it enough breath
and the fullness of time
to break the shell
and come forth into the day.
Your radiance suckles every blade of grass.

—TRADITIONAL EGYPTIAN HYMN

All their needs
Are satisfied.
If man, born in Tao,
Sinks into the deep shadow
Of nonaction
To forget aggression and concern,
He lacks nothing
His life is secure.
Moral: "All the fish needs
Is to get lost in water.
All man needs is to get lost
In Tao."

—WRITINGS OF CHUANG-TZU
(CLASSICAL TAOIST TEACHER)

CONTEMPLATION

Animals have much of the same needs we do. Yet you rarely hear them whine or growl in complaint.

Today the world is beautiful and flourishing and full. Ain't that enough?

DIVINITY

◇

The seed of God is in us
Now the seed of a pear tree
Grows into a pear tree
And a hazel seed
Grows into a hazel tree

A seed of God
Grows into God

—WRITINGS OF MEISTER ECKHART
(CHRISTIAN MYSTIC AND POET)

◇

In the beginning was God
Today is God
Tomorrow will be God
Who can make an image of God?
He has no body
He is as a word
Which comes out of your mouth
That word! It is no more
It is past and still it lives!
So is God.

—TRADITIONAL PYGMY TRIBAL WISDOM
(CENTRAL AFRICA)

CONTEMPLATION

Hindus rejoice at this time for it is Krishna's birthday! Singing and dancing, they celebrate Krishna as the eighth incarnation of the supreme God, Vishnu, the creator of all things. It is in the form of Krishna that God is most beloved by the people, for as Krishna he lived a life like ours on earth and revealed both his divine splendor and wisdom. Krishna is one of us. This is indeed worthy of the greatest celebration.

EVOLUTION

I died a mineral and became a plant.
I died a plant and rose an animal.
I died an animal and I was a man.
Why should I fear? When was I less by dying?
Yet once more I shall die a man, to soar
With the blessed angels; but even from angelhood
I must pass on. All except God perishes.
When I have sacrificed my angel soul,
I shall become that which no mind ever conceived.
O, let me not exist! for Non-Existence proclaims,
"To Him we shall return."

—WRITINGS OF RUMI (SUFI MYSTIC AND POET)

CONTEMPLATION

When the process of evolution takes place in the physical realm, the new being both transcends and includes the prior one. Plants are far more than minerals; yet they contain them.

When evolution takes place in the spiritual realm, the same transcending and inclusion occurs.

"When I was a child," Saint Paul reveals, "I thought like a child." But now . . .

Although we have evolved in spiritual maturity, and transcended spiritual infancy and childhood, we still retain childlike innocence and sincerity. Don't deny these qualities; use them to drive your further evolving.

DILIGENCE

◇

And those who in high thought and deep contemplation with ever-living power advance on the path, they in the end reach Nirvana, the peace supreme and infinite joy.

—DHAMMAPADA (BUDDHIST SACRED TEXT)

◇

What woman having ten pieces of silver, if she lose one piece, doth not light a candle, and sweep the house, and seek diligently till she find it?

—GOSPEL OF LUKE (CHRISTIAN NEW TESTAMENT)

◇

Now, as a spider mounting up by means of his thread (*tantu*) obtains free space, thus, assuredly, indeed, does that meditator, mounting up by means of *Om,* obtain independence (*svâtantrya*).

—MAITRI UPANISHAD (HINDU SACRED TEXT)

CONTEMPLATION

There are days when you just feel sluggish. Perhaps you want to skip your daily meditation or let the garden go. That's okay.

You don't always have to be superdiligent. But do a little bit anyway, just to keep up the pattern of diligence. Go to a new refreshing place and sit quietly. Give the flowers a light sprinkle. You've done your due diligence. Now give yourself a break.

DELAY

At that time the kingdom of heaven will be like ten virgins who took their lamps and went out to meet the bridegroom. Five of them were foolish and five were wise. The foolish ones took their lamps but did not take any oil with them. The wise, however, took oil in jars along with their lamps. The bridegroom was a long time in coming, and they all became drowsy and fell asleep.

At midnight the cry rang out: "Here's the bridegroom! Come out to meet him!"

Then all the virgins woke up and trimmed their lamps. The foolish ones said to the wise, "Give us some of your oil; our lamps are going out."

"No," they replied, "there may not be enough for both us and you. Instead, go to those who sell oil and buy some for yourselves."

But while they were on their way to buy the oil, the bridegroom arrived. The virgins who were ready went in with him to the wedding banquet. And the door was shut.

Later the others also came. "Sir! Sir!" they said. "Open the door for us!"

But he replied, "I tell you the truth, I don't know you."

Therefore keep watch, because you do not know the day or the hour.

— GOSPEL OF MATTHEW (CHRISTIAN NEW TESTAMENT)

The person of courage unflinchingly cuts straight through the barrier, unhindered even by Nata, the eight-armed demon king. In the presence of such valor, the twenty-eight Indian ancestors and six Chinese ancestors beg for their lives. If you hesitate, however, you'll be like someone watching a horse gallop past a window. With a blink, it is gone.

— WRITINGS OF WU-MEN (CLASSICAL ZEN
BUDDHIST TEACHER AND POET)

CONTEMPLATION

When you know where you want to go and where you want to be, there is never a reason for delay. Don't.

MURDER

The embodied Bodhisattva asked them again what they saw, and Savaripa finally replied, "I saw people just like us burning in hell." "Are you not afraid of being born there?" asked the Bodhisattva. "We are indeed afraid," they replied. "Is there any way we can be saved from such a fate?" "If there is a method, would you be willing to practice it?" "We are willing," they said. And so the Bodhisattva preached the Dharma to Savaripa and his wife:

"When you take a life, there are various kinds of karma produced. You will be reborn in hell. Killing gives rise to a disposition to further taking of life, with the inherent result that your own life is short. The outer reflection of all this is that you will be very unattractive.

"But if you refrain from taking life, you may well obtain enlightenment. When you do not have the desire to kill, the inherent result will be a long life. The outer reflection of all this is that you will be born with considerable personal magnetism."

—TRADITIONAL TIBETAN BUDDHIST TALE

CONTEMPLATION

The biblical command "Thou shalt not kill" is mistranslated. More accurately it is: "Thou shalt not murder."

There is a time for killing, and in fact this often occurs completely unintentionally—stepping on an unseen insect or washing one's hands of bacteria, for example.

Murder implies thought, planning, design. And it, too, happens frequently—the sarcastic remark that cuts to the quick or the self-mutilating denials of worthiness—unless we stop it.

Any murder kills enthusiasm, the feeling of connectedness in spirit with God; that's why it is the most serious of crimes.

EMERGENCE

◆

A very long time ago they were living down below. Down there every-thing was good; rain and fertility flourished. But because the chiefs grew bad, the rain stopped, the people became sick.

The chiefs responded to these events. They planned both a revenge upon the evildoers and an escape from their deteriorating condition. They heard sounds up above them, footsteps. Someone was walking up there. The village chief, Kik-mongwi, wanted to investigate. The chiefs, therefore, made a bird through song, sending it up with instructions to tell whoever was above that they, the people, wanted to come up. They planted a fir tree that failed to reach the surface, but a reed they planted alongside reached the top successfully.

The bird flew in spirals around the two ladders— the fir and the reed—up through the hole, but could find no one in the darkness above and returned exhausted. The chiefs made another bird messenger, Hum-mingbird, small but swift and strong. They gave him instructions to see who lived up there, if he was "kind" and "good" and "gentle." If so, they wished to come up. But Hummingbird also failed and returned, ex-hausted.

The chiefs then created Hawk, but he, too, could find no one above to tell of the conditions below—the bad hearts of the chiefs' "children"— and he came back equally exhausted. The chiefs revived each of these birds in sequence.

So they made a fourth bird, Motsni, a northern shrike, giving him the same message. He was stronger than the others, and he found the place where Oraibi is today, although "there were no houses there yet." Some-one was sitting there, and he moved his head to the side, telling the bird to sit down and inform him of his reason for coming. It was Masau'u, the Skeleton, who listened to Motsni's report from the chiefs. Masau'u told the bird, "Now this is the way I am living here. Now, if you are willing to live here that way, too, with me and share this life, why come, you are welcome." The bird returned to the chiefs with this message.

At that time many people gathered, and the chiefs led them up the reed ladder—the Kik-mongwi; the Flute chief; Horn chief; Agave chief; Singer chief; Wuwuchim chief; Rattlesnake chief; Antelope chief; Marau chief; Lagon chief; and the Warrior chief. The people followed, and when the news got around, everyone was clamoring to climb the reed. But fearing that too many two-hearts (sorcerers) would come to the surface, the village chief pulled up the reed, leaving a great number to fall back below the earth's surface.

The large number who had surfaced gathered by the rim of the opening, where the village chief told them that from then on they were to live good, single-hearted lives. They should follow Motsni wherever he instructed.

—TRADITIONAL HOPI TRIBAL STORY (NATIVE AMERICAN)

CONTEMPLATION

From the depths of our souls, we want to emerge. Perhaps there is some terrible trauma or long period of aridity that has gotten you down. Perhaps you have sent lovely bird messengers of hope to the surface seeking friends, guidance, and divine acceptance. Send again—but remember, the life on top is still a poor one. Come up and make it rich.

UNDERSTANDING

◇

When he felt that the day of his departure was drawing near, Bodhidharma called his four disciples to come and ordered them to state their original insights. Tao-fu was the first to respond: "According to my view, we should neither cling to words and letters nor dispense with them altogether, but only use them as an instrument of Tao." "You have got my skin," said the master. Then the nun Tsung-chih came forward, saying, "In the light of my present comprehension, it is like Ananda's viewing the Buddha land of Aksobhya, seeing it once and never again." "You have got my flesh," said the master. Tao-yu said, "The four elements are all empty; the five *skandhas* are all unreal. Looking from where I stand, there is not a thing that can be grasped." "You have got my bone," the master commented. Finally, it was Hui-k'o's turn to show his insight. But he did not open his mouth. Bowing reverently to the master, he kept standing in his place. The master remarked, "You have got my marrow"; and Hui-k'o came to be recognized as the Second Patriarch.

—TRADITIONAL ZEN BUDDHIST TALE

◇

A stone in the water does not comprehend how parched the hill is.
—TRADITIONAL HAUSA TRIBAL PROVERB (WEST AFRICA)

CONTEMPLATION

Stand beneath the moonlight
Stand under a tree
Stand with the birds as the shoreline
moves to and fro

Listen with an absent mind
Listen to the tree breathing and not breathing
Listen to the birds' silent attention
And an ocean of complexity

Hold the pulsating light in your hand
Hold the growing and dying leaves in your heart
Hold in view the flight that is yet to be
To the destination of certain perplexity

USEFUL

◇

It has been told that the tomb of Boland-Ashyan cured the sick, granted wishes, and was a boon to all who visited it. It became known as the "Sponge of Troubles."

Near the shrine was the town of Murghzur, where Faisal Nadim cooked food for locals and wayfarers alike. Although he lived so close to the holy tomb, Faisal himself never went there; but many, many pilgrims came to his kitchen, sat with him, and watched him at his work. These pilgrims initiated the Sufi lineage called the Nadimis, and those who visited the tomb and not Faisal's workplace were not understood as wise or saintly except by the ignorant.

Once the Sufi sage Khorram Ali was asked, "Why is it that the pious who visited such a holy and miraculous site were not transformed and yet those who attended Faisal's kitchen became saints?"

The sage answered thus: "A sponge absorbs and removes water that is not needed. But once done, this may, in certain circumstances, inhibit or preclude useful work. The sponge itself is quite insensitive, and its usefulness is relative to the judgment of the observer. A cook must know how to measure ingredients and prepare food that is digestible and nutritious. A cook may use a sponge, when necessary, to remove dirty water or whatever is in the way. Only the ignorant see the sponge and imagine it works by its own will."

—TRADITIONAL SUFI STORY

CONTEMPLATION

Spiritual work, especially on oneself, necessitates extraordinary sensitivity and attunement. If you soaked up everything you heard, including the constant self-barrage of prejudice and critique, you'd be virtually useless.

As it is, even with the best intention not to, you still absorb too much. Meditation, contemplative periods, silence, recreation—these squeeze the sponge.

SEPTEMBER

VISITING

In the last century a tourist visited the famous Polish rabbi Hafez Hayyim.

He was astonished to see that the rabbi's home was only a simple room filled with books. The only furniture was a table and a bench.

"Rabbi, where is your furniture?" asked the tourist.

"Where is yours?" replied Hafez.

"Mine? But I'm only a visitor here."

"So am I," said the rabbi.

—TRADITIONAL CHASSIDIC JEWISH ANECDOTE

The saintly Khidr journeyed to the palace and made his way to see the king. His appearance was so compelling that no one challenged him.

The king, Ibrahim ben Adam, asked Khidr, his unexpected visitor, what he was seeking. Khidr answered: "I am looking for a place to sleep in this hostel."

Ibrahim, the king, retorted: "This is no hostel, it is my palace."

Khidr inquired: "And whose was it before it was yours?"

"My father's."

"And before that?"

"His father's," Ibrahim said.

Khidr asked: "This place, which by your own declaration people are continuously visiting and leave-taking, you call something other than a hostel?"

—TRADITIONAL SUFI TALE

CONTEMPLATION

You have been granted, with your birth on this planet earth, extensive visiting rights. The establishment strongly requests you follow this guide:

1. *You may go anywhere you wish (as long as you pay the bills).*
2. *You must check in regularly.*
3. *Your visa may be revoked at any time with or without notice.*
4. *Most services are provided freely (ask management about details).*
5. *Enjoy your stay.*

EDUCATION

Confucius said, "It may be possible to study together without being able to go on the way together. It may be possible to go on the way together without being able to take a stand together. It may be possible to take a stand together without being able to plan together."

—ANALECTS (CLASSICAL CONFUCIANIST TEXT)

True learning induces in the mind service of mankind.

—ADI GRANTH (SIKH SACRED TEXT)

Knowledge makes a man honest, virtuous, and endearing to society. It is learning alone that enables a man to better the condition of his friends and relations. Knowledge is the holiest of holies, the god of the gods, and commands respect of crowned heads; shorn of it, a man is but an animal. The fixtures and furniture of one's house may be stolen by thieves; but knowledge, the highest treasure, is above all stealing.

—GARUDA PURANA (HINDU SACRED TEXT)

Know verily that knowledge is of two kinds: divine and satanic. The one welleth out from the fountain of divine inspiration; the other is but a reflection of vain and obscure thoughts. The source of the former is God Himself; the motive force of the latter the whisperings of selfish desire. The one is guided by the principle "Fear God; God will teach you"; the other is but a confirmation of the truth: "Knowledge is the most grievous veil between man and his Creator." The former bringeth forth the fruit of patience, of longing desire, of true understanding, and love; while the latter can yield naught but arrogance, vainglory, and conceit.

—WRITINGS OF BAHÁ'U'LLÁH (BAHÁ'Í FAITH)

"Some say that broad learning is an impediment in the study of Shinto; is that really so?"

"It is not extensive learning itself which is an impediment. It all depends on the mind of the scholar with such erudition, whether it becomes a benefit or a hindrance. Learning has as its original function knowledge of the way of mankind, becoming familiar with all the things within the realm, and producing human virtue. In spite of this fact, current scholarship concerns itself with matters of absolutely no value to the way of man, aiming merely for the approbation of fellow scholars, becoming merely a tenacious attachment to books, and thus dark and confused, without any illumination at all. Such is an evil to Shinto."

—PRECEPTS OF DIVINE LEARNING (SHINTO SACRED TEXT)

CONTEMPLATION

Do your educational activities lead you to yourself, to service with and for other people, to God?

This is the only education that has true meaning and the only education worthy of your efforts and sacrifices.

REWARDS

◆

On seeing that his own end is approaching, a father commands his son to come, and gathers together his relatives, and the kings, ministers, warriors, and citizens. When they are all assembled, he addresses them saying, "Now, gentlemen, this is my son, begotten by me. It is over fifty years since, from a certain city, he left me and ran away to endure loneliness and misery. His former name was so-and-so, and my name was so-and-so. At that time in that city I sought him sorrowfully. Suddenly in this place I met and regained him. This is really my son, and I am really his father. Now all the wealth which I possess belongs entirely to my son, and all my previous disbursements and receipts are known by this son."

When the poor son heard these words of his father, great was his joy at such unexpected news, and thus he thought, "Without any mind for or effort on my part, these treasures now come of themselves to me."

World-honored One! The very rich elder is the Tathagata, and we are all as the Buddha's sons. The Buddha has always declared that we are his sons. But because of the three sufferings, in the midst of births-and-deaths we have borne all kinds of torments, being deluded and ignorant and enjoying our attachment to trifles. Today the World-honored One has caused us to ponder over and remove the dirt of all diverting discussions of inferior things. In these we have hitherto been diligent to make progress and have got, as it were, a day's pay for our effort to reach Nirvana. Obtaining this, we greatly rejoiced and were contented, saying to ourselves, "For our diligence and progress in the Buddha-law what we have received is ample." . . . The Buddha, knowing that our minds delighted in inferior things, by his tactfulness taught according to our capacity, but still we did not perceive that we are really Buddha's sons. . . . Therefore we say that though we had no mind to hope or expect it, yet now the Great Treasure of the King of the Law has of itself come to us, and such things that Buddha-sons should obtain, we have all obtained.

—LOTUS SUTRA (BUDDHIST SACRED TEXT)

CONTEMPLATION

Though they are frequently initially unnoticed and sometimes completely unexpected, there are rewards for spiritual devotion.

They may be the seemingly simple—ease of breath, improved health, a certain lightness of heart restored.

Or they may be monumental—to the barren Hannah, the gift of a son, or to the servant Ali, the leadership of Islam.

The rewards of grace come more often to those who walk in it daily.

ADEPTS

◆

All methods aiming at the realization of awakening have their origin in your true nature. The true nature of everything is in your mind. Mind and matter are one, not two different things. Conditioning, servitude, and error do not truly exist. True and false, merit and sin, are illusory images. So is the law of cause and effect. As long as your activity is based on conceptual discrimination, it is not free. The free person sees all, because he knows that there is nothing to be seen. He perceives all, not being deceived by concepts. When he looks at things, he sees their true nature. When he perceives things, he penetrates their nature of interbeing. Thus, while living in the world, he possesses the secret of the arising and manifestation of phenomena. This is the only way to arrive at awakening. Free of errors caused by concepts, he lives in peace and freedom, even in the world of karma. Using skillful means, he realizes his calling of awakening in this conditioned world, without thinking whether the world is conditioned or unconditioned.

—WRITINGS OF CUU CHI (VIETNAMESE BUDDHIST MONK)

CONTEMPLATION

There's a very good reason why spiritual aspirants in so many traditions are called adepts. To move toward awakening and enlightenment requires great skill, right from the get-go. To think otherwise is simply arrogant or foolhardy. You wouldn't hire an unskilled mechanic to fine-tune your car's engine or an oafish carpenter to build an exquisite chair. Summon all your skills, and apply them to your great tasks.

MESSAGE

In Maharashtra there once lived a king named Shivaji, who had an elephant. One day his elephant ran amok and began destroying everything in his path. It so happened that a deluded one was just then returning from a lecture. The villagers tried to tell him not to go in that direction, saying, "One of His Majesty's elephants has run amok, and it is not quite safe to walk here. You may get crushed under his feet."

This fellow flared up and told them, "Look, you ignorant fools, you must see Rama in everyone. Everything there is, is Rama. You must have some insight, some knowledge in spiritual matters. Haven't you become aware of the fact that everything is Rama? I don't care about the elephant. But before I go, I am going to impart some true wisdom to you, and you must see Rama everywhere, and you must not make any distinctions."

The people thought this man was about as clever as the mad elephant, and there was no point in speaking to him any further, so they let him go. As he approached the elephant, the elephant lifted him up and threw him down several times, dashing him against the rocks. He began to howl in pain. Somehow the elephant was seized and put in chains before the fellow was killed. Now the deluded one who had claimed to be enlightened, instead of reaching the Sahasrar, reached the hospital.

After some time he recovered and returned and began to argue with his teacher. He said, "Look, you told me that everything is pervaded by Rama, and I approached the elephant considering it to be Rama, and look what he did to me."

The teacher said, "You fool. Why couldn't you see Rama in the people who told you not to go near the elephant?"

—TRADITIONAL HINDU TALE

CONTEMPLATION

The Grebo people of West Africa send this message: "Mosquito says, 'If you want a person to understand you, speak in his ears.'" God truly wants us to get all messages, so open your spiritual ears to them. And your eyes. . . . And your wise heart, too.

OVERCOMING

◇

Nothing in the world
is as soft and yielding as water.
Yet for dissolving the hard and inflexible,
nothing can surpass it.

The soft overcomes hard;
the gentle overcomes the rigid.
Everyone knows this is true,
but few can put it into practice.

—TAO TE CHING (CLASSICAL TAOIST TEXT)

◇

The snail has no hands
The snail has no feet
Gently the snail climbs the tree

—TRADITIONAL YORUBA TRIBAL PROVERB (WEST AFRICA)

◇

Rabbi Akiba, illiterate at forty, saw one day a stone's perforation where water fell from a spring, and having heard people say, "Waters wear down stones," he thought, "If soft water can bore through a rock, surely the iron-clad Torah should by sheer persistence, penetrate a tender mind"; and he turned to study.

—TALMUD (JEWISH SACRED TEXT)

CONTEMPLATION

An elephant pretty much goes where it wishes. It merely turns in a direction and by its sheer weight and bulk removes shrubbery and trees from its path. When joined by others of its kind, even a large patch of jungle becomes an easy obstacle to overcome.

This is why Hindus revere the Deity Ganesha, who bears the head of an elephant and its spiritual qualities as well. Carry memory, loyalty, and gentle devotion into your efforts. May you be blessed, like Ganesha, with auspicious success.

SPOIL

◇

A man was in dire need of funds, and the only way he could acquire them was to sell his house. He did not wish to give up the entire house, so he came to terms with the purchasers by which he retained unrestricted use of one room. He was permitted to store there any of his possessions.

Initially, he kept only small items there, and he came from time to time to the house and caused no disturbance. When he changed occupations, as he did occasionally, he brought his tools to the room also. The new owners made no protest to all this.

Finally, the man began to keep dead cats in the room, and because of the stench from their decomposition, the whole abode became uninhabitable.

The new owners went to the court for redress, but the judges ruled that the man had not breached the contract. The owners ended up re-selling the house, at a tremendous loss, to the original owner.

—WRITINGS OF HADRAT MUINUDIN CHISHTI
(SUFI MYSTIC)

CONTEMPLATION

The Sufis point out, and rightfully so, how even one unwilling or unready member of an order can spoil the efforts of the whole group.

So it is as well within each person. One powerful and unaddressed issue can sap your entire spiritual growth. It stinks, but it's true.

Eventually, you must deal with any serious concern that you're dwelling on. Working on what has begun to spoil, or better still what has yet to spoil, is an essential part of an active spiritual life. Go to it!

SEEKING

◆

A mouse wished to marry, but he desired a wife of rare virtue—whose beauty was without equal, whose body required no food, and whose heart would not pursue him when he went wandering.

First he went to the sun and said, "With everlasting love have I loved you. I will betroth you unto me."

The sun replied, "Just hours ago my face was darkened by the night. For the sun forever rises and sets. It is far better that you take a wife from your mother's kin and birthplace."

"No," said the mouse, "it is you I wish to wed."

"Always does the cloud conceal me," said the sun. "Go to her. She will not turn her face from you."

So the mouse went to the cloud. "This day have I labored and found my beloved, my beautiful one, my perfect one," declared the mouse. "By the sun's counsel I take you and will never forsake you."

"The One who watches upon the height of heights placed me in the power of the wind," replied the cloud, "and the wind shifts me east, west, north, and south. If you wed me, you will forever be a wanderer upon the earth. Forsake the handmaiden and take the mistress: Go to the wind."

So the mouse went to the wind in the desert. "Be not ashamed to marry a lowly creature like me," he said. "For you will be mine and I yours."

"Only a fool would marry me," said the wind, "for my breath is powerless against the wall. Go to her, for she will be your fortress in time of distress."

So the mouse went to the wall. "I come to you by the counsel of the sun and the cloud and the wind," said the mouse, "and I will betroth myself to you in loving-kindness and mercy."

"Not out of loving-kindness do you come but out of scorn—to mock me!" lamented the wall. "For although I am a wall and my breasts are like towers, the mice have made a hundred holes in my side! I can no more hold them back than a sieve can hold back water. If you wish to marry a worthy bride, go to the mice and wed one of them!"

So the mouse returned to his mother's birthplace and married one of his own kin. And his heart filled with joy at his good fortune.

—TRADITIONAL JEWISH TALE

CONTEMPLATION

Watch a cat. When they are seeking prey (like mice, for example), they stay right with what is in front of them. No detail is missed. They came; they sought; they pounced on.

That's that!

DEVIL

◈

Shall I inform you on whom it is that the devils descend? They descend on every lying, wicked person, into whose ears they pour hearsay vanities, and most of them are liars. And the poets—it is those straying in Evil, who follow them: do you not see them wandering distracted in every valley? They preach what they never practice.

—QUR'AN (HOLY BOOK OF ISLAM)

◈

Be sober, be watchful. Your adversary the devil prowls around like a roaring lion, seeking someone to devour.

—FIRST EPISTLE OF PETER (CHRISTIAN NEW TESTAMENT)

◈

The Essence of Mind or Suchness is the real Buddha,
While heretical views and the three poisonous elements [greed,
    anger, delusion] are Mara.
Enlightened by right views, we call forth the Buddha within us.
When our nature is dominated by the three poisonous elements
We are said to be possessed by the devil;
But when right views eliminate from our mind these poisonous
    elements
The devil will be transformed into a real Buddha.

—SUTRA OF HUI NENG (BUDDHIST SACRED TEXT)

CONTEMPLATION

Divine or devilish? It's hard to say sometimes, even when we're speaking honestly of ourselves. Both words hearken to the Indo-European understanding of Goddess (Devi) and God (Deva).

So true sages have always been wary of the devil, knowing how easily the devil mixes in the company of the spiritually self-acclaimed. This Sufi anecdote is right on the mark:

Once upon a time there was a dervish. As he was sitting in contemplation, he noticed that there was a sort of devil near him.

The dervish said: "Why are you sitting there, making no mis-chief?"

The demon raised his head wearily. "Since the theoreticians and would-be teachers of the Path have appeared in such numbers, there is nothing left for me to do."

PRECIOUSNESS

◇

And of Joseph he said, "Blessed of the Lord be his land, for the precious things of heaven, for the dew, and for the deep that coucheth beneath, and for the precious fruits brought forth by the sun, and for the precious things put forth by the moon, and for the chief things of the ancient mountains, and for the precious things of the lasting hills, and for the precious things of the earth and fullness thereof, and for the good will of him that dwelt in the bush: let the blessing come upon the head of Joseph, and upon the top of the head of him that was the prince of his brethren."

—BOOK OF DEUTERONOMY (HEBREW SCRIPTURES)

CONTEMPLATION

One has to be a princess or prince (like Joseph) to receive all the precious blessings of life.

It's not education or training or preparation that makes life's precious things available. You have to be a precious person; one who understands her or his great worth and who then can find the beauty and preciousness in all things.

This is an exalted and godly state.

GENEROSITY

◇

Once three merchants went on a journey. As the sun began to set on Friday evening, they decided to bury their money in a safe place, since it is forbidden to carry money on the Sabbath. But when they went to retrieve the money at the conclusion of the Sabbath, it was gone! Each accused the two others of having stolen it, but no one confessed to the theft.

So they presented their case to King Solomon.

Then the king told them this tale: "Once a girl and a boy became betrothed to each other when they were very young. They made a promise at that time that they would not marry anyone else without the other's permission. Soon after, the boy moved to a different city. When they grew up, the girl became engaged to another man but refused to marry him until she had obtained the consent of her childhood friend. So the girl and her fiancé filled several sacks with silver and gold and traveled to the city where the friend of her youth now lived.

"When the girl told her friend that she wished to marry a different man, he gladly gave his blessing to the couple, refusing to accept any money to release the girl from her childhood oath.

"Then the happy couple began their journey home, but were surprised along the way by an old thief who wished to steal both the girl and the money.

"'You are welcome to the money,' the girl said to the thief, 'but please spare me.' Then she told him about the mission they had just completed and added, 'If a young man like my friend can control his passion, how much easier it should be for an old man like you! Shouldn't you be filled with the fear of God at your age?'

"And the old thief took her words to heart and stole neither the girl nor the money, but let her and her fiancé go in peace.

"Now," said Solomon to his three listeners, "I have been asked to decide which of these three acted most nobly: the maid, the youth, or the thief?"

The first merchant said, "The maid, for she kept her oath."

The second merchant said, "The youth, for he controlled his passion and did not stand in the way of his friend's happiness."

The third merchant said, "The thief, of course! He could have kept the money and still let the girl go!"

Then Solomon pointed at the third merchant and declared, "There is your culprit! By his admiration of the thief, he has displayed his own greed and given himself away."

The man confessed his crime and showed the others where he had hidden the money.

—TRADITIONAL JEWISH TALE

CONTEMPLATION

Consider yourself a generous soul? Don't sneak away then when people around you are really in need.

Rabbi Shapiro, one of the spiritual leaders of the doomed Warsaw ghetto uprising in 1943, told his fellows this strange wisdom: "A Jew has to know how to do a favor." Please do.

BEAUTY

◆

One day the Creator was taking a rest, watching the village children at play. The children laughed and sang, yet the Creator was sad in his heart, for he thought, "They will grow old." Their hair will become silver and their skin wrinkled. The young hunters will lose strength and the lovely girls will be ugly and fat old women. And the wonderful flowers they play in, full of color, will fade. The leaves will fall. "Look, they are already turning yellow," and thinking about the winter to come, with little game and no green to be seen, the Creator's heart was all the more sad.

Yet the day was still warm and bright. The Creator saw the golden sunlight on the ground, the blue of the sky, the white of the corn being ground, and all the colors and, smiling, he said: "All these colors should be kept. I'll make something out of them, something for the children to see and have joy, and in this way there will be joy in my heart, too."

And so he did. He gathered a piece of sunlight, some blue from the sky, the white of the cornmeal, the gray shadows of the running children, yellow from the autumn leaves, green of pine needles, black from a beautiful girl's long hair, red, purple and orange from the flowers all around—all this the Creator put in his bag. Then, at the last he put the songs of the birds, too.

The Creator walked to a meadow where the children were playing and called to them: "Look, children. In this bag, there is a gift for you. Open it and you'll see."

The children opened it, and hundreds and hundreds of colored butterflies flew out, dancing on the children's hair, fluttering lightly from one flower to the next, and filling the air and sky. The children's hearts were full of joy, and they all said they had never seen anything so beautiful. Then the butterflies started to sing, and the children smiled as the songs were sung.

Then a songbird flew by, flew straight to the Creator's shoulder, and began scolding him. "It isn't right to give our songs to these new creatures. You promised us every bird would have his own song. And now you've gone and just handed them out. Isn't it enough these new pretty things you've made have all the colors of the rainbow?"

"Yes, you're right," the Creator agreed. "I made one song for each bird. The songs belong to you."

So the Creator took the songs away from the butterflies and now they fly quietly. The Creator said, "They're beautiful even so."

—TRADITIONAL PAPAGO TRIBAL STORY
(NATIVE AMERICAN)

CONTEMPLATION

This is a world of great beauty. The recent exploration of Mars, our closest relative of the planets, shows us how uniquely beautiful the Earth is. And we, of all the creatures here—the growing green things, the four-leggeds, the swimming, and the winged ones—are blessed with not only beauty but also the chance to see it. Walk the Beauty Path. It is a good way.

TESTING

◇

The people went to King Ratnapala and said to him, "You are the king. Is it proper for you to allow a disreputable system of religion to be practiced in your country? Even though Saraha, 'the Arrow-shooter,' is chief of fifteen thousand residences in Roli, he has lowered himself in caste by drinking wine, and therefore must be expelled."

The king, not wanting to expel a man who controlled fifteen thousand households, went to Saraha and said, "You are a Brahman; it is not fit that you drink wine." But Saraha replied, "I do not drink wine. Gather all the men and those Brahmans here, and I will take an oath to that effect." After they had gathered, Saraha stated, "If I had been drinking wine, let my hand burn. If I have not been drinking, may it not burn." He then put his hand in boiling oil, and it was not burned. "In truth, he does not drink wine," the king said. But the Brahmans said, "But truly he does drink wine."

So Saraha spoke as before. He drank molten copper and was not burned. "He still drinks," the Brahmans maintained. Saraha then said, "Whosoever sinks when entering the water, he is the one who drinks. If he does not sink, he does not drink." So he and another Brahman both entered the water. Saraha did not sink, but the other one did, so they finally said, "Saraha does not drink."

Similarly, Saraha was weighed on a scale: "Whoever is heavier does not drink," he said. They put three iron weights on the scale, each as heavy as a man, and still Saraha was heavier than the weights. He was heavier than even six of those weights. Finally the king said, "If anyone who has powers like these drinks wine, then let him drink."

—TRADITIONAL TIBETAN BUDDHIST TALE

CONTEMPLATION

Just when you've completed one test, here comes another.

The utmost test of people's spiritual character is how they handle their testers, who, often for arbitrary or self-serving reasons, impose repeated and unnecessary trials. Saraha was gracious. Jesus, too, even on the cross.

Make such graciousness a personal goal. Your examination starts now.

FAULT

One dark night, a thief, attempting to climb through the window of a house, fell to the ground when the window frame he was grasping came apart. The thief broke his legs.

He took the owner of the house to court. The owner said, "Don't sue me. Sue the carpenter who did the installation."

The carpenter in turn said, "The original builder didn't build the window opening the right way."

The builder was brought in, and he excused his faulty work by claiming, "A beautiful woman walking by drew my attention away."

The woman said, "It's not me that's beautiful. It was the dress I was wearing that day. It is very cleverly dyed, with beautiful colors and stripes."

"Ah," said the judge. "Now we know who's responsible for the thief's broken leg. Bring in the dyer."

When the dyer entered the courtroom, it turned out that he was the husband of the woman; and the truth be told—he was also the thief.

—TRADITIONAL SUFI TALE

Confucius said, "A faultless man I cannot hope ever to meet; the most I can hope for is to meet a man of fixed principles."

—ANALECTS (CLASSICAL CONFUCIANIST TEXT)

CONTEMPLATION

Some Jains are so concerned about being at fault in the death of any creature, even an insect, that they wear masks to prevent accidental inhalation. Obviously this fails; what about microscopic creatures?

Jains conduct ritual periods of introspection, fasting, confession and penance to come to terms with their unavoidable fault. This is a good practice for clearing and rebalancing; but don't go overboard with it and hurt yourself. That would be your fault!

FORGIVENESS

◇

Then Peter came up to him and said, "Lord, how many times shall my brother wrong me and I forgive him? Up to seven times?"

Jesus said to him, "I'm not telling you up to seven times, I'm telling you up to seventy-seven times.

"In this connection, the kingdom of the skies could be compared to a certain king who wanted to settle accounts with his slaves. As he started the settlement, they brought before him one who was indebted for ten million dollars. Since he didn't have it to pay back, the master ordered him and his wife and his children and everything he had to be sold in re-payment. So the slave fell down and bowed before him, saying, 'Have patience with me, and I will pay it all back to you.' And the master, feeling sorry for that slave, let him go and forgave him the loan.

"Then that slave went out and found one of his fellow slaves who owed him a hundred dollars, and seized him and started choking him, saying, 'If you owe it to me, pay up!'

"So his fellow slave fell down and pleaded with him, saying, 'Have patience with me, and I will pay you back.' But he wouldn't hear it, and instead went off and threw him in jail till he should pay the debt.

"So his fellow slaves, seeing these events, were most unhappy, and went and informed their master about everything that had happened. Then the master, calling him before him, said to him, 'Wretched slave, I let you off from your entire debt, because you pleaded with me. Shouldn't you also have pitied your fellow-slave, as I pitied you?' And in a rage the master handed him over to the torturers till he should pay back everything he owed. And that's what my heavenly father will do to you, if each of you does not forgive your brother from your hearts."

—GOSPEL OF MATTHEW (CHRISTIAN NEW TESTAMENT)

◇

Where there is forgiveness, there is God Himself.

—ADI GRANTH (SIKH SACRED TEXT)

◇

Moses son of 'Imran said, "My Lord, who is the greatest of Thy servants in Thy estimation?" and received the reply, "The one who forgives when he is in a position of power."

—HADITH OF BAIHAQI (ISLAMIC SACRED WRITINGS)

Why did the ancient Masters esteem the Tao?
Because, being one with the Tao, when you seek, you find; and when
    you make a mistake, you are forgiven.
That is why everybody loves it.

—TAO TE CHING (CLASSICAL TAOIST TEXT)

CONTEMPLATION

Jains have a holy day, Ksamavani, for universal forgiveness. Many Native American tribes have rituals of forgiveness in which everyone participates. Catholics have confession and forgiveness mediated by a priest.

We know that we need, for the sake of our souls, to both give and receive forgiveness on a regular basis. Okay, but how? Especially when the culprits (ourselves included) have committed such an egregious and seemingly unpardonable offense?

Noted spiritual psychologist and author M. Scott Peck puts it beautifully. In the criminal justice system, he tells us, a person must first be tried and convicted before an official pardon may be issued.

It is when we try to skip ahead and forgive first that we have the greatest difficulty. Make it easier for yourself; do the prep work of forgiveness.

SATISFACTION

◇

A holy one, a real sadhu, lived in a tiny shack far from other people. Every day, after his morning devotional rituals, he'd wash and hang out to dry his only possession, his loincloth. One day he discovered birds had pecked holes in it, and he went to the village to beg for a new one. A few days later the new loincloth met an identical fate. "Well," the villagers said, "you not only need a loincloth, but you need a cat to protect it from the birds." So the sadhu asked for and got a cat. Then he needed to beg for milk to feed the cat. After a time the villagers tired of supplying milk. "You need to keep a cow," they told the poor man. So he went and asked for a cow. Once he had the cow, he needed hay to feed the cow. His neighbors told him to stop begging and grow his own hay; there was plenty of untilled land to be had. So the sadhu became a farmer. Soon he had to build barns and hire laborers. Now he was a landholder and befitting such, he married, had children, and spent his days like all the other busy householders.

After a while, his guru came to visit the area and the now prosperous farm. Finding the farm filled with goods and buzzing with servants, the guru inquired of one: "An ascetic used to dwell in these parts. Do you know where he has gone?" Receiving no answer, the guru went to the main house where he ran into his surprised disciple. "What happened?" the guru asked. The sadhu fell at the feet of his master and pitifully said, "My Lord, it all started with a single loincloth."

—TRADITIONAL HINDU TALE

CONTEMPLATION

Satisfaction is elusive. Repeat: Satisfaction is elusive. We must keep telling ourselves this, for satisfaction of personal desires always appears right there, or just about right there, for the taking.

To dreamers and romantics (all of us, then), the full moon seems easy pickin's. Yet sometimes a full moon, even a full harvest moon, is totally eclipsed by the earth, and what was huge and bright and possibly ours simply vanishes.

We can chase it frantically if we wish, but surely it will be to no avail. Of course, in due time (often far more quickly than we imagined), it will come again.

An essential component of true satisfaction is allowance—allowance for all things, including yourself to, as the Shaker hymn says, "come round right."

SCRIPTURES

◆

The Taoist priest . . . looked around the middle hall and said, "You have a rare gem in your house; for when I entered I saw the radiance of a holy light. Where do you keep your treasure?"

Wan Teh-hsu answered, "In this poor dwelling there is nothing worthy of the name of a treasure."

The priest then took him by the hand and led him to the place where the Treatise on Response and Retribution lay, saying, "This holy book is the treasure. All the holy men of the three religions selected and compiled it to point out the way of virtue on which everyone should walk. If a man disciplines himself according to its instructions, the truth will shine forth in all its glory, and every letter in the sacred writing will emit rays of divine light. But if you recite the sacred text with a secret desire for profit or reward, selfishness will darken its native glory, and the writing will show no illumination."

—TREATISE ON RESPONSE AND RETRIBUTION
(CLASSICAL TAOIST TEXT)

◆

A thousand scriptures speak of His attributes and signs, His shrines, His paths, His greatness—O, witless people, that your hearts have not been won!

—TIRUMURAI (CLASSICAL HINDU TEXT)

CONTEMPLATION

If you hold to a certain holy scripture, hold to it powerfully. Read it; study it; meditate on it; share discussion of it; listen to its instruction and teaching.

Make sure your heart is won over, not to the scripture itself but to the Source to which all holy scripture directs you.

To do otherwise is self-serving and dark. The true purpose of scripture is unification and illumination of spirit.

CONCILIATION

◇

The Roman annals say such discord existed between two brothers that one of them maliciously laid waste the lands of the other. The emperor Julius, having heard of this, determined to punish the offender capitally. The latter, therefore, understanding what was meditated, went to the brother whom he had injured and besought forgiveness, at the same time requesting that he would screen him from the emperor's vengeance. But they who were present at the interview rebuked him and declared that he deserved punishment, not pardon. To which he made the following reply. "That prince is not worthy of regard who in war assumes the gentleness of a lamb, but in peace puts on the ferocity of a lion. Although my brother should not incline toward me, yet will I endeavor to conciliate him. For the injury I did him is sufficiently avenged in my repentance and bitterness of heart." This view of the case appeased the emperor and restored peace between himself and his brother.

—GESTA ROMANORUM (CLASSICAL CHRISTIAN TALES)

◇

I have just three things to teach:
simplicity, patience, compassion.
These three are your greatest treasures.
Simple in actions and in thoughts,
you return to the source of being.
Patient with both friends and enemies,
you accord with the way things are.
Compassionate toward yourself,
you reconcile all beings in the world.

—TAO TE CHING (CLASSICAL TAOIST TEXT)

CONTEMPLATION

An overriding compassion toward others will inevitably be accepted and conciliation brought about. Who would refuse?

We do—with ourselves. To reconcile with our brothers and sisters and the world itself, we must include ourselves, too.

You are your emperor. Accept your own olive branch of peace.

BARGAINING

◇

And the men turned their faces from thence, and went toward Sodom: but Abraham stood yet before the Lord. And Abraham drew near, and said, Wilt thou also destroy the righteous with the wicked? Peradventure there be fifty righteous within the city; wilt thou also destroy and not spare the place for the fifty righteous that are therein? That be far from thee to do after this manner, to slay the righteous with the wicked: and that the righteous should be as the wicked that be far from thee: Shall not the Judge of all the earth do right? And the Lord said, If I find in Sodom fifty righteous within the city, then I will spare all the place for their sake. And Abraham answered and said, Behold now, I have taken upon me to speak unto the Lord, who am but dust and ashes: Peradventure there shall lack five of the fifty righteous: wilt thou destroy all the city for lack of five? And he said, If I find there forty and five, I will not destroy it. And he spoke unto him yet again, and said, Peradventure there shall be forty found there. And he said, I will not do it for forty's sake. And he said unto him, O let not the Lord be angry, and I will speak: Peradventure there shall be thirty found there. And he said, I will not do it if I find thirty there. And he said, Behold now, I have taken upon me to speak unto the Lord: Peradventure there shall be twenty found there. And he said, I will not destroy it for twenty's sake. And he said, O, let not the Lord be angry, and I will speak yet but this once: Peradventure ten shall be found there. And he said, I will not destroy it for ten's sake.

And the Lord went his way as soon as he had left communing with Abraham; and Abraham returned to his place.

—BOOK OF GENESIS (HEBREW SCRIPTURES)

CONTEMPLATION

Every day we bargain, but in whose interest? In God's? Do we acknowledge that the one we bargain with has interests of her/his own just as valid and important as ours?

Bargain in good faith, and in Abrahamic spirit, stick to the bargains you've made.

SIGNS

Near the town of Coatepec in the province of Texcoco, a poor man was digging in his garden one day when an eagle swooped out of the air, seized him by the scalp, and carried him up toward the clouds, higher and higher, until the two of them were only a speck in the sky that quickly disappeared. Reaching a mountain peak, the man was taken into a dark cavern, where he heard the eagle say, "Lord of all power, I have carried out your command, and here is the poor farmer you told me to bring."

Without seeing who spoke, the man heard a voice say, "It is good. Bring him here," and without knowing who took his hand, he found himself being led into a dazzling chamber, where he saw King Montezuma lying unconscious, as if asleep. The man was told to sit next to the king, flowers were put in his hand, and he was given a smoking tube filled with tobacco.

"He is so drunk with pride that he closes his eyes to the whole world, and if you want to know how far it has carried him, hold your lighted smoking tube against his thigh, and you will see that he doesn't feel it."

Afraid to touch the king, the poor farmer hesitated. "Do it!" he was commanded. Then he held the hot tip of the tobacco against the king's thigh and saw that he felt nothing. He did not even stir.

"Now go back where you came from and tell Montezuma what you have seen and what I ordered you to do. So that he will believe you, have him show you his thigh. Then point to the spot where you touched him, and he will find a burn. Tell him that the Lord of Creation is angry and that because of his arrogance his rule is about to end. The time is short. Say to him, 'Enjoy what is left!'"

The poor farmer stood amazed, but with his digging stick still in his hand, he went straight to Mexico and asked to speak to Montezuma.

—TRADITIONAL AZTEC STORY

CONTEMPLATION

Signs and wonders may be right before you. Anything and anyone can bring warning or guidance to you. For the sake of your spiritual well-being, do not be dismissive or flippant like Montezuma or the pharaoh who was confronted by Moses. You will be cut off.

TURNING

◆

Whoever was heedless before and afterward is not; such a one illumines this world like the moon freed from the clouds.

Whoever, by a good deed, covers the evil done, such a one illumines this world like the moon freed from the clouds.

—DHAMMAPADA (BUDDHIST SACRED TEXT)

◆

God's world is great and holy. Among the holy lands in the world is the Holy Land of Israel. In the land of Israel, the holiest city is Jerusalem. In Jerusalem the holiest place was the Temple, and in the Temple the holiest spot was the holy of holies.

There are seventy peoples in the world. Among those holy peoples is the people of Israel. The holiest of the people of Israel is the tribe of Levi. In the tribe of Levi, the holiest are the priests. Among the priests, the holiest was the high priest.

There are seventy languages in the world. Among the holy languages is the holy language of Hebrew. Holier than all else in this language is the Holy Torah, and in the Torah the holiest part is the Ten Commandments. In the Ten Commandments the holiest of all words is the Name of God.

Every spot where a person raises their eyes to heaven is a holy of holies. Every person, having been created by God in God's own image and likeness, is a high priest. Every day of a person's life is a Day of Atonement, and every word that a person speaks with sincerity is the Name of the Lord.

—TRADITIONAL JEWISH COMMENTARY

CONTEMPLATION

In every person's life, outer and inner, there are special times of harvest. Only then can we see what we have accomplished and what we have not.

The fruit of the vine may then be turned into wine for spiritual sustenance and refreshment. Seeds may be collected and protected, so that once planted these seeds may turn into new life.

The opportunity to turn toward real spiritual maturity, with all the responsibilities this entails, is ever-present for us. Accept this as a farmer accepts this year's crop.

INVITATION

Jesus said, "A man had received visitors. And when he had prepared the dinner, he sent his servant to invite the guests. He went to the first one and said to him, 'My master invites you.' He said, 'I have claims against some merchants. They are coming to me this evening. I must go and give them my orders. I ask to be excused from the dinner.' He went to another and said to him, 'My master has invited you.' He said to him, 'I have just bought a house and am required for the day. I shall not have any spare time.' He went to another and said to him, 'My master invites you.' He said to him, 'My friend is going to get married, and I am to prepare the banquet. I shall not be able to come. I ask to be excused from the dinner.' He went to another and said to him, 'My master invites you.' He said to him, 'I have just bought a farm, and I am on my way to collect the rent. I shall not be able to come. I ask to be excused.' The servant returned and said to his master, 'Those whom you invited to the dinner have asked to be excused.' The master said to his servant, 'Go outside to the streets and bring back those whom you happen to meet, so that they may dine.'"

—GOSPEL OF THOMAS
(APOCRYPHAL CHRISTIAN TEACHING)

When invited to stay in the Buddha's hut, we always refuse.
We are too used to sleeping among the rushes.

—WRITINGS OF TRAN THAI TONG
(CLASSICAL VIETNAMESE BUDDHIST TEACHER)

CONTEMPLATION

In the Islamic world, ever since the time of the Prophet Muhammad, people are called to prayer—vocally. The call is loud and unmistakable.

Allah, Muslims say, is most compassionate and merciful. This must be so, for the call to prayer, to God, comes, regardless of our habitual inattention or excuses, every day again.

Whatever you do, don't remove yourself completely out of earshot.

EMPTINESS

◇

Once there was a proud astronomer, who journeyed to see the teacher of the most noble physician Avicenna. This sage's name was Kushyar, but when the astronomer came, full of his knowledge, Kushyar would not agree to teach him in any way.

Sadly, the astronomer readied to depart. Then Kushyar told him, "It is your belief that you know so very much that makes you like a vessel completely full of water. And because of this fullness, like the vessel, you cannot allow any more in. But the fullness is only that of vanity, regardless of how you feel about it, and the truth is that you are really empty."

—TRADITIONAL SUFI TALE

◇

We shape clay into a pot, but it is the emptiness inside that holds whatever we want.

—TAO TE CHING (CLASSICAL TAOIST TEXT)

CONTEMPLATION

The trees are emptying of leaves. If the old leaves, having lost vitality and the ability to generate sustenance from the sun, hung on, the tree would be sapped.

Where would it find the energy to produce new leaves in the spring and become full again?

PERSPECTIVE

◆

Lord Krishna wanted to test the wisdom of his kings. One day he summoned a king called Duryodana. Duryodana was well known throughout his kingdom for his cruelty and miserliness, and his subjects lived in terror. Lord Krishna said to King Duryodana, "I want you to go and travel the world over and find for me one truly good man." Duryodana replied, "Yes, Lord," and obediently began his search. He met and spoke with many people, and after much time had passed he returned to Lord Krishna saying, "Lord, I have done as you have asked and searched the world over for one truly good man. He is not to be found. All of them are selfish and wicked. Nowhere is there to be found this good man you seek!"

Lord Krishna sent him away and called another king called Dhammaraja. He was a king well known for his generosity and benevolence and well loved by all his people. Krishna said to him, "King Dhammaraja, I wish for you to travel the world over and bring to me one truly wicked man." Dhammaraja also obeyed, and on his travels he met and spoke with many people. After much time had passed he returned to Krishna saying, "Lord, I have failed you. There are people who are misguided, people who are misled, people who act in blindness, but nowhere could I find one truly evil man. They are all good at heart despite their failings!"

—TRADITIONAL HINDU TALE

CONTEMPLATION

Your life and happiness are largely determined by your perspective.
This notice tells the "tail":

> Lost dog, missing one paw; old and toothless; one ear bitten off; answers to the name "Lucky."

Though there are all kinds of people in this world, with the right attitude we can consider ourselves lucky indeed to be here. We have such intriguing neighbors!

LIFE SPAN

◇

Jesus said, "There was a rich man who had much money. He said, 'I shall put my money to use so that I may sow, reap, plant, and fill my store-house with produce, with the result that I shall lack nothing.' Such were his intentions, but that same night he died. Let him who has ears hear."

—GOSPEL OF THOMAS
(APOCRYPHAL CHRISTIAN TEACHING)

◇

When Zeus created Man, he made him short-lived. When winter came, Man, making use of his intelligence, built himself a house; and one day a horse, who could no longer stand the freezing rain and cutting wind, came to the house and begged for shelter. The Man said that he would admit the horse on one condition: that he give him a portion of the years allotted to him by Zeus. The horse willingly agreed. A little later an ox appeared, driven to the house by the cruel weather. The Man demanded the same entrance fee from the ox, who paid without protest. Finally a dog, half-dead with cold, came by and yielded a number of his years in order to gain admittance. The result of these transactions was this: During the time allotted them by Zeus, Men are unspoiled and good; when they are using the years given by the horse, they are proud and hard to manage; when they reach the years of the ox, they are able leaders; and at the end of their lives, having fallen back upon the dog years, they become ill-tempered scolds.

—FABLE OF AESOP (CLASSICAL GREEK)

CONTEMPLATION

Every year, around this time of Yom Kippur, the Day of Atonement, pious Jews (and those who become pious just for the occasion) pray that they will once again be entered by God in the Book of Life.

If so, they believe one more year will be added. But in life and in death, it is quality, not quantity that matters.

The good King Hezekiah, sorely ill and on the verge of death, went before God and was granted many more years of life—more years to keep "walking in truth and with a perfect heart." More years to "do that which is good in thy sight."

INVOCATION

◇

And it is told, it is said,
that Quetzalcoatl invoked
Someone who was deified,
in the innermost of heaven:
She of the starry skirt.
He who makes things shine;
Lady of our flesh, Lord of our flesh;
She who supports the earth,
He who covers it with cotton.
Toward that place he directed his plea,
thus it was known;
toward the Place of Duality,
above the nine levels of heaven.
And it was known that
he invoked the One who dwelt there,
made supplications,
living in meditation and retirement.

—TRADITIONAL AZTEC HYMN

◇

The sun shall be turned into darkness, and the moon into blood, before the great and the terrible day of the Lord come.

And it shall come to pass, that whosoever shall call on the name of the Lord shall be delivered.

—BOOK OF JOEL (HEBREW SCRIPTURES)

◇

When a man begins to call on the sacred name, a lotus flower begins to grow in Paradise for him.

—WRITINGS OF FA-CHAO (CLASSICAL CHINESE TEACHER)

CONTEMPLATION

Invoke the Goddess, the God, within your own being. This One lives in meditation and flourishes when named.

You will be surprised not only at its beauty, but at its potency.

Discover the true name; although this may change for you and in you over time, the invocation will remain true. Speak the name, and find grace.

ANTICIPATION

If a man dies, will he live again?
All the days of my hard service
I will wait for my renewal to come.
You will call and I will answer you;
you will long for the creature your hands have made.

—BOOK OF JOB (HEBREW SCRIPTURES)

Then he made this comparison: "Once there was someone who had a fig tree planted in his orchard and came looking for the fruit and found none. So he said to the gardener, 'This is three years now I've been coming to look for some fruit on this fig tree and not finding any. Cut it down: why should it even take up space?'

"But he answered, 'Master, leave it alone this one year more, while I dig around the roots and give it manure, to see if it bears fruit in the future; if not, you can cut it down.'"

—GOSPEL OF LUKE (CHRISTIAN NEW TESTAMENT)

CONTEMPLATION

Waiting and anticipating are two different things. When you wait, you are not sure that what you're waiting for—a job offer, a marriage proposal, an acceptance to a school—will actually come. When you anticipate, you expect what you're anticipating to actualize.

Elie Wiesel, Nobel laureate, observes that romance, up to very recent times, was based on anticipation. Couples, for example, did not kiss until many, many months had passed. How delicious this anticipation can be, when one is certain of the beloved!

GIFTING

But on the other hand, those who were obviously important in the world should not look down upon their brethren who have entered the religious community from a condition of poverty. They should be prouder of their life together with their poor brothers than of the social status of their rich parents. The fact that they have contributed some of their resources to the community is no reason for them to have a high opinion of themselves. Nor should they take greater pride by sharing their riches with the community than by enjoying them in the world. For whereas all vices express themselves in evil acts, pride lurks also in our good works in order to destroy even them. And what good is it to dispense gifts to the poor and even become poor oneself if giving up riches makes a person prouder than he was when he possessed a fortune?

—WRITINGS OF AUGUSTINE
(CLASSICAL CHRISTIAN TEACHER)

There are seven kinds of offering that can be practiced by even those who are not wealthy. The first is the physical offering. This is to offer service by one's labor. The highest type of this offering is to offer one's own life. . . . The second is the spiritual offering. This is to offer a compassionate heart to others. The third is the offering of eyes. This is to offer a warm glance to others, which will give them tranquillity. The fourth is the offering of countenance. This is to offer a soft countenance with a smile to others. The fifth is the oral offering. This is to offer kind and warm words to others. The sixth is the seat offering. This is to offer one's seat to others. The seventh is the offering of shelter. This is to let others spend the night at one's home. These kinds of offering can be practiced by anyone in everyday life.

—TEACHING OF THE BUDDHA

CONTEMPLATION

In the Runic (Pagan) calendar, the half-month of Gyfu begins today. The significance of Gyfu, of gifting, is that it unifies giver and receiver on both a personal and communal level.

As you can't give what you don't have, don't try. Give well, and easily.

PROTECTOR

◆

To you did the soul of the ox complain:
"For whom did you create me? Who made me?
Fury and violence oppress me, and cruelty and tyranny.
I have no shepherd other than you: then obtain good pastures for me."
Then spoke the Wise Lord himself, he who understands the prayers
    in his soul:
"No master has been found, no judge according to Righteousness,
For the breeder and the herdsman has the creator fashioned you.

The ordinance of sprinkling the water of the cattle, for the welfare
    of the ox,
And the milk for the welfare of men desiring food,
This has the Wise Lord, the Holy One,
Fashioned by his decree, in accord with Righteousness."

The ox-soul:
"Whom hast thou, as Good Mind, who may take care of us?"

"I know but this one, Zarathustra Spitama, the only one who has
    heard our teaching;
He will make known our purpose, O Wise One, and that of Right-
    eousness.
Sweetness of speech shall be given to him."

And then moaned the ox-soul: "That I should have to be content
With the powerless word of a man without strength for a guardian,
I who wish for a strong master!
Will he ever be, he who shall help him with his hands?"

—AVESTA (ZOROASTRIAN SACRED TEXT)

CONTEMPLATION

Whose job is it to protect the animals and other created beings? God's?
    We must be the Zarathustra Spitamas of our time and place.
    But here's an overlooked factor: When we speak to these issues, our speech must be, like Zarathustra's, sweet. In this way, a certain protection is afforded from a renewed cycle of recrimination and attack.

APPRECIATION

◇

Nothing meant more to Nahum of Chernobyl than celebrating Sukkot with great joy. And nothing enhanced his joy like a lovely *etrog* fruit from the Holy Land. But one year there was a drought in Israel, and there were very few *etrogim* available for the holiday. Only one man in Chernobyl had an *etrog*—Moshe Haim, the wealthiest man in town.

Desolate to be without an *etrog* for the holiday, Nahum decided that he must buy Moshe Haim's *etrog*. But he was a very poor man. What could he possibly offer Moshe Haim, the richest man in Chernobyl? The only things of value that Nahum owned were the Baal Shem Tov's phylacteries—these *tefillin* he had inherited from the Master. Surely he could not part with those! But how could he welcome the Festival of Joy without an *etrog*?

Then Nahum reached a decision. Seizing the *tefillin,* he ran to Moshe Haim's house and said to him, "I would like to buy your *etrog!*"

"You!" scoffed the rich man. "You could never afford it!"

Then Nahum held out the *tefillin*. "Would you accept these in exchange? They once belonged to the Baal Shem Tov."

Moshe Haim gasped when he saw what was in Nahum's hand. The holy Besht's *tefillin!*

"Very well," he said, trying to conceal his excitement. "I will sell you my *etrog*," and he placed the gleaming yellow fruit in Nahum's outstretched hand.

Overjoyed, Nahum ran home to show the *etrog* to his wife.

"Where did you get that?" cried his wife when she saw the *etrog*. "We don't even have enough food for the holiday!"

"I traded the Baal Shem Tov's *tefillin* for it," announced Nahum.

Enraged, his wife grabbed the *etrog* out of Nahum's hand and flung it to the ground, breaking off the *pittum* and thus making it unusable for the holiday.

Nahum's face flushed with anger, then suddenly grew calm. "Yesterday," he said, "we owned a priceless treasure—the Besht's *tefillin*. Today we owned another priceless treasure—a beautiful *etrog*. Now we have neither. But we still have each other. Let's not fight. Good *yontov!*"

—TRADITIONAL CHASSIDIC JEWISH TALE

The man with one eye thanks God only after he has seen a blind man.

—TRADITIONAL HAUSA TRIBAL PROVERB (WEST AFRICA)

CONTEMPLATION

To be appreciated, you first must be in an appreciative frame of mind yourself. Can you find joy amidst hardship? Then you will be like the true follower of spirit the Buddha described as "shining among blind mortals as the fragrant lotus growing in the garbage by the roadside, bringing joy to all who pass by."

OCTOBER

WELCOME

◆

Then some of the believers who belonged to the party of the Pharisees stood up and said, "The Gentiles must be circumcised and required to obey the law of Moses."

The apostles and elders met to consider this question. After much discussion, Peter got up and addressed them: "Brothers, you know that some time ago God made a choice among you that the Gentiles might hear from my lips the message of the gospel and believe. God, who knows the heart, showed that he accepted them by giving the Holy Spirit to them, just as he did to us. He made no distinction between us and them, for he purified their hearts by faith. Now then, why do you try to test God by putting on the necks of the disciples a yoke that neither we nor our fathers have been able to bear? No! We believe it is through the grace of our Lord Jesus that we are saved, just as they are."

The whole assembly became silent as they listened to Barnabas and Paul telling about the miraculous signs and wonders God had done among the Gentiles through them. When they finished, James spoke up: "Brothers, listen to me. Simon has described to us how God at first showed his concern by taking from the Gentiles a people for himself. The words of the prophets are in agreement with this, as it is written:

> After this I will return and rebuild David's fallen tent.
> Its ruins I will rebuild,
> and I will restore it,
> that the remnant of men may seek the Lord,
> and all the Gentiles who bear my name,
> says the Lord, who does these things
> that have been known for ages.

"It is my judgment, therefore, that we should not make it difficult for the Gentiles who are turning to God."

—BOOK OF ACTS (CHRISTIAN NEW TESTAMENT)

CONTEMPLATION

A great Sufi master, it is told, was refused welcome by the scholars and religionists of a city renowned for its holy teachers. He was not of their nation, and they did not accept him.

One day, in the middle of winter, when no such flowers bloomed, he came to the city with a gift—and a sign. A fragrant rose.

One should not put obstacles in the way of sincere seekers. Welcome them as you would welcome the return of a most beloved—with sweetness and pleasure.

BREATHING

◆

He himself gives all life and breath and everything else. In him we live and move and have our being.

—BOOK OF ACTS (CHRISTIAN NEW TESTAMENT)

◆

There is this one way, monks, for the purification of beings, for the overcoming of sorrow and misery, for the destruction of pain and grief, for winning the right path, for the attainment of Nirvana. And how, monks, does a monk live contemplating body in the body? Here a monk, having gone to the forest, sits down cross-legged, keeping his body erect and setting up mindfulness in front of him. Mindful he breathes in, mindful he breathes out. Breathing in long, he knows, "I breathe in long." Breathing out long, he knows, "I breathe out long." Breathing in short, he knows, "I breathe in short." Breathing out short, he knows, "I breathe out short." "Experiencing the whole body I shall breathe out," thus he trains himself.

—SATIPATTHANA SUTTA (BUDDHIST SACRED TEXT)

CONTEMPLATION

Breathing is the one essential function of life that you cannot stop. You can refuse drink. You can fast, as Buddha, Jesus, and many other ascetics have done, for very long periods. To live, you must literally take things, water or food, in your own hands and bring them intentionally and willfully into yourself.

Breath is different. It is given to you as your first and most precious gift. Like any gift, it then belongs to you, and you may manage and use it. Take this in deeply.

THOUGHT

◆

There was a man who wandered throughout the world seeking his deepest desire. He wandered from one city to another, from one realm to another, looking for fulfillment and happiness, but in all his wanderings he never came to it. Finally one day, tired from his search, he sat down underneath a great tree at the foot of a mountain. What he did not know is that this was The Great Wish Fulfilling Tree. Whatever one wishes for when seated underneath it immediately becomes true.

As he rested in his weariness, he thought to himself, "What a beautiful spot this is. I wish I had a home here," and instantly before his eyes a lovely home appeared. Surprised and delighted, he thought further, "Ah, if only I had a partner to be here with me, then my happiness would be complete," and in a moment a beautiful woman appeared calling him "husband" and beckoning to him. "Well, first, I am hungry," he thought. "I wish there was food to eat." Immediately a banquet table appeared, covered with every wonderful kind of food and drink, main courses, pastries, sweets of every variety. The man sat down and began to feast himself hungrily, but part way through the meal, still feeling tired, he thought, "I wish I had a servant to serve me the rest of this food," and sure enough a manservant appeared.

Finishing the meal, the man sat back down to lean against this wonderful tree and began to reflect, "How amazing it is that everything I wish has come true. There is some mysterious force about this tree. I wonder if there is a demon who lives in it," and sure enough no sooner than he thought this than a great demon appeared. "Oh, my," he thought, "this demon will probably eat me up," and that is just what it did.

—TRADITIONAL HINDU TALE

CONTEMPLATION

Whether you think it's true or not, thoughts have power. Great power.

Thoughts, pleasant and unpleasant, provocative and mundane, are continuously streaming through a person's mind. Yogis in the Hindu Vedic tradition knew from direct contemplative experience how difficult (and sometimes laughable) it was to quiet chattering thoughts. In the Rig Veda, they wrote:

Our thoughts wander in all directions and many are the ways of men: the cartwright hopes for accidents, the physician for the cripple, the priest for a rich patron and the frog for a pond to plunge into. For the sake of Spirit, O Mind, let go of these wandering thoughts.

You must practice; don't even think about it.

RELEASE

◇

So free am I, so gloriously free
Free from three petty things—
From mortar, from pestle and from my twisted cord,
Freed from rebirth and death I am
And all that has held me down
Is hurled away.

—THERIGATHA (BUDDHIST SACRED TEXT)

◇

The thunderstorm breaks, and the whole of nature breathes freely again.

—I CHING (CLASSICAL CHINESE TEXT)

◇

On the throne of many hues, Immortal Aphrodite, child of Zeus, weaving wiles—I beg you not to subdue my spirit, Queen, with pain or sorrow.

In your chariot yoked with swift, lovely sparrows bringing you over the dark earth,

Come to me now again, release me from this pain, everything my spirit longs to have fulfilled, fulfill, and you be my ally.

—WRITINGS OF SAPPHO
(ANCIENT GREEK PRIESTESS AND POET)

CONTEMPLATION

There are days where you must howl to the heavens or run wildly on the sandy shores of the lake. Today may be one of those days, or perhaps you felt this way recently, or maybe you sense a day like this soon upcoming.

Take the offer. Like an unexpected pouring-out, long after the peak of summer's heat, it feels great!

ALLOWING

◆

So Jacob sent word to Rachel and Leah to come out to the fields where his flocks were. He said to them, "I see that your father's attitude toward me is not what it was before, but the God of my father has been with me. You know that I've worked for your father with all my strength, yet your father has cheated me by changing my wages ten times. However, God has not allowed him to harm me. If he said, 'The speckled ones will be your wages,' then all the flocks gave birth to speckled young; and if he said, 'The streaked ones will be your wages,' then all the flocks bore streaked young. So God has taken away your father's livestock and has given them to me."

Then Rachel and Leah replied, "Do we still have any share in the inheritance of our father's estate? Does he not regard us as foreigners? Not only has he sold us, but he has used up what was paid for us. Surely all the wealth that God took away from our father belongs to us and our children. So do whatever God has told you."

Then Jacob put his children and his wives on camels, and he drove all his livestock ahead of him, along with all the goods he had accumulated in Paddan Aram, to go to his father Isaac in the land of Canaan.

When Laban had gone to shear his sheep, Rachel stole her father's household gods. Moreover, Jacob deceived Laban the Aramean by not telling him he was running away. So he fled with all he had, and crossing the river, he headed for the hill country of Gilead.

On the third day Laban was told that Jacob had fled. Taking his relatives with him, he pursued Jacob for seven days and caught up with him in the hill country of Gilead.

Then Laban said to Jacob, "What have you done? You've deceived me, and you've carried off my daughters like captives in war. Why did you run off secretly and deceive me? Why didn't you tell me, so I could send you away with joy and singing to the music of tambourines and harps? You didn't even let me kiss my grandchildren and my daughters goodbye. You have done a foolish thing. I have the power to harm you; but last night the God of your father said to me, 'Be careful not to say anything to Jacob, either good or bad.' Now you have gone off because you longed to return to your father's house. But why did you steal my gods?"

—BOOK OF GENESIS (HEBREW SCRIPTURES)

CONTEMPLATION

What is allowed and what isn't?

Jacob, in this story, had had enough—literally, in the sense of sheep and cattle, and enough as well of his father-in-law Laban's conniving ways—to put up with things in Aram no more. God said move on and he did.

Laban, too, listened, albeit much more reluctantly, to God's instructions to let Jacob and his family be.

Still he pursued them. And he could not help but ask about his precious idolatrous statues.

When God gives allowance, it really is no longer a personal matter.

SUPERNATURAL

◆

Akiva used to teach, "It is always good to say: 'Everything God does is for the best.'"

Once Akiva went out walking, and he came to a town. He wanted to stay there for the night, but they wouldn't give him lodgings.

He said, "Everything God does is for the best."

He went out to the field and slept there overnight. He had with him a candle, a rooster, and a donkey. During the night, the wind blew the candle out, a cat came and ate the rooster, and a lion came and ate the donkey. But Akiva said, "Everything God does is for the best."

That same night an army passed by where Akiva was sleeping and captured the town, killing most of the inhabitants.

"How right I was to say that everything God does is for the best!" exclaimed Akiva, "for had they let me stay in the town, I would surely have been killed! And had my candle been lit or had the rooster crowed or the donkey brayed when the army passed this way, that, too, would have brought about my end!"

—TRADITIONAL JEWISH TALE

CONTEMPLATION

How we hanker after supernatural intervention in our lives!

This is well and good in two distinct and related ways: first of all, we (our limited selves) are not the only power in this realm, and it is appropriate we recognize this truth; secondly, when we validate supernatural powers beyond our normal ones, it opens these transpersonal forces to us.

We can be (and are) so much more than we naturally think.

SWEETNESS

◆

May the wind blow sweetness,
the rivers flow sweetness,
the herbs grow sweetness,
for the People of Truth!

Sweet be the night,
sweet the dawn,
sweet be earth's fragrance,
sweet be our Heaven!

May the tree afford us sweetness,
the sun shine sweetness,
our cows yield sweetness—
milk in plenty!

—RIG VEDA (HINDU SACRED TEXT)

◇

A man traveling across a field encountered a tiger; he fled, the tiger after him. Coming to a precipice, he caught hold of the root of a wild vine and swung himself down over the edge. The tiger sniffed at him from above. Trembling, the man looked down to where, far below, another tiger was waiting to eat him. Only the vine sustained him.

Two mice, one white and one black, little by little started to gnaw away the vine. The man saw a luscious strawberry near him. Grasping the vine with one hand, he plucked the strawberry with the other. How sweet it tasted!

—TRADITIONAL ZEN BUDDHIST ANECDOTE

CONTEMPLATION

It's early October. In parts of the north, many of the fall fruits are coming to the peak of their sweetness. In parts of the south, the trees may be devoid of fruits altogether.

Yet sweetness is gathering there, too, drawn into the sap of the trees from the good earth below and saved for the fruits-to-be.

Spiritual life is like this. There are sudden bursts of sweet realization and delight. And there is the often unacknowledged, yet deliciously sweet taste of devoted practice.

OCTOBER 8
ZEALOT

◇

Where is he who set
his Holy Spirit among them,
who sent his glorious arm of power
to be at Moses' right hand,
who divided the waters before them,
to gain for himself everlasting renown,
who led them through the depths?
Like a horse in open country,
they did not stumble;
like cattle that go down to the plain,
they were given rest by the Spirit of the Lord.
This is how you guided your people
to make for yourself a glorious name.
Look down from heaven and see
from your lofty throne, holy and glorious.
Where are your zeal and your might?
Your tenderness and compassion are withheld from us.

—BOOK OF ISAIAH (HEBREW SCRIPTURES)

CONTEMPLATION

We don't typically see zeal and tenderness as companions and partners. We associate God's zealousness with destruction and religious zealots with at least offensiveness, if not brutality.

The great teacher and mythologist Joseph Campbell saw and understood both faces of zeal. He wrote:

> Instead of clearing his own heart the zealot tries to clear the world. The laws of the City of God are applied only to his in-group (tribe, church, nation, class, or whatnot) while the fire of a perpetual holy war is hurled (with good conscience, and indeed a sense of pious service) against whatever uncircumcised, barbarian, heathen, "native," or alien people happens to occupy the position of neighbor. . . .

> The good news, which the World Redeemer brings and which so many have been glad to hear, zealous to preach, but reluctant, apparently, to demonstrate, is that God is love, that He can be, and is to be, loved, and that all without exception are his children.

OCTOBER 9
STRANGERS

All the people of the whole world are equally brothers and sisters.
There is no one who is an utter stranger. The souls of all people are
equal, whether they live on the high mountains or at the bottoms of the
valleys.

—OFUDESAKI (TENRIKYO SACRED TEXT)

I have given each being a separate and unique way
of seeing and knowing and saying that knowledge.
What seems wrong to you is right for him.
What is poison to one is honey to someone else.
The ocean diver doesn't need snowshoes!
The Love-Religion has no code or doctrine,
Only God.

—WRITINGS OF RUMI (SUFI MYSTIC AND POET)

You are a blacksmith if you heat
You are a washerman if you beat,
A weaver if you lay the warp
A Brahman if you read the scriptures
Is anyone in this world born through the ear?
Therefore, whoever realizes the divine nature is high born.

—BASAVANNA (CLASSICAL HINDU WRITINGS)

CONTEMPLATION

*Bow to each other. In India this greeting tells the other person, stranger and
well-known friend alike, that the God in you acknowledges the God in her / him.*

*Even a brief glance at anyone in the world will reveal differences in style,
coloration, and constitution. Every individual, every culture for that matter,
speaks and worships in ways that are strange, often very strange to us.*

*Yet in truth, when we turn and really look at ourselves or those closest to us,
don't we find the same strangeness?*

This is what we have in common. This is what makes us, ultimately, friends.

SACRIFICE

◇

I have talked to you, talked, dark Lifter of Mountains,
About this old love, from birth after birth.
Don't go, don't, Lifter of Mountains,
Let me offer a sacrifice—myself—beloved, to your beautiful face.
Come, here in the courtyard, dark Lord,
The women are singing auspicious wedding songs;
My eyes have fashioned an altar of pearl tears,
And here is my sacrifice: the body and mind
Of Mira, the servant who clings to your feet, through life after life, a
Virginal harvest for you to reap.

—WRITINGS OF MIRABAI
(HINDU MYSTIC AND POET)

CONTEMPLATION

Abraham, the father of the Jews, was called on by God to make an incomprehensible sacrifice. God asked that Abraham bring his only son, Isaac, to the sacrificial altar. How, if Isaac were dead, would Abraham's promise from God to be the father of multitudes be fulfilled? For Abraham and Sarah, having had the miraculous birth of Isaac in their old age, were surely to have but one son. Nonetheless, Abraham brought Isaac, bound and subdued, to the altar and prepared to kill him. But God intervened. He accepted a ram found in a thicket in place of Isaac, and Abraham's promise was fulfilled.

As time went on, the form of sacrifice became refined. Animals, plant foods, then incense took their place on the altar. Eventually some came to understand that God did not require these material sacrifices but only a willing spirit. Jewish tradition honors those who have had this willingness to give up that which they had to give. What of Ruth, the grandmother of David, who found herself widowed and poor after the death of her Jewish husband? Although a Moabitess by birth, and considered an alien by the Jewish community, Ruth gave up the comfort and security of her homeland to follow her mother-in-law Naomi to an unknown future. Naomi had asked Ruth not to come with her, but Ruth, because of her great love for Naomi, would not stay. Back in Israel, Ruth, with happiness in her heart, went each day to the fields to harvest what little she could to sustain Naomi and herself. Her sweet sacrifice did not go unnoticed. Boaz, kin of Naomi, soon fell in love with the hardworking woman he saw in his fields and married her.

Sacrifice is not, as we fear, always fatal, then. It is simply the process of making the world about us, and in us, sacred ground.

WORM

Do not tell yourself in your heart of hearts that you are greater than your neighbor, because you serve God so very fervently. You are no different from the rest of the creatures who were created for the service of God. And how could you be more admirable than the worm? For it serves its Maker with all its power and strength.

—TRADITIONAL CHASSIDIC JEWISH TEACHING

This is how a human being can change:

There's a worm addicted to eating grape leaves.
     Suddenly, he wakes up,
call it Grace, whatever, something
wakes him, and he's no longer
a worm.
     He's the entire vineyard,
and the orchard too, the fruit, the trunks,
a growing wisdom and joy
that doesn't need
to devour.

—WRITINGS OF RUMI (SUFI MYSTIC AND POET)

CONTEMPLATION

At this time, Hindus complete the celebration of Dassehra, the ten-day festival that honors especially the watchful Goddess Durga and the hero-God Rama. Both are known as conquerors of demons, and thus Dassehra celebrates the transformation of evil.

Be like the worm. Conquer your evil habits by chewing on them bit by bit. Leave good, improved soil of the soul behind. Go on to the next bit . . . and worm your way to salvation.

READINESS

◇

A wild boar was busily sharpening his tusks on the trunk of a tree. The fox asked why he was putting himself to such trouble when there were no hunters in the vicinity and no danger in sight. The wild boar replied: ". . . Won't have time to sharpen my tusks when danger comes."

—FABLE OF AESOP (CLASSICAL GREEK)

◇

Hanina ben Dosa and his wife were very poor. Every Friday his wife would burn twigs in her oven to make smoke so that her neighbors would not know she had no bread to bake.

One Friday afternoon one of her neighbors, a meddlesome, mean-spirited woman, decided to embarrass Hanina's wife. "I know that the oven is empty," she said to herself. "I will go and see for myself."

When she knocked on the door, Hanina's wife ran into her bedroom. The neighbor came into the house and peered into the oven. How surprised she was to find it full of baking bread!

"Hurry, woman!" she cried. "Bring your breadshovel, or the loaves will be burned to cinders!"

But Hanina's wife was already on her way with the long, wide paddles in her hands, for being Hanina ben Dosa's wife, she was quite used to miracles.

—TRADITIONAL JEWISH TALE

◇

The stick that is at your friend's house will not drive away the leopard.

—TRADITIONAL GANDA TRIBAL PROVERB
(CENTRAL AFRICA)

CONTEMPLATION

The hour, Muhammad said, will not surprise the one who says: Allah, Allah. Are you ready for anything—from disaster to miracles?

Sharpen your study; perform your rituals; keep good friends close by. Be on your mark.

JOURNEYING

◈

Thrice was I beaten with rods, once was I stoned, thrice I suffered shipwreck, a night and a day I have been in the deep;

In journeyings often, in perils of waters, in perils of robbers, in perils by mine own countrymen, in perils by the heathen, in perils in the city, in perils in the wilderness, in perils in the sea, in perils among false brethren;

In weariness and painfulness, in watchings often, in hunger and thirst, in fastings often, in cold and nakedness.

—PAUL'S SECOND EPISTLE TO THE CORINTHIANS
(CHRISTIAN NEW TESTAMENT)

◈

You are to wander,
entering and departing
from strange villages . . .
Perhaps you will achieve nothing anywhere.
It may be that the things you carry with you
and your items of trade
find no favor in any place . . .
But do not turn back, keep a firm step . . .
Something you will achieve;
Something the Lord of the Universe will assign to you.

—SAYING OF CHILAM BALAM (MAYAN PRIEST)

CONTEMPLATION

In journeying, it is the intention that determines the result. Paul, the itinerant preacher, wanted only to tell the world of Jesus; though he suffered much, he fulfilled his assignment. Is there anyone today in the world who has not heard of Jesus?

Other journeyers' intentions have not been so clear; nor have they been so open to God's instructions. Columbus came looking for spices and gold to what was for him a wholly new world. He returned, by most accounts, infected with disease. Had he listened to the wisdom of indigenous people, like the priest Chilam Balam, his journey might have brought blessing.

JOY

Chuang-tzu and his close friend Hui-tzu were enjoying each other's company on the shores of the Hao. Chuang-tzu said, "The flashing fish are out enjoying each other, too, swimming gracefully this way and that. Such is the joy of fish!"

"You're no fish," said Hui-tzu. "How could you know their joy?"

"You're no Chuang-tzu," said Chuang-tzu. "How could you know I don't know the joy of fish?"

"If 'I am no Chuang-tzu,'" said Hui-tzu, "means 'I don't know Chuang-tzu,' then to be consistent, you don't know the joy of fish if you aren't a fish!"

"Let's go back to the beginning," said Chuang-tzu. "Your own question, 'How could you know the joy of fish?' already made an assumption about my knowing it! I don't have to jump in the water to know!"

—WRITINGS OF CHUANG-TZU
(CLASSICAL TAOIST TEACHER)

Two paths lie in front of man. Pondering on them, the wise man chooses the path of joy; the fool takes the path of pleasure.

—KATHA UPANISHAD (HINDU SACRED TEXT)

CONTEMPLATION

The poet Ghalib noted, "For the raindrop, joy is entering the river." Perhaps yours, like Chuang-tzu's, is watching fish. What are you waiting for? Take the path like a river straight to the sea!

REPOSE

"O Mummu, my vizier, who rejoicest my spirit,
Come hither and let us go to Tiamat!"
They went and sat down before Tiamat,
Exchanging counsel about the gods, their firstborn.
Apsu, opening his mouth,
Said unto resplendent Tiamat:
"Their ways are verily loathsome unto me.
By day I find no relief, nor repose by night.
I will destroy, I will wreck their ways,
That quiet may be restored. Let us have rest!"
As soon as Tiamat heard this,
She was wroth and called out to her husband.
She cried out aggrieved, as she raged all alone,
Injecting woe into her mood:
"What? Should we destroy that which we have built?
Their ways are indeed troublesome, but let us attend kindly!"

—TRADITIONAL BABYLONIAN HYMN

The repose of the sage is not what the world calls repose. His repose is the result of his mental attitude. All creation could not disturb his equilibrium: hence his repose.

When water is still, it is like a mirror, reflecting the beard and the eyebrows. . . . And if water thus derives lucidity from stillness, how much more the faculties of the mind? The mind of the sage being in repose becomes the mirror of the universe, the speculum of all creation.

Repose, tranquillity, stillness, inaction—these were the levels of the universe, the ultimate perfection of Tao. Therefore wise rulers and sages rest therein.

Repose, tranquillity, stillness, inaction—these were the source of all things. Keep to this when coming forward to pacify a troubled world, and your merit shall be great and your name illustrious, and the empire united into one. In your repose you will be wise; in your movements powerful. By inaction you will gain honor; and by confining yourself to the pure and simple, you will hinder the whole world from struggling with you for show.

—WRITINGS OF CHUANG-TZU
(CLASSICAL TAOIST TEACHER)

CONTEMPLATION

It is tempting to think as Apsu did: "Let's eliminate the trouble or troublemakers and obtain repose." But the trouble is found in one's own restlessness.

Follow Tiamat's advice. Be kind, especially to yourself, and let true repose develop.

LIONIZATION

◆

The rabbi of Chelm and one of his Talmud students were spending the night at the inn. The student asked the servant to wake him at dawn because he was to take an early train. The servant did so. Not wishing to wake the rabbi, the student groped in the dark for his clothes, and in his haste he put on the long rabbinical gabardine. He hurried to the station, and as he entered the train, he was struck dumb with amazement as he looked at himself in the compartment mirror.

"What an idiot that servant is!" he cried angrily. "I asked him to wake me. Instead he went and woke the rabbi!"

—TRADITIONAL JEWISH TALE

◆

While walking down the path with a student, a Sufi master was attacked by a vicious dog. The offended disciple shouted at the dog: "How dare you treat my master in this way?"

The teacher said: "Compared with you, this dog is surely less fickle. He barks at people out of habit and his natural predilections. You take me as your master and yet remain wholly ignorant and unobservant of the many worthy and radiant souls we have met in the course of our journeying to this day. You fixed your gaze solely on me and gave them no notice."

—TRADITIONAL SUFI ANECDOTE

CONTEMPLATION

How easy to make our favorite spiritual teacher or religious leader the one and only!

We read their books (or the ones about them), and if we know how they look and dress, we try to imitate them. We believe in our lionization of them, that they are what we are supposed to be and nothing else.

It's a great thing to have true spiritual masters in our world and, if you're really lucky, in your midst, but your spiritual life and its fulfillment are still up to you and always will be.

Aesop relates that "a snide fox one day disparaged a lioness for giving birth to only one cub at a time. 'Yes, only one,' she replied, 'but it's a lion!'"

Lionize yourself.

GREED

◇

Three young men were entrusted by their chief with a fine cow. On their journey they prepared to slaughter the cow for dinner. One said, "I want all the blood for myself." To drink the blood, he placed himself under the cow's throat. But in slaughtering the cow, the young man's throat was accidentally cut as well, and he died.

Two were left. One decided he would go to the river for water to cook the cow for dinner. Walking backward so that he could keep an eye on his companion, he fell into the river and was instantly devoured by an alligator.

Now there was only one man remaining. He cooked the cow and put a fine pot of soup up to boil. As the soup cooked, a red deer, pursued by hunters, stepped into the pot, and most of the soup's fat stuck to its feet. The young man could not let this rich fat go running off just like that, so he chased the deer and, catching it, licked all the fat off the deer's feet.

Meanwhile, a pregnant woman found what seemed to be an abandoned pot of soup. She ate as much as she could, then gave birth to her baby. She put the baby on top of a large bowl and filled the bowl with soup and meat. When she reached her village and unloaded her treasure, the meat was all gone. The baby had eaten it all!

—TRADITIONAL WEST AFRICAN TALE

CONTEMPLATION

Those who pursue the path of greed have got to be very careful. The junk-bond dealers and savings and loan swindlers must watch their associates as closely as the young man who fell into the river. And they can never know when they may, like that unfortunate man, find themselves up to their neck in alligators. Their lives, as the Bhagavad Gita tells it, are "nectar at the beginning, poison at the end."

In the land of the Kogi, people possess very little. The people of this five-thousand-year-old civilization, secluded in the Colombian rain forests, still own only the most primitive tools and technology. Yet they possess a profound understanding of the interconnectedness of the inner world and the outer world. Those who have visited this real-life Shangri-La bring back this message: "They see us as moral idiots, greedy beyond all understanding. . . . The highest morality is understanding that for everything taken something must be given back. . . . The Kogi demand an ethical revolution on our part, in which greed and selfishness are tempered by awe and by a sensitivity to the earth as a living—and now perhaps dying—totality."

Greed is a tremendous burden to carry. Yet we don't all have to take vows of poverty to lighten the load on ourselves and our planet. Mahatma Gandhi, who himself lived a life of extreme simplicity and austerity, did not require the same of his millions of followers. He asked them only to simplify their everyday lives, which by our standards were already incredibly simple and austere. Even in the 1930s Gandhi realized, "There is enough for everyone's need, but there is not enough for everyone's greed."

CONSEQUENCES

◆

A king went hunting one day and, in the heat of the chase, became separated from the hunting party. In a forest clearing, the king was relieved to discover a small garden, where, he hoped, he might find refreshment, for he had become terribly thirsty.

The gardener did not acknowledge the king as the king, for he wore no royal clothing, but only that which hunters wear. The king asked for drink, and the gardener went forthwith to the orchard, picked some pomegranates, and squeezed a cupful of juice for him.

The king quickly emptied the cup and, still dry-mouthed, requested that an additional cup be brought to him. The gardener complied and returned to the orchard.

While the gardener was gone, the king ruminated, "This seems to be quite a rich place. Just think, it took only a few minutes to produce a large cup of pomegranate juice, and the gardener will soon be back with another. I ought to impose a very heavy tax indeed on such a property."

But the gardener did not return quickly; he delayed for more than an hour. The puzzled and perturbed king asked himself, "How is it the gardener could get the first cup full in just a few minutes and in over an hour be unable to squeeze out for me the second one?"

The king waited. When the gardener eventually brought the next cup of juice, not quite as full as the first, the king demanded an explanation for the delay.

The gardener, unrecognized by the king but in truth a Sufi master, answered, "You, O King, maintained a good intention when you made your original request for refreshment. However, when I went to procure the second cup, your good-heartedness altered. I know of no other explanation for the sudden diminishing of the pomegranates' juiciness."

—TRADITIONAL SUFI TALE

CONTEMPLATION

Whether we like it or not, there are consequences not only of our actions but of our thoughts and attitudes as well. This may be a daunting prospect, but in truth this law of cause and effect has a huge upside. Want another delicious cup of pomegranate juice? Think and act positively.

SEEDS

◇

Four medicine men, born of the same mother, smoked together. This was the first time that men had ever smoked, and they sang and prayed together as they did so.

The brothers, who called the sacred weed *nawak'osis,* were meant to teach its use to the people. But *nawak'osis* made them powerful and wise and clear-minded, and they did not want to share it with others. They planted the sacred weed in a secret place that only they knew. They guarded the songs and prayers and rituals that went with smoking. They formed a Tobacco Society, just the four of them.

So there was anger, there was war, there was restlessness of spirit, there was impiety. *Nawak'osis* was meant to calm anger, to make men worship, to make peace, to ease the mind. But without the sacred herb, unity and peace were lacking.

A young man called Bull-by-Himself said to his wife: "These four powerful ones have been given something good to share with the people, but they are keeping it for themselves. So things are bad. I must find a way to plant and reap the sacred weed they call *nawak'osis.*

"There are four powerful men in our tribe," said Bull-by-Himself, "who have the medicine and the knowledge but keep them from us."

"Ah," said the man-beavers, "that is wrong. This sacred weed is meant to be shared. Here is what you must do."

The following night the beavers came as they had promised. They brought with them the sacred weed *nawak'osis.* The tops of the stalks were covered with little round seeds, and the man-beavers put the seeds into the medicine bundle the woman had prepared.

"It's planting time now," said the beavers. "Don't touch *nawak'osis* before you're ready to plant. Choose a place where there is not too much shade and not too much sunlight. Mix plenty of brown earth with plenty of black earth, and keep the soil loose. Say the prayers we have taught you. Then you, Bull-by-Himself, must take a deer horn and with its point make holes in the earth—one hole for each seed. And you, his wife, must use a buffalo-horn spoon to drop one seed into each hole. Keep singing the songs we taught you all the while. Then both of you dance lightly over this earth, tamping down the seeds. After that you just wait for *nawak'osis* to grow. Now we have taught you everything. Now we go."

Bull-by-Himself and his wife planted the sacred weed as they had been told. The four medicine-men brothers said to one another: "What can this man Bull-by-Himself and his wife be planting? Their songs sound familiar." They sent somebody to find out, and this person came back saying: "They are planting *nawak'osis*, doing it in a sacred manner."

Thus with the help of the beaver people, Bull-by-Himself and his wife brought the sacred tobacco to the tribes, who have been smoking it in a sacred manner ever since.

—TRADITIONAL SIKSIKA TRIBAL TALE
(NATIVE AMERICAN)

CONTEMPLATION

It takes prayer, care, and harvesting just to get the seeds you need. In all of this and in the planting is found salvation—good medicine.

To Meister Eckhart, Christian mystic and priest, it was revealed:

The seed of God is in us. Given an intelligent and hardworking farmer, it will thrive and grow up to God, whose seed it is; and accordingly its fruits will be God-nature.

COMMAND

◆

Be generous in prosperity, and thankful in adversity. Be worthy of the trust of thy neighbor, and look upon him with a bright and friendly face. Be a treasure to the poor, an admonisher to the rich, an answerer of the cry of the needy, a preserver of the sanctity of thy pledge. Be fair in thy judgment, and guarded in thy speech. Be unjust to no man, and show all meekness to all men. Be as a lamp unto them that walk in darkness, a joy to the sorrowful, a sea for the thirsty, a haven for the distressed, an upholder and defender of the victim of oppression. Let integrity and uprightness distinguish all thine acts. Be a home for the stranger, a balm to the suffering, a tower of strength for the fugitive. Be eyes to the blind, and a guiding light unto the feet of the erring. Be an ornament to the countenance of truth, a crown to the brow of fidelity, a pillar of the temple of righteousness, a breath of life to the body of mankind, an ensign of the hosts of justice, a luminary above the horizon of virtue, a dew to the soil of the human heart, an ark on the ocean of knowledge, a sun in the heaven of bounty, a gem on the diadem of wisdom, a shining light in the firmament of thy generation, a fruit upon the tree of humility.

—WRITINGS OF BAHÁ'U'LLÁH (BAHÁ'Í FAITH)

CONTEMPLATION

Confucius said, "Without recognizing the ordinances of Heaven, it is impossible to be a superior man." Once you do understand, you can follow through and be in command yourself.

UNKNOWN

◇

"As when a lump of salt is thrown into water and therein being dissolved it cannot be grasped again, but wherever the water is taken it is found salt, in the same way, O Maitreyi, the supreme Spirit is an ocean of pure consciousness boundless and infinite. Arising out of the elements, into them it returns again: there is no consciousness after death." Thus spoke Yajnavalkya.

Thereupon Maitreyi said: "I am amazed, O my Lord, to hear that after death there is no consciousness."

To this Yajnavalkya replied: "I am not speaking words of amazement; but sufficient for wisdom is what I say.

"For where there seems to be a duality, there one sees another, one hears another, one feels another's perfume, one thinks of another, one knows another. But when all has become Spirit, one's own Self, how and whom could one see? How and whom could one hear? How and whom could one know? How can one know him who knows all? How can the Knower be known?"

—BRIHADARANYAKA UPANISHAD (HINDU SACRED TEXT)

CONTEMPLATION

Buddha refused to get involved in philosophical disputes about abstractions. But he was questioned so frequently about Nirvana that he gave this answer (in the form of a question, of course) regarding the knowable and unknowable.

When the candle-flame of ego is snuffed out (the literal meaning of Nirvana), where does the flame go?

LAW

◈

The night passes; it is never to return again.
The night passes in vain
for one who acts not according to the law.

—UTTARADHYAYANA SUTRA (JAIN SACRED TEXT)

◈

The God of old bids us all abide by his injunctions.
Then shall we get whatever we want,
Be it white or red.

—TRADITIONAL AKAN TALKING-DRUM PRAYER
(WEST AFRICA)

◈

Oh how I love your Law! It is my meditation all the day.

—PSALM 119 (HEBREW SCRIPTURES)

CONTEMPLATION

Governments proclaim, "Ignorance of the law is no excuse," hoping by a single simple maxim to overcome the principal problem of law enforcement—one must know the law in order to abide by it.

Laws, religious or otherwise, may start out as relatively simple declarations (King Hammurabi's code or the Ten Commandments, for example), but it usually doesn't take too long before the injunctions and rules proliferate in both number and detail. The five holy books attributed to Moses, the Torah (also known as the Law), came to hold more than five hundred specific commandments, some as particular as the proper color (red) for sacrificial cattle and the intolerable color (white) found on a leper's skin.

No matter how devoted or studious a person may be, it is not possible to be fully compliant with any body of law.

What then are we to do? Taoists laugh and shake their heads. "The fewer laws the better," they say. "That way people won't be breaking the law all the time and getting punished. Left alone, most people will do good anyway."

Many Jews choose to embrace the Law given to them, celebrating the holy day, Simchas Torah (the Joy of the Law), with great pleasure and zest.

Whether you view "the Law" as principles of universal harmony and unity or as a compendium of instructions and mandates, it's still a good idea to get right with the Law.

Open your practice today!

THEFT

Said the Great Maggid to Rabbi Zusya, his disciple: "I cannot teach you the ten principles of service. But a little child and a thief can show you what they are.

"From the child you can learn three things:
He is merry for no particular reason.
Never for a moment is he idle.
When he needs something, he demands it vigorously.
"The thief can instruct you in seven things:
He does his service by might.
If he does not finish what he has set out to do in one night, he devotes the next night to it.
He and those who work with him love one another.
He risks his life for slight gains.
What he takes has so little value for him that he gives it up for a very small coin.
He endures blows and hardship and it matters nothing to him.
He likes his trade and would not exchange it for any other."

—TRADITIONAL CHASSIDIC JEWISH ANECDOTE

CONTEMPLATION

Little children are often thieves. This is because they have not yet learned that such-and-such good thing "does not belong to you."

To them, and professional thieves as well, everything is up for grabs.

There is great merit in applying this attitude in spiritual matters. With the good cheer of a child and the passionate abandon of a thief, you can obtain unlimited wealth of the soul.

COMMUNITY

◆

Community: irrationals unified by hope of the impossible.

—WRITINGS OF MULLAH DO-PIAZZA (SUFI TEACHER)

◆

If I am not for myself, who then will be for me?
If I am only for myself, who am I? And if not now, when?

—TEACHINGS OF HILLEL (JEWISH RABBI)

◆

The pebbles are the strength of a wall.

—TRADITIONAL BUJI TRIBAL PROVERB (WEST AFRICA)

CONTEMPLATION

On his journey on the road less traveled, M. Scott Peck discovered: "In and through community lies the salvation of the world. Nothing is more important. Yet it is virtually impossible to describe community meaningfully to someone who has never experienced it—and most of us have never had an experience of true community. The problem is analogous to an attempt to describe the taste of artichokes to someone who has never eaten one."

Most indigenous peoples sat (and still sit) in circles. From the earliest age a child experiences herself or himself as an equal part of something much larger, yet self-contained and whole.

Reconnect to this. Join a circle or circles. You'll know which ones are right for you; true community tastes good!

CONFUSION

Once a man receives this fixed bodily form, he holds on to it, waiting for the end. Sometimes clashing with things, sometimes bending before them, he runs his course like a galloping steed, and nothing can stop him. Is he not pathetic? Sweating and laboring to the end of his days and never seeing his accomplishment, utterly exhausting himself and never knowing where to look for rest—can you help pitying him? I'm not dead yet! he says, but what good is that? His body decays, his mind follows it—can you deny that this is a great sorrow? Man's life has always been a muddle like this. How could I be the only muddled one, and other men not muddled?

—WRITINGS OF CHUANG-TZU
(CLASSICAL TAOIST TEACHER)

CONTEMPLATION

Chuang-tzu must have been really confused to ask if he was the only one confused by the confusion of this confused world.

When the winds are whipping, as they very well might be today, they tend to stir an already anxious mind to greater states of befuddlement.

This is the time simply to stop: If your meditation or prayer practice is strong, go to it. Another alternative is to allow your mind to flutter and flap away and just be an objective witness to it all. Clearly an opportunity.

ENTROPY

◆

The king of Adja, Adjahosu, had everything. One day when he went to see his diviner, he said: "You must divine something for me. I am too rich and do not know what it is to be poor. I want to know what it is to be poor."

The diviner told him, after he divined, to bring a drum, a gong, and rattles. "When you have them, tell your hunters to catch a giraffe."

The diviner instructed them to tie the gong, drum, and rattles about the neck of the giraffe and told the man to get on its back. Then they took a cloth and tied him in place, and the diviner gave him a little stick to strike the drum with. When he beat the drum, the giraffe ran away with him into the bush.

They passed through brush and thorny bushes until they were in the middle of the forest, when the cloth became so torn that the king fell off the animal. He did not know where his house was; he was completely lost.

One day, when the king's sons came home, they said to the eldest brother: "Look, we were at a market in the field of Adjahosu, and we saw a black man whom they call Adjahosu. And an old woman commanded him to sell wood." The older brother said, "Good, we will go to the next market there."

He placed himself where his younger brothers had been and after a time saw an old woman accompanied by a man, who was carrying her cloths. When the man put the cloths down, he took his bush knife and entered the forest nearby. In a short time, he saw the man returning with wood, which he put down beside his mistress. After this the woman said, "You can eat," and gave him something to eat.

As he was eating, his son approached him. When he recognized his child, he began to cry, and the son did, too.

The son led his father to the old woman and asked her, "Where did you find this man?"

She answered: "I was looking for indigo leaves. One day I saw him alone in the bush."

The son took the man and said, "Now you will sell him to me."

She said, "If I sell him now, who will carry my load to my house?"

The son said, "I will buy him and give you the money, and you can buy another carrier with this money."

"Let me be! This old one here, what will you do with him?"

The son replied: "This is not an old one to me. He is my father. I beg you to sell him to me."

The old woman said, "Since he is your father, take him."

So his son took Adjahosu home and bathed him and gave him fresh clothes. After that Adjahosu summoned all his people before him to speak to them. He said: "Because I myself am very very rich, I wanted to know what is poverty. Now I say to you, my sons and my family, never ask to be poor."

—TRADITIONAL WEST AFRICAN TALE

CONTEMPLATION

Things always deteriorate and lose energy. Entropy is a universal law of physics and is sure to happen whether you ask for it or not. Don't go asking for it, or you'll end up in a sorry state, like poor King Adjahosu. The only hope, Buddha tells us, lies in spiritual practice.

Those who have not practiced spiritual disciplines in their youth, he points out, pine away like old cranes in a lake without fish.

REALIZATION

◇

I am the justness of plants
I am the courage of the wild boar
I am the salmon leaping
I am the stillness of the lake
I am the word of wise inquiry
I am the spear-point of battle
I am the divinity who created the crown of fire.
Who pours light on the meeting in the mountains?
Who tells the ages of the moon?
Who teaches where sets the sun?
Who, if not I?

—ORTHA NAN GAIDHEAL (TRADITIONAL GAELIC SONG)

CONTEMPLATION

The great realization is the realization of who you are.

All of us are someone at birth; only some of us fill into and expand upon our essential nature; very, very few of us realize who we are at heart and act from this inner self.

The story is told of a Zen Buddhist priest. A civil war was raging, and the conquering general, known for the terror he brought, was approaching the town. Everyone had fled; not a soul remained except the monk.

When the soldiers reported the monk's presence in the temple, the outraged general hastened there. He stormed into the sacred place, drew his sword, and stared at the solitary priest. "Don't you know who I am?" he bellowed. "I am the one who can slice you to pieces without blinking an eye!"

The master monk was calm and matter-of-factly responded, "And I, sir, am the one who can be sliced into pieces without blinking an eye."

The general realized who he was faced with and withdrew without a word.

MEASURING

◆

But thou hast lifted up thyself against the Lord of heaven; and they have brought the vessels of his house before thee, and thou, and thy lords, thy wives, and thy concubines, have drunk wine in them; and thou hast praised the gods of silver, and gold, of brass, iron, wood, and stone, which see not, nor hear, nor know: and the God in whose hand thy breath is, and whose are all thy ways, hast thou not glorified: Then was the part of the hand sent from him; and this writing was written. And this is the writing that was written, MENE, MENE, TEKEL, UPHARSIN. This is the interpretation of the thing: MENE; God hath numbered thy kingdom, and finished it. TEKEL; Thou art weighed in the balances, and art found wanting. PERES; Thy kingdom is divided, and given to the Medes and Persians.

Then commanded Belshazzar, and they clothed Daniel with scarlet, and put a chain of gold about his neck, and made a proclamation concerning him, that he should be the third ruler in the kingdom.

In that night was Belshazzar the king of the Chaldeans slain.

—BOOK OF DANIEL (HEBREW SCRIPTURES)

CONTEMPLATION

We try to measure everything—from the tiniest subatomic particle to the time and space of the universe. Measure yourself on occasion: a spiritual checkup.

How's the meditation going? More profound and less restless than a few months ago? The purpose of such measuring is to enable you to make adjustments and fine-tune your practice, not to judge yourself. You are the only true arbiter of your own spiritual development.

PRESUMPTION

◆

Once upon a time when Brahmadatta was reigning in Benares, the Bodhisattva was a maned lion and dwelled at Gold Den in the Himalayas. Bounding forth one day from his lair, he looked north and west, south and east, and roared aloud as he went in quest of prey. Slaying a large buffalo, he devoured the prime of the carcass, after which he went down to a pool and, having drunk his fill of crystal water, turned to go toward his den. Now a hungry jackal, suddenly meeting the lion and being unable to make his escape, threw himself at the lion's feet. Being asked what he wanted, the jackal replied, "Lord, let me be thy servant." "Very well," said the lion, "serve me, and you shall feed on prime meat."

Lying one day in his den, the lion told the jackal to scan the valleys from the mountaintop, to see whether there were any elephants or horses or buffaloes about, or any other animals of which he, the jackal, was fond. If any such were in sight, the jackal was to report and say with due obeisance, "Shine forth in thy might, Lord." Then the lion promised to kill and eat, giving a part to the jackal. From that time on, the jackal used to climb the heights, and whenever he espied below beasts to his taste, he would report it to the lion and, falling at his feet, say, "Shine forth in thy might, Lord." Hereon the lion would nimbly bound forth and slay the beast, even if it were a rutting elephant, and share the prime of the carcass with the jackal. Glutted with his meal, the jackal would then retire to his den and sleep. Thenceforth the lion's leavings fell to the jackal, and he grew fat.

Now as time went on, the jackal grew bigger and bigger until he grew haughty. "Have not I, too, four legs?" he asked himself. "Why am I a pensioner day by day on others' bounty? Henceforth *I* will kill elephants and other beasts, for my own eating. The lion, king of beasts, kills them only because of the formula, 'Shine forth in thy might, Lord.' I'll make the lion call out to me, 'Shine forth in thy might, jackal,' and then I'll kill an elephant for myself." Said the lion, "Jackal, only lions can kill elephants, nor has the world ever seen a jackal able to cope with them. Give up this fancy, and continue to feed on what I kill." But say what the lion could, the jackal would not give way and still pressed his request. So at last the lion gave way and, bidding the jackal couch in the den, climbed the peak and thence espied an elephant in rut. Returning to the mouth of the cave, he said, "Shine forth in thy might, jackal." Then from Gold Den the jackal nimbly bounded forth, looked around him on all four sides, and thrice raising its howl, sprang at the elephant, meaning to fasten on its head. But missing his aim, he alighted at the elephant's feet. The infuriated brute raised its right foot and crushed the jackal's head, trampling the bones into powder. Then pounding the carcass into a mass and dunging upon it, the elephant dashed trumpeting into the forest.

—TRADITIONAL BUDDHIST TALE

CONTEMPLATION

Think you can do what your boss does; what your teacher does; what your clergyperson does just because you've associated with them and done a few things in the same field?

One does not become a spiritual lion in a season or two. One does not become a spiritual lion through a special formula.

When you've got real claws and teeth, roar all you want.

ESCAPE

One morning when Solomon was in the hall of justice, one of his followers came running to him in fear. His face was pale, his lips blue, and his hands were trembling.

"What is it that disturbs you?" asked the king.

"It was Death, Death bumped into me in the courtyard and looked upon me with rage and vengeance."

"Come now," said Solomon, "ask any boon."

"O protector of our lives, I beg thee to loan me your swiftest horse, the one that even leaves the wind behind, that he may carry me to Hindustan and save me from the jaws of Death."

"Take the horse; but also know, dear servant, that it is your spiritual poverty that you fear. Greed and ambition are the Hindustan you seek."

The next day, when Solomon held audience in his courtyard, he asked Death why he looked upon his servant with such scorn.

Death spoke: "I accidentally bumped him, and when I saw him, I stared in wonder, for God commanded me to take his soul tonight in Hindustan, and I knew if he even had a hundred wings, he could not get to Hindustan in time for me to claim him."

—TRADITIONAL JEWISH TALE

CONTEMPLATION

If you are fleeing from something, what is it really? Quite often you'll find it is something far different than you imagined.

As the days get colder, use this time to be still and examine your anxieties. There is escape to be found from imagined frights.

PROSPERITY

◇

Yea, and there was continual peace among them and exceedingly great prosperity . . . because of their heed and diligence which they gave unto the word of God.

—BOOK OF MORMON

◇

The blessing of the Lord, it maketh rich, and he addeth no sorrow with it.

—BOOK OF PROVERBS (HEBREW SCRIPTURES)

◇

As long as you watch the way
As long as your steps are steady
As long as your wisdom is unimpaired—
So long will you reap profit.
As long as the moon of prosperity is waxing
And as long as Death does not knock at your door,
Continue to live chastely,
And let your actions benefit all.

—WRITINGS OF NAGARJUNA AND SAKYA PANDIT
(BUDDHIST TEACHERS)

CONTEMPLATION

The incarnated God Krishna, charioteer to Arjuna, his doubting soldier friend, promises him that all faithful efforts at meditation will accumulate: like layers of gold plating, they will eventually make Arjuna rich and resplendent in his spiritual nature.

Mother Teresa carries to the West from India a twist on this Krishnan message. "We are here," she tells us, "not to be successful, but faithful," emphasizing in a different way the superseding importance of the process to the result.

As another great soul (Jesus of Nazareth) put it: Seek you first the kingdom of heaven, and all else will surely be added.

You are assured prosperity by every authority. It is for you.

NOVEMBER

SAINTS

◇

A young man once came to a great rabbi and asked him to make him a rabbi.

It was wintertime then. The rabbi stood at the window looking out upon the yard while the rabbinical candidate was droning into his ears a glowing account of his piety and learning.

The young man said, "You see, Rabbi, I always go dressed in spotless white like the sages of old. I never drink any alcoholic beverages; only water ever passes my lips. Also, I perform austerities. I have sharp-edged nails inside my shoes to mortify me. Even in the coldest weather, I lie naked in the snow to torment my flesh. Also daily, the *shammes* gives me forty lashes on my bare back to complete my perpetual penance."

And as the young man spoke, a white horse was led into the yard and to the water trough. It drank, and then it rolled in the snow, as horses sometimes do.

"Just look!" cried the rabbi. "That animal, too, is dressed in white. It also drinks nothing but water, has nails in its shoes, and rolls naked in the snow. Also, rest assured, it gets its daily ration of forty lashes on the rump from its master. Now, I ask you, is it a saint, or is it a horse?"

—TRADITIONAL JEWISH TALE

CONTEMPLATION

Catholics acknowledge all sorts of saints. There are mystic saints, like Saint Teresa of Ávila, from whom Mother Teresa of Calcutta took her sacred name. There are teaching saints, like Saint Thomas Aquinas, a great theologian who helped develop ideas of religious education and scholarship. There are martyr saints, like Saint Stephen, who declared his faith openly and unashamedly even at the great Temple in Jerusalem itself.

So many ways to be a saint. Pick one.

AFTERLIFE

◇

I came to drink with my friend
And find him I could not.
O Death, who taketh away Life
And giveth no day at court,
A day will come and I shall see him again.
Aye, I shall see him . . .
For I too am going toward death.

I say to you say
The wives you have,
The passion you know of them
Goes with you.

I say to you say
The drinks you drink,
The pleasure of them
Goes with you.

I say to you say
The pipes you smoke,
The quiet they bring
Goes with you.

Come, then
Dance all the colors of Life
For a lover of pleasure
Now dead.

—TRADITIONAL DAHOMEY TRIBAL SONG (WEST AFRICA)

CONTEMPLATION

One day, the Mullah Nasreddin was walking through a cemetery, when he fell into an old grave. "How would it feel to be really dead?" he wondered. In this frame of mind he heard a noise, and it occurred to him that it must be the Angel of Reckoning coming to take him. In truth, it was only a caravan passing nearby.

Nasreddin leaped out of the grave and, stumbling, spooked the entire train of camels. It took the camel drivers a great while to recapture their beasts and, frustrated, they beat Nasreddin for having caused such a problem.

By the time he got home, Nasreddin was in quite a state. His wife asked him why he looked the way he did and why he was so late.

"I have been dead," Nasreddin said matter-of-factly.

She could not resist. "Well, then," she asked, "what is it like?"

"Oh, it's all right," Nasreddin answered, "as long as you don't upset the camels."

As an old rabbi says, "Anything's possible," and if this applies anywhere, it surely does to questions of the afterlife. Our Dahomean friends and Nasreddin thought they had it figured out. Perhaps the afterlife is like other unknown-before-they-happen life experiences—birth, a new school, marriage: we'll know only when we get there.

So what do we do now?

Elisabeth Kübler-Ross, noted as an authority on dying and death and life after life, summed it up very nicely: "Live it up!"

AWAKE

It is said that soon after his enlightenment, the Buddha passed a man on the road who was struck by the extraordinary radiance and peacefulness of his presence. The man stopped and asked, "My friend, what are you? Are you a celestial being or a god?"

"No," said the Buddha.

"Well, then, are you some kind of magician or wizard?"

Again the Buddha answered, "No."

"Are you a man?"

"No."

"Well, my friend, what then are you?"

The Buddha replied, "I am awake."

—TRADITIONAL BUDDHIST TALE

The night watchman of the village spied the Mullah Nasreddin opening his own bedroom window and climbing in.

"What are you doing?" the watchman asked. "Have you been locked out?"

"Be quiet," Nasreddin ordered. "They tell me I'm a sleepwalker. I'm going in to catch myself asleep and find out if it's true."

—TRADITIONAL SUFI TALE

CONTEMPLATION

Even on a brisk morning, you may not feel fully awake. And if you do feel awake, does that make it so? Might you find yourself surprised at some task to be so sluggish, so stupid, so asleep?

Awakening is not a process subject to vagaries; it requires practice, attention, and dear friends to shake you out of slumber now and again.

ABSURDITY

◇

The inhabitants of a small village in Upper Burma were ignorant and foolish, but there was one who was less ignorant but more foolish than the others. The villagers, however, regarded him as their Wiseman and consulted him on all matters that puzzled them from time to time.

One night a rogue elephant wandered into a sugarcane field belonging to a villager and ate up all the sugarcane. The following morning the owner of the field discovered the loss and was mystified to see the elephant's tracks. It never entered his mind that the tracks were those of an elephant. So he went and fetched the Village Wiseman. The Village Wiseman looked carefully at the elephant tracks and sat down and pondered the whole day. Just as the sun was setting, he stood up and announced with a smile, "I have solved the mystery. There are two problems to be considered. First, how could anyone steal the sugarcane without leaving any footprints? Second, what are those large round marks on the ground? The explanation is this: The thief tied a winnowing tray to each foot, came walking across the field, and carried away the sugarcane on his shoulders."

—TRADITIONAL BURMESE BUDDHIST TALE

CONTEMPLATION

Anything can happen. We know that sometimes even the craziest and most absurd events take place.

Must there be an explanation for everything? This is where both science and religion get into trouble, persistently proposing (and defending) dogmatic solutions and attacking those who don't accept them. Once in a while, just let the elephant wander off. That makes sense.

INSPIRATION

Consider the divine spirit in the human soul
This spirit is not easily satisfied
It storms the firmament
and scales the heavens
trying to reach the Spirit that drives the heavens
Because of this energy
everything in the world grows green,
flourishes,
and bursts into leaf.
But the spirit is never satisfied.
It presses on,
deeper and deeper into the vortex,
further and further into the whirlpool,
the primary source
in which the spirit has its origin.
This spirit seeks to be
broken through by God.
God leads this spirit
into a desert
into the wilderness and solitude of the divinity
where God is pure unity
and where God gushes up within himself.

—WRITINGS OF MEISTER ECKHART
(CHRISTIAN MYSTIC AND POET)

CONTEMPLATION

*Jnana (higher knowledge), among Jain students and scholars in India, is cele-
brated at this time. For all we "know," the Sanskrit word* jnana *may have common
roots with the Greek term* gnosis, *both indicating a way to true knowledge.*

*Without taking in, breathing in the spirit (inspiration), all knowledge of
self, of others, of God, is dead. With inspiration, the oddest thoughts can come
gushing forth, bringing unexpected new growth even in ostensibly barren times
and places.*

Wherever you are inspired to be, be!

Wherever you are inspired to go, go!

LOVE

So when they had dined, Jesus saith to Simon Peter, Simon, son of Jonas, lovest thou me more than these? He saith unto him, Yea, Lord; thou knowest that I love thee. He saith unto him, Feed my lambs.

He saith to him again the second time, Simon, son of Jonas, lovest thou me? He saith unto him, Yea, Lord; thou knowest that I love thee. He saith unto him, Feed my sheep.

He saith unto him the third time, Simon, son of Jonas, lovest thou me? Peter was grieved because he said unto him the third time, Lovest thou me? And he said unto him, Lord, thou knowest all things; thou knowest that I love thee. Jesus saith unto him, Feed my sheep.

—GOSPEL OF JOHN (CHRISTIAN NEW TESTAMENT)

Without *kâma* (love) a person has no wish for worldly profit, without kâma a person does not strive after the Good; therefore kâma stands above. . . . For the sake of *kâma,* the rishis (holy ones) even give themselves up to asceticism, eating the leaves of trees, fruits, and roots, living on the air. . . . Traders, farmers, herders, craftspeople, as also artists, and those that carry out actions consecrated to the gods, give themselves up to their works because of *kâma.* Others again take to the sea filled with *kâma.* Without *kâma* the manifold workings of the world would not be thinkable. As honey is the sweet juice from the flower, so *kâma* is.

—TRADITIONAL HINDU TEACHING

CONTEMPLATION

*Love, M. Scott Peck professes, is not a feeling but an activity. "Feed my sheep,"
Jesus told Simon Peter, not feel sorry, or sad or glad, or appreciative about
them.*

*And as we are to fulfill the two imperative commandments—to love God
with all our being and to love our neighbors as ourselves—this means action.*

*The Divine Krishna tells the Hindu counterpart to Peter, Arjuna, what happens
when we love like this:*

*Seek the Divine with your whole being
I truly love you*

No one renders to me service
More precious than this one
Nor will there ever be anyone
Whom I love more on earth.

You will come to me
I promise it to you surely.
I love you.

SLANDER

◇

Once there was a man who had three daughters, one a thief, one a lazy good-for-nothing, and the third a slanderer. A man came and wished to marry the three daughters to his three sons.

"No," said their father, "for they are unworthy."

But the other man persisted, and the three couples were married.

The father of the three sons put the thieving daughter in charge of all his money and the lazy daughter in charge of all his servants. And each morning he came to the daughter who was a slanderer to inquire about her health.

After some time, the girls' father came to visit them.

"Thank you, Father, for sending me to this house," said the daughter who had once been a thief. "For I have repented of my evil ways."

The second daughter likewise praised her father, for she too had changed her wicked ways.

But the third daughter said, "May you be cursed, Father, for sending me here! For you have married me to two husbands, not to one. As soon as the son goes to work each morning, the father comes to force himself upon me. If you do not believe me, hide under the bed and see for yourself."

So the next morning, the father hid under his daughter's bed as soon as her husband left for work. A few moments later the father-in-law came into the room and kissed his daughter-in-law on the forehead as he did every day.

"Leave me alone!" she cried. "My father is here!"

At that her father came out from under the bed and killed him. When the sons heard of this, they came and killed their father-in-law. Then they killed the slanderer herself.

So it is that slander slays three: the one who spreads the slander, the one who listens to it, and the one who is slandered.

—TRADITIONAL JEWISH TALE

CONTEMPLATION

A wise rabbi said this about badmouthing: "If it's true what you're saying about the other, it's sad for them. If it's not true, it's sad for you."

Wouldn't you rather have in your mouth the good taste of good words?

AVAILABILITY

People were also bringing babies to Jesus to have him touch them. When the disciples saw this, they rebuked them. But Jesus called the children to him and said, "Let the little children come to me, and do not hinder them, for the kingdom of God belongs to such as these. I tell you the truth, anyone who will not receive the kingdom of God like a little child will never enter it."

As Jesus approached Jericho, a blind man was sitting by the roadside begging. When he heard the crowd going by, he asked what was happening. They told him, "Jesus of Nazareth is passing by."

He called out, "Jesus, Son of David, have mercy on me!"

Those who led the way rebuked him and told him to be quiet, but he shouted all the more, "Son of David, have mercy on me!"

Jesus stopped and ordered the man to be brought to him. When he came near, Jesus asked him, "What do you want me to do for you?"

"Lord, I want to see," he replied.

Jesus said to him, "Receive your sight; your faith has healed you." Immediately he received his sight and followed Jesus, praising God. When all the people saw it, they also praised God.

—GOSPEL OF LUKE (CHRISTIAN NEW TESTAMENT)

CONTEMPLATION

Jesus was a great soul, open and available to those who sought to be with him. He gave comfort, healing, teaching to those who were considered undeserving or unreachable.

Even for Jesus, availability was a two-way street. He needed others, like the despised tax collector Zacchaeus, to make themselves and their resources available to him. "I must stay at your house," he told the astonished Zacchaeus, and so it came to be.

Today, we are blessed. Many great souls from around the world have made themselves available to us. When you go to meet them, be like the eager Zacchaeus—make yourself available to them and their work.

WORLDLINESS

◆

Little by little, wean yourself. This is the gist of what I have to say. From an embryo, whose nourishment comes in the blood, move to an infant drinking milk, to a child on solid food, to a searcher after wisdom, to a hunter of more invisible game.

Think how it is to have a conversation with an embryo. You might say, "The world outside is vast and intricate. There are wheat fields and mountain passes, and orchards in bloom. At night there are millions of galaxies, and in sunlight the beauty of friends dancing at a wedding."

You ask the embryo why he, or she, stays cooped up in the dark with eyes closed. Listen to the answer.

There is no "other world." I only know what I've experienced. You must be hallucinating.

—WRITINGS OF RUMI (SUFI MYSTIC AND POET)

◆

I climb the road to Cold Mountain,
The road to Cold Mountain that never ends.
The valleys are long and strewn with stones;
The streams broad and banked with thick grass.
Moss is slippery, though no rain has fallen;
Pines sigh, but it isn't the wind.
Who can break from the snare of the world
And sit with me among the white clouds?

—WRITINGS OF HAN-SHAN (BUDDHIST POET)

CONTEMPLATION

There's an upside to worldliness—we're here already. If you have an aversion to the world and an accompanying desire to return to what you think is a blissful womb-world awaiting you, then you are as obsessively attached to the world as the businesspeople or scientists you scoff at.

It's not what you make of the world that's really important; it's what it makes of you. The world—its gravity and buoyancy, its exuberant growth and fetid decay, its amazing inhabitants—shapes the very heart and soul of you.

ACCUMULATION

If good does not accumulate, it is not enough to make a name for a man. If evil does not accumulate, it is not strong enough to destroy a man. Therefore, the inferior man thinks to himself, "Goodness in small things has no value," and so neglects it. He thinks, "Small sins do no harm," and so does not give them up. Thus, his sins accumulate until they can no longer be covered up and his guilt becomes so great that it can no longer be wiped out.

—TEACHING OF CONFUCIUS (CLASSICAL CHINESE)

When a man grows aware of a new way in which to serve God, he should carry it around with him secretly, and without uttering it, for nine months, as though he were pregnant with it, and let others know of it only at the end of that time, as though it were a birth.

—TRADITIONAL CHASSIDIC JEWISH TEACHING

CONTEMPLATION

Just as icicles grow in size by adding layers, so do we accumulate a spiritual body of bulk and import.

It is the methodical stewards of moral and spiritual practice who eventually become so added-to that they burst with new spiritual power.

Joseph, the boy given the coat of many colors, was such a person. He lived a life of virtue. (He refused the immoral advances of his protector's wife, for one thing.) And as Joseph added to God's glory with such acts, God added to Joseph's life—a noble wife, two sons who became princes of Israel, and the governorship of Egypt.

The name Joseph means "God adds to"; God did and still does.

AGE

A man who does not learn from life grows old like an ox: his body grows, but not his wisdom.

I have gone through many rounds of birth and death, looking in vain for the builder of this body. Heavy indeed is birth and death again and again! But now I have seen you, house-builder, you shall not build this house again. Its beams are broken; its dome is shattered: self-will is extinguished; nirvana is attained.

—DHAMMAPADA (SACRED BUDDHIST TEXT)

CONTEMPLATION

Age, in and of itself, has no merit.

In some countries, today is the day of remembering and honoring veterans of war. Many of these people are well advanced in age and sometimes so feeble, they can no longer join their comrades-in-arms in annual parades.

We may feel compassion or even pity for them. They're so old and they fought for us, too.

But have they learned peace? If so, hold no concern for them but rather ask yourself, "Have I or am I finding peace?"

NOVEMBER 12
PROPERTY

Some children were playing beside a river. They made castles of sand, and each child defended his castle and said, "This one is mine." They kept their castles separate and would not allow any mistakes about which was whose. When the castles were all finished, one child kicked over someone else's castle and completely destroyed it. The owner of the castle flew into a rage, pulled the other child's hair, struck him with his fist, and bawled out, "He has spoiled my castle! Come along all of you and help me to punish him as he deserves." The others all came to his help. They beat the child with a stick and then stamped on him as he lay on the ground. . . . Then they went on playing in their sand castles, each saying, "This is mine; no one else may have it. Keep away! Don't touch my castle!" But evening came, it was getting dark, and they all thought they ought to be going home. No one now cared what became of his castle. One child stamped on his, another pushed his over with both hands. Then they turned away and went back, each to his home.

—YOGACHARA BHUMI SHASTRA (BUDDHIST SACRED TEXT)

CONTEMPLATION

If anything is held as sacred in today's world, it is property—private property. Laws and police enforcement protect it, and a global system of finance has been established to procure it.

Isn't this all a bit too much? After all, the tide will eventually come in and wash it away.

Too much attention paid to prosperity and ownership can be very destructive to your good nature. Enjoy what you have, but don't let it spoil you.

CONSISTENCY

◇

Those who are devoted to the perfection of wisdom should expect therefrom many advantages here and now. They will not die an untimely death, nor from poison, or sword, or fire, or water, or staff, or violence. When they bring to mind and repeat this perfection of wisdom, the calamities which threaten them from kings and princes, from kings' counselors and kings' ministers, will not take place. If kings, etc., would try to do harm to those who again and again bring to mind and repeat the perfection of wisdom, they will not succeed; because the perfection of wisdom upholds them.

—PERFECTION OF WISDOM IN EIGHT THOUSAND LINES
(BUDDHIST SACRED TEXT)

◇

One who has a true hold on life, when he walks on land does not meet tigers or wild buffaloes; in battle he is not touched by weapons of war. Indeed, a buffalo that attacked him would find nothing for his horns to butt, a tiger would find nothing for its claws to tear, a weapon would find no place for its blade to lodge.

—TAO TE CHING (CLASSICAL TAOIST TEXT)

◇

You will not fear the terror of the night,
nor the arrow that flies by day,
nor the pestilence that stalks in darkness,
nor the destruction that wastes at noonday.
A thousand may fall at your side,
ten thousand at your right hand;
but it will not come near you.
You will only look with your eyes
and see the recompense of the wicked.
Because you have made the Lord your refuge,
the Most High your habitation,
no evil shall befall you.
You will tread on the lion and the adder,
the young lion and the serpent you will trample under foot.

—PSALM 91 (HEBREW SCRIPTURES)

CONTEMPLATION

Most of us have heard some version of the story of Daniel in the lion's den. Most of us believe it is a simple tale of God's grace in action, saving poor Daniel at the last moment from the ravenous jaws of the beast, as if God and Daniel were characters in an old-fashioned melodrama.

The words of a gospel song tell the real story: "And Daniel prayed every morning, noon, and night." It was Daniel's consistency with God that made him and God ready to face the lions.

SWORD

◈

Damocles was an envious nobleman in the court of the ruler of Syracuse, Dionysius. Damocles coveted both the ruler's opulent lifestyle and the fawning respect the other courtiers gave the king. Although Dionysius was a mean-spirited and despicable person, Damocles was so taken by what the king had that he flattered Dionysius constantly and said to his friends, "If only I could be king for even one day, how wonderful that would be." This fervent wish (like all such prayers) reached the ears of His Highness, and Dionysius decided to grant Damocles' desire.

"Tomorrow," Dionysius decreed, "a great banquet will be held. All the court must attend. But in my stead will sit Damocles on the throne, with all the glory and honor due a king of Syracuse." So the next day there reigned "King" Damocles, dressed in royal robes, and indulging himself in all the rich food and drink and resplendent praise that the subjects of Syracuse could muster. Damocles was having a grand time, when he happened to notice out of the corner of his eye a huge (and seemingly very sharp) sword hanging by a single hair from the ceiling directly above his "royal" head! Of course, he wanted to run, but Dionysius would have none of it—after all, a bargain was a bargain. "Now," he told the frightened Damocles, "you know what goes with the position you wanted so badly."

—ANCIENT GREEK STORY

◈

During the short aeons of swords,
They meditate on love,
Introducing to nonviolence
Hundreds of millions of living beings.

In the midst of great battles
They remain impartial to both sides;
For bodhisattvas of great strength
Delight in reconciliation of conflict.

—DISCOURSE OF VIMALAKIRTI (BUDDHIST SACRED TEXT)

CONTEMPLATION

Swords cut many ways. Most of us try our best to avoid places and positions in which swords and swordplay may be manifest.

The early members of the Sikh community, living in an Indian culture torn between Hinduism and Islam, sought peace and brotherhood among people of faith. Their first guide, Nanak, born on this day, not only preached nonviolence, he actively worked to keep potential combatants from initiating bloodshed.

Yet, not too many generations later, after suffering severe persecution and attacks, the Sikhs themselves were compelled to carry swords for defense. And they still do so today.

Similarly, the principal founder of the Taoist religion, Chang Tao-ling, carried an unsheathed sword, ready at any time to confront nature spirits, ghosts, and otherworldly beings who, in their confusion and misery, had entered this world. His sword moved them to return to their rightful place where these beings could find happiness.

Swords cut many ways. Let the swords in your life move you to courage, right action, and happiness.

KEY

"But what about you?" he asked. "Who do you say I am?"

Simon Peter answered, "You are the Christ, the Son of the living God."

Jesus replied, "Blessed are you, Simon son of Jonah, for this was not revealed to you by man, but by my Father in heaven. And I tell you that you are Peter, and on this rock I will build my church, and the gates of Hades will not overcome it. I will give you the keys of the kingdom of heaven; whatever you bind on earth will be bound in heaven, and whatever you loose on earth will be loosed in heaven." Then he warned his disciples not to tell anyone that he was the Christ.

—GOSPEL OF MATTHEW (CHRISTIAN NEW TESTAMENT)

His are the keys of the heavens and the earth.

—QUR'AN (HOLY BOOK OF ISLAM)

CONTEMPLATION

A Buddhist tale of keys:

Nan-ch'uan was the abbot and teacher, Chao-chou his favorite among numerous fellow monks and students. Subtly, they colluded to help enlighten the novices.

Assigned to duty as a stoker in the kitchen, Chao-chou one day got a huge fire burning, then closed all the doors firmly. The kitchen filled with smoke.

He called out, "Fire, fire!" and soon a throng of monks came to the rescue. When the entire community had assembled at the kitchen door, Chao-chou said, "Say the right word, then I will open the door." No one spoke; but in the hubbub, Nan-ch'uan slipped a key through a slot in the door to Chao-chou inside. He opened the door.

Your spiritual life and the power you derive from it, the noted Interfaith Minister June Radicchi relates, are "an inside job." Turn the key.

UGLINESS

A princess once said to Rabbi Joshua ben Hananiah, "It is true that you are a sage, but why are you so ugly? Imagine God pouring wisdom into such an ugly vessel as yours!"

Rabbi Joshua answered, "Tell me, O Princess, in what sort of vessels does your father keep his wine?"

"In earthen jars, of course," answered the princess.

Rabbi Joshua pretended to be amazed.

"How can that be?" he exclaimed. "Everybody keeps wine in earthen jars, but your father, after all, is the king! Surely he can afford finer vessels!"

"In what sort of vessels do you think my father ought to keep his wine?"

"For a king, gold and silver vessels would be more fitting."

The princess then went to her father and said, "It is not fitting that a king like you should keep his wine in earthen jars like the commonest man."

The king agreed and ordered that all his wine should be poured into gold and silver vessels. This was done, but before long the wine turned sour.

Angered, the king asked his daughter, "From whom did you get the advice you gave me?"

"From Rabbi Joshua ben Hananiah."

So the king sent for Rabbi Joshua.

"What made you give my daughter such wicked advice?" he asked angrily.

Rabbi Joshua then told him how the princess had referred to him as "wisdom in an ugly vessel," and that he had wanted to prove to her that beauty is sometimes a handicap.

The king remonstrated: "Aren't there people who combine in themselves both beauty and great talents?"

Rabbi Joshua answered, "Rest assured—had they been ugly, their talents would have been better developed."

—TRADITIONAL JEWISH TALE

CONTEMPLATION

In some ways each of us is considered ugly by others. If we internalize this judgment, it can disfigure and cripple us.

In the natural world, plants and animals possess no such standards of measurement to determine beauty and ugliness. The only standard is effectiveness.

Saint Paul was described as "little in stature, with a bald head and crooked legs . . . with eyebrows meeting and a nose somewhat hooked." Not pretty, but could he get the job done!

All devotion, all prayer, all divine aspiration and effort are beautiful.

SECRETS

It is as if some man goes into an intimate friend's house, gets drunk, and falls asleep. Meanwhile his friend, having to go forth on official duty, ties a priceless jewel within the man's garment as a present, and then departs. The man, being asleep, knows nothing of this. On arising he travels onward until he reaches some other country where, striving for food and clothing, he labors diligently, undergoes exceeding great hardship, and is content even if he can obtain but a little. Later, his friend happens to meet him and speaks thus—"Tut! Sir! How is it you have come down to this, merely for the sake of food and clothing? Wishing you to be in comfort and able to satisfy your five senses, I, formerly in such a year and month and on such a day, tied a priceless jewel within your garment. Now as of old it is present there, yet you in ignorance are slaving and worrying to keep yourself alive. How very stupid! Go you now and exchange that jewel for what you need, and forever hereafter live as you will, free from poverty and shortage."

—LOTUS SUTRA (BUDDHIST SACRED TEXT)

Whether you like it or not, whether you know it or not, secretly Nature seeks and hunts and tries to ferret out the track in which God may be found.

—WRITINGS OF MEISTER ECKHART
(CHRISTIAN MYSTIC AND POET)

O splendid jewel, serenely infused with the Sun!
He formed the Word in you as a human being,
And therefore you are the jewel that shines most brightly.

—WRITINGS OF HILDEGARD VON BINGEN
(CHRISTIAN MYSTIC AND POET)

CONTEMPLATION

It is not as if God, Goddess, the devil, or any other powers (demonic or otherwise) that you might believe in are playing some bizarre trick on you, hiding the secret of universal truth and success from you.

In Judaism, God is sometimes called melech ha olam—*king of the universe. Yet* olam, *typically translated as "universe," has another root meaning— "the hidden." This interpretation leads us to consider the universe and the ultimate powers of it as not obvious and absolute but shadowed and relative.*

Albert Einstein knew this. He devoted his full imagination to the search for the ultimate revelation of truth—from the microcosmic (atomic and subatomic realms) to the macrocosmic (expanding galaxies and the nature of light itself). By the end of his illustrious life, he had yet to find the one Unified Field Theory that explained all the secrets. Still he chuckled with goodwill and good humor knowing that "God does not play dice with the world."

Children understand. You do too when deeply in meditation or deeply in love. There is a secret. There isn't. Who's telling?

CONFESSION

A certain king, named Asmodeus, established an ordinance by which every malefactor taken and brought before the judge should distinctly declare three truths, against which no exception could be taken, or else be capitally condemned. If, however, he did this, his life and property should be safe. It chanced that a certain soldier transgressed the law and fled. He hid himself in a forest, and there committed many atrocities, despoiling and slaying whomsoever he could lay his hands upon. When the judge of the district ascertained his haunt, he ordered the forest to be surrounded, and the soldier to be seized and brought bound to the seat of judgment. "You know the law," said the judge. "I do," returned the other: "if I declare three unquestionable truths, I shall be free; but if not, I must die." "True," replied the judge: "take then advantage of the law's clemency, or undergo the punishment it awards without delay." "Cause silence to be kept," said the soldier undauntedly. His wish being complied with, he proceeded in the following manner. "The first truth is this. I protest before ye all that from my youth up I have been a bad man." The judge, hearing this, said to the bystanders, "He says true?" They answered, "Else he had not now been in this situation." "Go on, then," said the judge; "what is the second truth?" "I like not," exclaimed he, "the dangerous situation in which I stand." "Certainly," said the judge, "we may credit thee. Now then for the third truth, and thou hast saved thy life." "Why," he replied, "if I once get out of this confounded place, I will never willingly reenter it." "Amen," said the judge, "thy wit hath preserved thee; go in peace." And thus he was saved.

My beloved, the king is Christ. The soldier is any sinner; the judge is a wise confessor. If the sinner confess the truth in such a manner as not even demons can object, he shall be saved, that is, if he confess and repent.

—*GESTA ROMANORUM* (CLASSICAL CHRISTIAN TALES)

CONTEMPLATION

When the Catholic conquistadors came to what was for them a new world, they soon found that the Aztecs had a format and procedure for confession almost identical to their own. The penitent confessed not to Jesus but to her or his "Father and Mother" Quetzalcoatl.

Find your own way to regularly confess. It's strange, but however you do it, it will save you.

RELIGION

Religion is basically virtue, which is grounded ultimately in the spiritual nature of man.

—KUNDAKUNDA (JAIN SACRED TEXT)

My religion is to have nothing to be ashamed of when I die.

—WRITINGS OF MILAREPA (TIBETAN BUDDHIST TEACHER)

Give reverence to your tradition's God, who the whole world and all that lives pervades.

—NATCHINTANAI (CLASSICAL HINDU TEXT)

Our religion is the traditions of our ancestors, the dreams of our old men, given them by the Great Spirit, and the visions of our sachems [chiefs], and is written in the hearts of our people.

—SAYING OF SEATHL (NATIVE AMERICAN CHIEF)

CONTEMPLATION

Whether you are a member of a religion of one or one billion, this religion is yours.

A religion is not better or worse because it has numerous adherents or followers around the world. Every religion started with one person.

Today we can no longer afford to be dismissive of anyone's religion, for our own sake and for the sake of universal peace.

The great Sufi teacher Bawa Muhaiyaddeen taught:

We must open everything each religion has. We have to open each of the religions. If we open the religions and look inside, then we will see only one point, one family, one God, and one truth. God's story, the story of mankind, and the point of truth will be inside. There will be no discrimination, no differences, no separation, and no hell inside. There will be only one light inside.

RESISTANCE

"Come now, let us reason together," says the Lord. "Though your sins are like scarlet, they shall be as white as snow; though they are red as crimson, they shall be like wool. If you are willing and obedient, you will eat the best from the land; but if you resist and rebel, you will be devoured by the sword." For the mouth of the Lord has spoken.

—BOOK OF ISAIAH (HEBREW SCRIPTURES)

God gives nothing to those who keep their arms crossed.

—TRADITIONAL BAMBARA TRIBAL PROVERB (WEST AFRICA)

CONTEMPLATION

Resistance to Divine Will is not only futile, it can be devastating to one's soul. Stress, illness, and sometimes even death follow upon stubborn refusal to do what one knows is right and good.

Resistance to human or societal will is not only possible, it is also, in certain circumstances, essential.

Christians were right to resist persecution from the Roman authorities and continue their worship. So were the pagans Praetextatus and Paulina, who guarded the ancient Greek Eleusinian mysteries and resisted the orders of the newly Christianized emperor Valentinian to suppress these venerable mystical rituals.

Mahatma Gandhi and Martin Luther King, Jr., were right with their God in resisting political oppression and prejudice that was unofficially and officially ordained by their nations.

You, too, are right to resist any abuse or compulsion against conscience.

BLESSING

Blessed are You, Adonoy, our God and God of our fathers,
God of Abraham, God of Isaac, and God of Jacob,
Great, mighty, and awesome God, Highest God,
Doer of good, kind deeds, Master of all,
Who remembers the love of the Patriarchs and brings a redeemer to
    their children's children for His name's sake, with love.
King, Helper, Rescuer, and Shield.
Blessed are You, Adonoy, Shield of Abraham.

—TRADITIONAL JEWISH PRAYER

CONTEMPLATION

Pandora's box was not a box but a sacred honey-vase. What poured out when it was opened were not the terrible ills of the world but universal blessing.

A person may be blessed with many things—a loving family, abundant vitality, intelligence, wealth, numerous abilities and charms—and each of us is blessed with many of these things and others as well.

When you know these blessings, that they are in you, joined to you in spirit and soul, you know God.

GRIEF

◆

The Tibetan teacher Marpa lived on a farm with his family a thousand years ago. On the farm there also lived many monks who came to study with this great teacher. One day Marpa's oldest son was killed. Marpa was grieving deeply when one of the monks came to him and said, "I don't understand. You teach us that all is an illusion. Yet you are crying. If all is an illusion, then why do you grieve so deeply?" Marpa replied, "Indeed, everything is an illusion. And the death of a child is the greatest of these illusions."

—TRADITIONAL BUDDHIST TALE

◆

Don't Grieve.
Anything you lose comes around in another form.
The child weaned from mother's milk
now drinks wine and honey mixed.
God's joy moves from unmarked box to unmarked box,
from cell to cell.
As rainwater,
down into flowerbed.
As roses, up from ground.
Now it looks like a plate of rice and fish,
Now a cliff covered with vines,
Now a horse being saddled.
It hides within these,
till one day it cracks them open.

Fa'ilatun, fa'ilatun, fa'ilatun fa'ilat
There's the light gold of wheat in the sun,
and the gold of bread made from wheat . . .
I have neither, I am only talking about them
as a town in the desert looks up
to stars on a clear night.

—WRITINGS OF RUMI (SUFI MYSTIC AND POET)

CONTEMPLATION

When you've had a great loss, grieve first. Enlightenment can (and will) come later. When Kisa Gotami's young son died, she ran grief-stricken to Buddha for help in bringing the child back to her and life. Others laughed at her; Buddha took her seriously. He instructed her to make the rounds of the city and, "in whatever house no one has died," fetch grains of mustard seed. By the time Kisa Gotami, empty-handed, returned to Buddha's presence, she was enlightened about both suffering and grief.

DEVOTION

◆

A woman of Chaoch'eng who was over seventy years old had an only son. One day he went into the mountains and was eaten by a tiger. The old woman grieved and grieved, ready to give up her life. Then with vociferous cries she complained to the local authorities.

"How can a tiger be subject to the law?" said the magistrate with a smile. This only aggravated the old woman's tantrum, and when the magistrate scolded her, she would not be intimidated. Because he felt sorry for her, he kept his own temper and even ended by agreeing to have the beast apprehended.

Day and night Li Neng and his hunters now stalked the mountain hollows in hopes of catching a tiger. But more than a month passed without success, and the agent was given a severe beating of one hundred strokes. Having nowhere to turn for redress, he presented himself at the shrine east of the town. There he called on his knees for the local deity, crying until he had no voice.

Soon a tiger came up. Li Neng was aghast, expecting to be eaten. But the tiger entered the shrine and, looking steadily at the agent, sat down on its haunches in the doorway. Li Neng called to the tiger as though it were a deity: "If it was you who killed the woman's son, then you should submit to my arrest." Then the agent took out a rope and tied it around the tiger's neck. The tiger dropped his ears and accepted the rope, and the agent led the beast to the magistrate's office. The magistrate asked the tiger, "That woman's son—you ate him?" The tiger nodded.

"Those who take life must die," continued the magistrate. "That law stands from oldest times. Besides, the poor woman had only one son. How do you suppose she'll survive the years that remain to her? However, if you should be able to serve as her son, I shall spare you." Again the tiger nodded.

When the morrow dawned, the old woman opened her gate to find a deer's carcass, which she took and sold for her daily necessities. This became a custom, though sometimes the tiger would bring money or silk in his mouth and flip it into her yard. And so the woman became quite well-to-do- -far better cared for than when her son was alive. Eventually the tiger would come and lie under the eaves of her house the whole day, and the people and livestock no longer feared it.

After several years the old woman died, whereupon the tiger came and bellowed in the front hall. The woman had saved up enough for an ample burial service, and her kinsmen laid her to rest. When the mound over the tomb was completed, the tiger suddenly bounded up. The mourners fled, and the tiger went straight to the front of the tomb, roared thunderously for a long while, and then departed. Local people set up a shrine to the loyal tiger by the eastern outskirts of the township, where it remains to this day.

—TRADITIONAL CHINESE TALE

CONTEMPLATION

The first Chassidic master, the Baal Shem Tov, said, "If we had power over the ends of the earth, it would not give us that fulfillment of existence which a quiet devoted relationship to nearby life can give us." And nearby loved ones.

A Chinese legend tells of two lovers. So devoted were they in life that death could not separate their spirits. In recognition of their devotion, the Gods transformed them into butterflies and made it so they would be together incarnation after incarnation.

CLEAVING

◇

Pappus ben Yehudah asked him, "Master, aren't you afraid of the Romans?"

Akiva answered, "Let me tell you a story: Once a fox was walking along the shore when he saw fish darting back and forth in the water. 'What are you fleeing?' he asked them. 'The fishermen's nets,' they replied. 'Why not come out onto the shore?' suggested the sly fox. 'Once your ancestors and mine lived side by side upon the land.' But the fish replied: 'If we are in danger in the sea where we live, how much greater will the danger be in a place that spells our death!'"

"So it is with us," Akiva told Pappus. "If we are in danger when we study Torah, which is our Tree of Life, imagine our danger if we no longer cling to it!"

In a few days Akiva was arrested and imprisoned. They led him out for execution just at the time for reciting the morning *Sh'ma*. As the Roman executioners were tearing his flesh from his body with iron combs, he continued to recite his prayers.

His disciples cried, "Master, even now? This far?"

Akiva answered, "All my life I wondered how I could fulfill the commandment to love God with all my soul. Would I ever be able to give up my soul to serve God? Now that I have the opportunity, should I not seize it?"

He reached the end of the *Sh'ma* and held the word "One" to his last breath. And then he died.

The angels cried, "Is this the Torah and is this her reward?"

A voice burst forth from heaven, "Happy are you, Akiva, for you have inherited the joy of eternity!"

—TRADITIONAL JEWISH TALE

CONTEMPLATION

Feel in your heart. Feel the person, the teacher, the faith that you most love. Cleave to this one with all your heart now and always.

COVENANT

◆

When Abram was ninety-nine years old, the Lord appeared to him and said, "I am God Almighty; walk before me and be blameless. I will confirm my covenant between me and you and will greatly increase your numbers."

Abram fell facedown, and God said to him, "As for me, this is my covenant with you: You will be the father of many nations. No longer will you be called Abram; your name will be Abraham, for I have made you a father of many nations. I will make you very fruitful; I will make nations of you, and kings will come from you. I will establish my covenant as an everlasting covenant between me and you and your descendants after you for the generations to come, to be your God and the God of your descendants after you. The whole land of Canaan, where you are now an alien, I will give as an everlasting possession to you and your descendants after you; and I will be their God."

Then God said to Abraham, "As for you, you must keep my covenant, you and your descendants after you for the generations to come."

—BOOK OF GENESIS (HEBREW SCRIPTURES)

CONTEMPLATION

To complete this covenant, God asks—no, commands—a piece of flesh (circumcision) of Abraham and all his male descendants. Similar sacrifices of animals had marked tribal covenants, between man and man and man and his God, for millennia.

By Jesus' time, it was understood by many that God required a "circumcised" heart as a symbol of covenant making.

Women have had another take on all this. On this day, in some traditional pagan cultures, women gather together in worship circles (covens) to celebrate—mystery, life, and death. It's a day of merrymaking! Nothing of the flesh is harmed, and the covenant of spirit is renewed.

COMPASSION

◇

The prophet Muhammad (peace be upon him) was teaching, reciting from the Qur'an to an assembly of earnest listeners out in the desert sand not too far from their tents when a sickly cat walked straight to Muhammad (peace be upon him), sat down on the hem of his exquisite and precious robe, and went to sleep.

All day the prophet Muhammad (peace be upon him) spoke and conversed with the believers, the sun rising to its fullest and falling again, and none of the party, nor the prophet Muhammad (peace be upon him) stirred. The cat as well remained asleep and still, healing in the way cats do, in the protection of the prophet Muhammad (peace be upon him) and the succor of his robe.

At last, the day was coming to its end, and all, as well the prophet Muhammad (peace be upon him), were now to return to their dwelling places for the night.

Without a word, the prophet Muhammad (peace be upon him) took a knife, cut off the hem of his robe on which the sick cat still lay sleeping, by this act destroying the finest of robes, and left the cat undisturbed.

—TRADITIONAL MUSLIM TALE

CONTEMPLATION

It is one thing to talk about compassion, about loving one's neighbor. . . . Compassion is about feeling and action. In the Gospels, Jesus is said to be compassionate; the Greek word used is splanchnizomai—"*moved in one's bowels*"—*which means he really felt it! Among the Tsalagi (Cherokee) people, and traditionally in Native American culture, Dhyani Ywahoo, spiritual elder, tells us: Prayer is action. What benefit is it, she asks, if one knows how to grow corn but does not share this knowledge? What benefit is it if one has food and does not bring it to the sick and elderly?*

GRATITUDE

Glorified art Thou, O Lord my God! I yield Thee thanks for having enabled me to recognize the Manifestation of Thyself. . . . Again I thank Thee for having empowered me to be steadfast in Thy love, and to speak forth Thy praise and to extol Thy virtues, and for having given me to drink of the cup of Thy mercy that hath surpassed all things visible and invisible. Thou art the Almighty, the Most Exalted, the All-Glorious, the All-Loving.

—WRITINGS OF BAHÁ'U'LLÁH (BAHÁ'Í FAITH)

Bless the Lord, O my soul. O Lord my God, thou art very great; thou art clothed with honor and majesty.

Who coverest thyself with light as with a garment: who stretchest out the heavens like a curtain: Who layeth the beans of his chambers in the waters: who maketh the clouds his chariot: who walketh upon the wings of the wind: Who maketh winds his messengers; flaming fire his ministers; Who laid the earth upon its foundations, that it should not be removed forever.

Thou coveredst it with the deep as with a garment: the waters stood above the mountains. He watereth the hills from his chambers: the earth is satisfied with the fruit of thy works.

He causeth the grass to grow for the cattle, and herb for the service of man: that he may bring forth food out of the earth; and wine that maketh glad the heart of man, and oil to make his face to shine, and bread which strengthened man's heart.

The trees of the Lord are full of sap; the cedars of Lebanon which he hath planted; Where the birds make their nests: as for the stork, the fir trees are its house. The high hills are a refuge for the wild goats; and the rocks for the conies.

He appointed the moon for seasons: the sun knoweth its going down. Thou makest darkness, and it is night: wherein all the beasts of the forest do creep forth. The young lions roar after their prey, and seek their meat from God. The sun ariseth, they gather themselves together, and lay them down in their dens. Man goeth forth unto his work and to his labor until the evening.

O Lord, how manifold are thy works! In wisdom hast thou made them all: the earth is full of thy riches.

—PSALM 104 (HEBREW SCRIPTURES)

CONTEMPLATION

Does it take a special day to give thanks?

The story is told of a very learned rabbi, who finding on his journeys an ignorant Jew, stayed to instruct the man in righteous ways of thanksgiving.

No matter how much this poor man studied, he, to the great rabbi's consternation, just could not catch on. For weeks this went on.

Finally one morning at dawn the rabbi peeked in the fellow's window to check if he was properly preparing for morning prayers. The man had just woken up. In full voice he cried out, "Thank you, God! I see I am alive again this morning!" The rabbi left without a word.

The Tsalagi (Cherokees) give prayer-thanks every morning, too, to Aqteshna Ana, the Dew-on-the-Grass. Always there, always fresh on the soles of one's feet, always a reminder to hold a grateful heart.

HOPE

Because you have made the Lord your refuge
The Most High your habitation,
No evil shall befall you
No scourge come near your tent
For he will give his angels charge of you
To guard you in all your ways.

—PSALM 91 (HEBREW SCRIPTURES)

There is a body outside the body
Which has nothing to do with anything produced by magical arts.
Making this aware energy completely pervasive
Is the living, active, unified original spirit.
The bright moon congeals the gold liquid,
Blue lotus refines jade reality.
When you've cooked the marrow of the sun and moon
The pearl is so bright, you don't worry about poverty.

—WRITINGS OF SUN BU-ER (ANCIENT TAOIST TEACHER)

CONTEMPLATION

In the north the first snows, perhaps even heavy ones, have fallen. Some Native American tribes call this period "Blanket," for the earth is beginning to be covered over for the winter. How can we, at this time, hope?

Peter Gomes, minister to the Harvard University community, addresses this problem point-blank. "Hope," he claims, "is based on experience, the experience of what God has done. . . . . . It does not operate out of ignorance as is commonly believed, but out of knowledge."

Can you not remember, even as Job did in the most pathetic of circumstances, a whole litany of good and great things that have come to you? Can you see the earth, cleared of snow and ice, and breathing freely once again? Good, you have hope!

MONEY

◇

Running after that cur, money,
I have forgotten you, O Lord.
What a shame! I have time only for making money, not for you.
How can a dog who loves rotten meat, relish the nectar?

—DHAMMAPADA (BUDDHIST SACRED TEXT)

◆

After Jesus and his disciples arrived in Capernaum, the collectors of
the two-drachma tax came to Peter and asked, "Doesn't your teacher pay
the temple tax?"

"Yes, he does," he replied.

When Peter came into the house, Jesus was the first to speak. "What
do you think, Simon?" he asked. "From whom do the kings of the earth
collect duty and taxes—from their own sons or from others?"

"From others," Peter answered.

"Then the sons are exempt," Jesus said to him. "But so that we may not
offend them, go to the lake and throw out your line. Take the first fish
you catch; open its mouth, and you will find a four-drachma coin. Take it
and give it to them for my tax and yours."

—GOSPEL OF MATTHEW (CHRISTIAN NEW TESTAMENT)

CONTEMPLATION

*There's a wonderful Jack Benny joke about (of course) money. Benny is confronted
at gunpoint by a robber who demands, "Your money or your life." After a long
pause—a very long pause—Benny squeaks out, "I'm thinking, I'm thinking."*

*Jesus didn't have to think. He knew that the Scriptures professed "Money an-
swers all things," and in certain circumstances, like due taxes, it is the only answer.*

*Think about this as well. Jesus didn't get up and run around frantically to
get the money either, losing himself in the process. For God's sake, Jesus and the
money he used had a definite purpose.*

MORNING

Earth our mother, breathe forth life
   all night sleeping
   now awaking
   in the east
   now see the dawn

Earth our mother, breathe and waken
   leaves are stirring
   all things moving
   new day coming
   life renewing

Eagle soaring, see the morning
   see the new mysterious morning
   something marvelous and sacred
   though it happens every day
   Dawn the child of God and Darkness

—TRADITIONAL PAWNEE TRIBAL PRAYER
(NATIVE AMERICAN)

CONTEMPLATION

What would make this morning special?

Imagine that the person you most want to have breakfast with in the entire world is showing up in your kitchen this morning.

Or that they're going to give you a lifetime bonus check at work this very morning.

Or that the cure for a dreadful disease will be discovered and announced on the morning of this day.

Now, imagine. The most luminous and nearby star has perched itself right above your house. Someone who loves you dearly is waiting to kiss you and give well-wishes. A magnificent pulsating energy inspires you throughout your whole being.

Good morning.

DECEMBER

HEART

Once Rabbi Yohanan ben Zakkai said to his five disciples: "What is the most desirable thing to strive for in life?"

Rabbi Eliezer said: "A good eye."

Rabbi Joshua said: "A good friend."

Rabbi Yose said: "A good neighbor."

Rabbi Simeon said: "Wisdom to foretell the future."

Rabbi Eleazar said: "A good heart."

Rabbi Yohanan then said to his five disciples: "The words of Eleazar please me most, because his thought includes all the rest."

At another time Rabbi Yohanan asked his disciples: "What is the thing that man should avoid most in life?"

Rabbi Eliezer said: "An evil eye."

Rabbi Joshua said: "An evil friend."

Rabbi Yose said: "A bad neighbor."

Rabbi Simeon said: "One who borrows money and doesn't return it."

Rabbi Eleazar said: "A bad heart."

Rabbi Yohanan then said: "The words of Eleazar please me most because his thought includes all of yours."

—TRADITIONAL JEWISH TEACHING

The highest sage shares his moral possessions with others.

The next in wisdom shares his material possessions with others.

The man who because of his own wisdom looks down on others has never won men's hearts.

The man who in spite of his own wisdom is humble to others has never failed to win men's hearts.

—BOOK OF LIEH-TZU (CLASSICAL TAOIST TEXT)

CONTEMPLATION

Today is World AIDS day; in some future tomorrow there will be a cure for AIDS, but people of the world will still be suffering, from disease, malnutrition, poverty, and assuredly a lack of love.

Mother Teresa loved and served those in suffering. She once noted: "This is a gift of love, but I've been told I cannot give the gift of peace because I don't give peace to anyone."

It may seem strange that such heartfelt labors as Mother Teresa's with the sick and the poor disturbed many people. But on reflection, this makes sense; giving your heart is an act that shakes up the spirit. Yet ultimately, peace does come to the wholehearted.

EXPERIENCE

If saying Ram [God] gave liberation
    saying candy made your mouth sweet,
    saying fire burned your feet,
    saying water quenched your thirst,
    saying food banished hunger,
    the whole world would be free.

—WRITINGS OF KABIR
(CLASSICAL INDIAN MYSTIC AND POET)

Before practicing Zen, rivers were rivers and mountains were mountains. When I practiced Zen, I saw that rivers were no longer rivers and mountains no longer mountains. Now I see that rivers are again rivers and mountains are again mountains.

—TRADITIONAL ZEN BUDDHIST TEACHING

The fish trap exists because of the fish; once you've gotten the fish, you can forget the trap. The rabbit snare exists because of the rabbit; once you've gotten the rabbit, you can forget the snare. Words exist because of meaning; once you've gotten the meaning, you can forget the words. Where can I find a man who has forgotten words so I can have a word with him?

—WRITINGS OF CHUANG-TZU
(CLASSICAL TAOIST TEACHER)

CONTEMPLATION

Baba Hari Dass has spoken no words for going on fifty years. The leader of a yoga-based community, he nonetheless teaches every day, writing on the experience of pleasure and pain, devotion and spiritual practice.

In response to his students' questions, he often refers to the practice of Bogah yoga—the yoga of everyday experience.

There is plenty enough experience to go around today and every day. We need only be present (and do whatever makes us present) to have a great experience of life!

DO-GOODERS

◇

What does it profit, my brethren, if a man says he has faith but has not works? Can his faith save him? If a brother or sister is ill clad and in lack of daily food, and one of you says to them, "Go in peace, be warmed and filled," without giving them the things needed for the body, what does it profit? So faith by itself, without work, is dead.

—EPISTLE OF JAMES (CHRISTIAN NEW TESTAMENT)

◇

Be mindful of your duty [to God], and do good works; and again, be mindful of your duty, and believe; and once again: be mindful of your duty, and do right. God loves the doers of good.

—QUR'AN (HOLY BOOK OF ISLAM)

◇

Anything evil refrain from doing; all good deeds do! So will you be released forever from the influence of evil stars, and always be encompassed by good guardian angels.

—TRACT OF THE QUIET WAY (TAOIST SACRED TEXT)

CONTEMPLATION

An additional, typically unacknowledged responsibility goes along with doing a good deed—creating no new obligation for the recipient. A Jewish legend tells of a very good and charitable man who, when granted favor by his angel, asked only that a holy shadow would fall over his good deeds. And so it came to be; the boon was given, and all were blessed.

HOSPITALITY

◇

Ijapa the tortoise was on a journey. He was tired and hungry, for he had been walking a long time. He came to the village where Ojola the boa lived, and he stopped there, thinking, "Ojola will surely feed me, for I am famished."

Ojola greeted him, saying, "Enter my house, and cool yourself in the shade, for I can see you have been on the trail."

They sat and talked. Ijapa smelled food cooking over the fire.

Ojola said, "Let us prepare ourselves. Then we shall eat together."

Ijapa went outside. When he came in again, he saw the food in the middle of the room and smelled its odors. But Ojola the boa was coiled around the food. There was no way to get to it. Ojola's body was long, and his coils lay one atop the other, and there was no entrance through them. Ijapa's hunger was intense.

Ojola said, "Come, do not be restless. Sit down. Let us eat."

Ijapa said, "I would be glad to sit with you. But you, why do you surround the dinner?"

Ojola said, "This is our custom. When my people eat, they always sit this way." The boa went on eating while Ijapa again went around and around, trying to find a way to the food. Ojola finished eating. He said, "What a pleasure it is to eat dinner with a friend."

Ijapa left Ojola's house hungrier than he had come. He brooded on his experience with Ojola. He decided that he would return the courtesy by inviting Ojola to his house to eat with him. He told his wife to prepare a meal for a certain festive day. And he began to weave a long tail out of grass. When it was finished, he fastened it to himself with tree gum.

On the festival day, Ojola arrived. They greeted each other at the door, Ijapa saying, "You have been on a long journey. You are hungry."

Ojola was glad. He went to the spring to wash. When he returned, he found Ijapa already eating. Ijapa's grass tail was coiled several times around the food. Ojola could not get close to the dinner. Ijapa ate with enthusiasm.

Ojola went around and around. It was useless. At last he said, "Ijapa, how did it happen that once you were quite short but now you are very long?"

Ijapa said, "One person learns from another about such things." Ojola then remembered the time Ijapa had been his guest.

—TRADITIONAL YORUBA TRIBAL TALE (WEST AFRICA)

CONTEMPLATION

In a letter to the Hebrews, Saul the Jew, turned Paul the wandering Christian, gave this instruction: "Do not neglect to show hospitality to strangers, for thereby some have entertained angels unawares." Seen any angels at your door recently?

ADVENTURE

◇

I live as I please.
I wander where I like;
I go in and out each day
According to my pleasure;
I move where
My inclination leads me;
I assume all the forms
Which it pleases me to assume;
I hold in my right hand
The Lapis stone;
I wear in my right ear
The flower of Ankham for ornament;
I am flourishing,
I am prosperous;
I am a perennial youth
In the garden of immortality.

—TRADITIONAL EGYPTIAN HYMN

CONTEMPLATION

Have you arrived?

The root meaning of adventure *is "coming to." Adventure, then, is a process, and the attitude of adventurous people is that of openness.*

In Christian circles this period in December leading up to Christmas is called Advent. The truly adventurous are open to finding a new and perhaps unexpected Christ-child, the Wonder-child within us all.

DELIGHT

◆

May it be delightful my house;
From my head may it be delightful;
To my feet may it be delightful;
Where I lie may it be delightful;
All above me may it be delightful;
All around me may it be delightful.

—TRADITIONAL DINÉ TRIBAL CHANT (NATIVE AMERICAN)

◆

Thus saith the Lord, Let not the wise man glory in his wisdom, neither let the mighty man glory in his might, let not the rich man glory in his riches: But let him that glorieth glory in this, that he understandeth and knoweth me, that I am the Lord who exercise loving-kindness, judgment, and righteousness, in the earth: for in these things I delight, saith the Lord.

—BOOK OF JEREMIAH (HEBREW SCRIPTURES)

CONTEMPLATION

Gan-Heden, *translated as "Garden of Eden," really means this: a universal realm of unpassing time and delight. This is our place! The most delightful place!*

Still we are not meant to dwell there constantly or permanently. Rabbi Aaron of Karlin understood this. When, because of his righteousness, the heavenly powers offered him freely all the delights of the world, he refused. "I'll accept," he said, "but first I want to sweat for them!"

Ah, delight upon delight!

CAREGIVERS

Lord, I am grateful to You that in Your mysterious love You have taken away from me all earthly wealth, and that You now clothe and feed me through the kindness of others.

Lord, I am grateful to You that since You have taken away from me the sight of my eyes, You care for me now through the eyes of others.

Lord, I am grateful to You that since you have taken away from me the strength of my hands and heart, you care for me now through the hands and hearts of others.

Lord, I pray for them, that You will reward them in Your love, that they may continue to faithfully serve and care until they come to a happy end in eternity with You.

—WRITINGS OF MECHTHILD OF MAGDEBURG
(CHRISTIAN MYSTIC AND POET)

CONTEMPLATION

All of us are caregivers, whether it be to our own children or parents, our partners, or in some additional capacity as friends or volunteers. When we pray for those who care for us, we also pray for ourselves. Caregivers must have great strength. Pray for strength.

DECEMBER 8
SUFFERING

Rabbi Yohanan said, "The Israelites are compared to an olive tree, because as the olive yields its oil only by hard pressure, so the Israelites do not return to righteousness except through suffering."

—TALMUD (JEWISH SACRED TEXT)

Yet the suffering
Involved in my awakening will have a limit
It is like the suffering of having an incision made
In order to remove and destroy greater pain.
But the Supreme Physician does not employ
Common medical treatments such as these
With an extremely gentle technique,
He remedies all the greatest sins.

—SHANTIDEVA, GUIDE TO THE BODHISATTVA'S
WAY OF LIFE (BUDDHIST SACRED TEXT)

We rejoice in our sufferings, knowing that suffering produces endurance, and endurance produces character, and character produces hope, and hope does not disappoint us, because God's love has been poured into our hearts.

—PAUL'S EPISTLE TO THE ROMANS
(CHRISTIAN NEW TESTAMENT)

CONTEMPLATION

Everyone and everything suffers. Even the physicists, in expostulating the Second Law of Thermodynamics, acknowledge that energy always and inevitably dissipates. For living things, this means suffering.

We humans have two choices—to suffer unconsciously or to suffer consciously. We can merely resign ourselves to our fates (the Greeks saw these as demigods) and suffer the natural consequences, or with superhuman surrender, will, and effort make from simple olives sacred oil and the source of holy light.

ILLUMINATION

Which are the mountains not clothed with your beams?
Which are the regions not warmed by the brightness of your light?
Brightener of gloom, illuminator of darkness,
Dispeller of darkness, illuminator of the broad earth.

—TRADITIONAL BABYLONIAN HYMN

He who dwells in the light, yet is other than the light, whom the light does not know, whose body is the light, who controls the light from within—He is the *atman* within you.

—YAJUR VEDA (HINDU SACRED TEXT)

I, the highest and fiery power, have kindled every living spark and I have breathed out nothing that can die. . . . I flame above the beauty of the fields, I shine in the waters; in the sun, the moon and the stars, I burn. . . . All living things take their radiance from me.

—WRITINGS OF HILDEGARD VON BINGEN
(CHRISTIAN MYSTIC AND POET)

CONTEMPLATION

Aristides, a general and politician in ancient Greece, had an epiphany. "There came," he reported, "from Isis a light and other unutterable things conducing to salvation." Now such illumination does not generally come to military leaders unless they are wide-eyed spiritual seekers, too.

Judas Maccabee, the Israelite rebel leader who overthrew the Greeks and restored the eternal light in the Temple, may have had his own illumination. It is not recorded, but the shining victory he brought about is celebrated still today—as Chanukah.

You shine on, too, and make your own victories of illumination. We can always use more light!

DECEMBER 10
HOLDING

◊

By you have I been held from the womb.

—PSALM 71 (HEBREW SCRIPTURES)

◊

One day the venerable guru and his disciple were out for a peaceful walk when they came upon a distraught woman sitting on the riverbank. Politely the old man inquired if they could be of help. The woman thanked them for their offer. She needed desperately to cross the river but was paralyzed with fear of being drowned in the rushing water. Without hesitation the old guru picked the young woman up in his arms and carried her to the other shore. The woman went happily on her own way. After a few hours on the forest path, the young disciple broke the silence. "Tell me," he said to the old master, "how did it feel to hold such a beautiful woman? Her arms and thighs pressed around you, her breasts against your chest with every breath, her eyes gazing into yours—how did it feel?" The young man panted his question.

The old guru stayed silent for a little while. Then, facing his disciple, he whispered, "You can say much better than I how it feels to carry such a woman. For I put her down hours ago at the riverbank, but you are still holding her in your arms."

—TRADITIONAL HINDU TALE

◊

Throw away holiness and wisdom, and people will be a hundred times happier.

—TAO TE CHING (CLASSICAL TAOIST TEXT)

CONTEMPLATION

They seem to hold on to nothing, the self-directed (and often self-proclaimed) saints and holy ones. They head for the forest and give up society; but do they really? They forgo a regular diet and rely on morsels from benefactors; but are they free from hunger? They hold out in monasteries and caves in complete silence; but are they, in truth, still?

Monks and nuns form new societies, whose rules are often much stricter than the ones they leave. They have given up food, but not the effort to obtain it;

they hunger as well for enlightenment and liberation, and attempt to keep their minds from holding them in unholier states of being.

The great ones do not hold to such extreme measures. They use them when required and otherwise live naturally, held within the heart of the universe. You do the same.

HEAVEN

◇

A big, tough samurai once went to see a little monk. "Monk," he said in a voice accustomed to instant obedience, "teach me about heaven and hell!"

The monk looked up at this mighty warrior and replied with utter disdain, "Teach you about heaven and hell? I couldn't teach you about anything. You're dirty. You smell. Your blade is rusty. You're a disgrace, an embarrassment to the samurai class. Get out of my sight. I can't stand you."

The samurai was furious. He shook, got all red in the face, was speechless with rage. He pulled out his sword and raised it above him, preparing to slay the monk.

"That's hell," said the monk softly.

The samurai was overwhelmed. The compassion and surrender of this little man who had offered his life to give this teaching to show him hell! He slowly put down his sword, filled with gratitude, and suddenly peaceful.

"And that's heaven," said the monk softly.

—TRADITIONAL ZEN BUDDHIST TALE

CONTEMPLATION

How and where do we find heaven? The word heaven comes from an old English word heofon, *"to cover."*

Heaven, then, is found when someone uncovers the truth with you and folds you in its embrace. Heaven, then, is ubiquitous—it's even, as Jesus said, inside us—and available.

CONCEPTION

When one begins to apply this magic, it is as if, in the middle of one's being, there were a nonbeing. When in the course of time the work is finished, and beyond the body there is another body, it is as if, in the middle of the nonbeing, there were a being. Only after a completed work of a hundred days will the Light be real, then only will it become spirit-fire. After a hundred days there develops by itself in the middle of the Light, a point of the true Light-pole. Suddenly there develops the seed pearl. It is as if man and woman embraced and a conception took place.

—THE SECRET OF THE GOLDEN FLOWER
(CLASSICAL TAOIST TEXT)

Whenever two are linked this way, there comes another from the Unseen world. It may be through birth, if nothing prevents conception, but a third does come, when two unite in love, or in hate. The intense qualities born of such joining appear in the spiritual world.

—WRITINGS OF RUMI (SUFI MYSTIC AND POET)

CONTEMPLATION

Whenever one has intercourse (sexual or otherwise) with another being, something of essence is shared. Tremendous, primordial, universal power is unleashed.

This is why spiritual masters are so circumspect about who they share their innermost wisdom with. Jesus told parables—even to his closest disciples.

Choose your spiritual mates carefully; there's the children to think about!

PRETENSE

The champion archer of Salimia constantly complained. The people of his town had no reputation for archery, and his excellence was largely unrecognized and little understood. "They cannot know," became his bitter refrain, and everyone in Salimia was convinced of his unhappiness.

One day, a wandering Sufi master stopped in the teahouse, and the patrons, sympathetic to their champion's plight, told the master about him.

"Ah," the master said, "this fellow very well may believe he is indeed suffering a miserable fate, but in truth God has been most kind and generous to him. Had he grown up in a place where talent in archery was common, he would be constantly apprehensive about being bested.

"If he really wanted to find competitors of his ilk, there would be no real obstacle to finding them.

"Until a man—and those who listen to him—hear the message that is not said, and dismiss the spoken one, he will be chained."

—TRADITIONAL SUFI TALE

A hunter asked a woodcutter whether he had seen any lion tracks in the area. "Matter of fact," replied the woodcutter, "I can lead you right to the lion himself." At this the hunter turned pale and stammered: "It's—it's the tracks I'm looking for, not—not the lion."

—FABLE OF AESOP (CLASSICAL GREEK)

CONTEMPLATION

It's not so much that people lie; rather, they pretend. There's not much to be done about it except . . . what about yourself?

You have the power, like a master gardener with a pair of finely honed pruning shears, to simply cut all pretense away. Did you exaggerate? Admit it. Snip! Boast inordinately? Snap! Gardening this way can be such fun!

TENACITY

◇

Thereupon Naropa exchanged his load of wood for a black antelope's pelt, took up the habit of a yogin, and finally set out in search of the yogin Tilopa.

Naropa wandered through the land but did not find him. Finally, after a long search, he met Tilopa on the road. Naropa did reverence and circumambulated Tilopa, saying, "O guru, are you in good health?" "I am not your guru, and you are not my student," said Tilopa. And in anger he began to thrash Naropa, but Naropa's faith only increased.

Naropa then gathered alms in a clay pot and presented them in front of his guru—who became angry and beat him as before. Naropa's faith increased even more. He ate the remaining food and made circumambulation. Naropa brought alms again in the evening, and the next morning he went out for more. In this way, for twelve years, he did reverence before the guru without despairing, although the guru did not speak any words to him except in anger.

One day Naropa was begging alms where a wedding was taking place. He received great amounts of food of many different kinds and a quantity of a very tasty dish called "green patasa," which had eighty-four different ingredients. He gave this dish to his guru. The guru ate it and was so pleased that he said: "My son, where did you get such food? Who gave it to you?"

Naropa felt the extraordinary joy that is obtained in the first bodhisattva stage. He thought to himself: "For twelve years I stayed near my guru and he did not even say 'Who are you?' Now he has said 'My son.'" As he reflected on this, Naropa became very happy. "Son," said Tilopa, "go get me some more of this delicious dish."

—TRADITIONAL TIBETAN BUDDHIST TALE

CONTEMPLATION

We give up far too easily when it comes to spiritual concerns. Not so other concerns: should we work extra hours for three months to get the crop in or to complete an office project? Sure. There's a visible reward in front of us; so, sure, we'll do it.

But if a spiritual teacher we've heard about (and really want to see) is vis-

iting the area; "Well, it's a weekend"; "She'll come back sometime"; "I'll read the book." No tenacity.

And now for the rest of Naropa's story. Four times he brought the special dish for the master and was received graciously. But the tenacious Naropa was not done yet. Ashamed to ask for the fifth serving, he stole the pot and presented it to the guru, who was most pleased.

Naropa was initiated and in turn obtained great spiritual powers, which he used to the benefit of countless beings. They say he finally went to the heavenly realm of the Dakas.

COMPROMISE

◇

The Lion fell in love with the farmer's daughter and asked for her hand in marriage. The farmer did not like the idea of marrying his daughter to a ferocious beast; nor, for that matter, did he like the idea of refusing him. He told the Lion that, though he considered him a son-in-law after his own heart, his daughter was naturally alarmed by his long teeth and claws, and that he could not grant his consent to the marriage until the Lion had had both teeth and claws removed. Because the Lion was in love, he agreed to the double sacrifice. But when he appeared at the farmer's cottage to claim his bride, he was greeted with scorn and driven away with a stout stick.

—FABLE OF AESOP (CLASSICAL GREEK)

◇

One night a king dreamed that he saw a king in paradise and a dervish in the hellish realm.

The king demanded: "What is the meaning of this? I should have thought that the positions would be the other way around."

A voice answered: "The king is in heaven because he respected dervishes. The dervish is in hell because he compromised with kings."

—WRITINGS OF IBN EL ARABI (SUFI TEACHER)

CONTEMPLATION

Compromising your true nature is never acceptable or advantageous.

The Dalai Lama didn't. When the Chinese came to Tibet in the early 1950s, the then teenage leader of his people could have stayed and tried to work something out with the Chinese. It had been tried before.

No. He fled to India in order to preserve Tibetan religion and culture. Take no chances with what is similarly precious and vital to you.

MASK

When Moses came down from Mount Sinai with the two tablets of the Testimony in his hands, he was not aware that his face was radiant because he had spoken with the Lord. When Aaron and all the Israelites saw Moses, his face was radiant, and they were afraid to come near him. But Moses called to them; so Aaron and all the leaders of the community came back to him, and he spoke to them. Afterward all the Israelites came near him, and he gave them all the commands the Lord had given him on Mount Sinai.

When Moses finished speaking to them, he put a veil over his face. But whenever he entered the Lord's presence to speak with him, he removed the veil until he came out. And when he came out and told the Israelites what he had been commanded, they saw that his face was radiant. Then Moses would put the veil back over his face until he went in to speak with the Lord.

—BOOK OF EXODUS (HEBREW SCRIPTURES)

CONTEMPLATION

If you wish to command in good faith, you cannot conceal your intentions.

If you wish to command only attention, then the masking you do will be self-serving. You'll hide what you're afraid others won't like and put on a phony face of what you think they will.

It is never in your best interest, or that of those around you, to mask your true self. Let it show radiantly! Just find the right time and place to do it.

FAIRNESS

◇

Once there was a man who went out into the forest looking for a runaway horse. At one point he had to climb across a gap in the mountain, where he saw that a large snake had got its tail caught under some large rocks.

The snake said to the man, "If you help free me, I'll see that you get your just reward!"

So the man took his staff and pried the rocks apart so the snake could get out.

The man asked what his just reward might be.

"Death," said the snake. "Death is your just reward."

The man said that he'd never heard of that before, and he'd like to ask the first living creature they met if the snake really was right about this.

They walked along until they met a bear. The man asked the bear what one's just reward ought to be, and the bear answered that it was death.

But the man said, "Let's walk a little farther and ask someone else."

After a while they met a wolf. The man asked him what one's just reward ought to be.

The wolf answered, "Death. That's one's just reward."

"Well!" said the snake. "Let's get on with it."

"No," said the man. "I want to hear one more judge in the case, whoever it might be."

A little while later they met a fox, and the man asked him what, in his opinion, was a just reward.

"I don't think we ought to make a final judgment in this case until we have examined it thoroughly. To begin with, what actually happened?"

"Well," said the man, "the snake had got its tail caught in a rock crevice."

Then the fox said, "I think we'd better go back to the spot and take a look."

And so they did. When they arrived, the fox asked the man to use his staff to pry the rocks apart again, and he told the snake to place his tail just where it had been when he'd got it caught. When the tail was again in place, the fox told the man to let go of the staff.

"Now I'm stuck even worse than I was before."

And the fox said, "Well then, you might as well just stay here, so that the two of you will be even again."

—TRADITIONAL NORTHERN EUROPEAN STORY

CONTEMPLATION

A true-life tale about fairness:

Once a Bahá'í pilgrim bearing gifts of silver was accosted by thieves just as the devotee was nearing arrival at his beloved 'Abdu'l Bahá's home in Haifa. As the robbers were about to take off with the loot, the man cried out that the silver was meant for his master. The thieves immediately returned all the silver to the astonished pilgrim; 'Abdu'l Bahá had fed them, clothed them, and given shelter to their families.

'Abdu'l Bahá's rewards went far beyond the return of the silver. He was honored by political and religious leaders throughout the world for his charitable work. But beyond even this, 'Abdu'l Bahá was loved, genuinely loved. Not only did his fellow Bahá'ís cherish him, but the entire city of Haifa did as well. Even the Muslim and Christian communities, who were generally antagonistic to the Bahá'í message, embraced the man. When he died, thousands came to be part of 'Abdu'l Bahá's last service.

ANSWERS

The Mullah Nasreddin one day addressed his congregation from the pulpit in the following words: "I beseech you to tell me truly, O brethren! O true believers! if what I am going to say to you is already known to you."

And the answer came, as in one voice, from his congregation, that they did not know, and that it was not possible for them to know, what the Mullah was going to say to them. "Then," quoth the preacher, "of what use to you or to me is an unknown subject?" And he descended from the pulpit and left the mosque.

On the following Friday his congregation, instead of having decreased, had greatly increased, and their anxiety to hear what he was going to say was felt in the very atmosphere.

The Mullah ascended the pulpit and said, "O brethren! O true believers! I beseech you to tell me truly if what I am going to say to you is already known to you."

The answer that came to the Mullah was so spontaneous as to suggest prearrangement. They all shouted, "Yes, Mullah, we do know what you are going to say to us."

"That being the case," quoth the Mullah, "there is no need either of you wasting your time or of me wasting my time." And descending from the pulpit, he left the mosque. His congregation, having prayed, also left gradually, one by one and in groups.

On the following Friday the Mullah Nasreddin again mounted the pulpit and saw that his mosque was so crowded that not a nook or corner in it was empty. He addressed his congregation in exactly the same manner. "O brethren! O true believers!" said he, "I ask you to tell me truly if what I am going to say is already known to you."

And again the answer of his numerous congregation had evidently been prepared beforehand, for one half of them rose and said, "Yes, Mullah, we do know what you are going to say to us," and the other half rose and said, "O Mullah, how could we poor ignorant people know what you intend to say to us?"

Nasreddin answered, "It is well said; and now if the half that knows what I am going to say would explain to the other half what it is, I would be deeply grateful, for, of course, it will be unnecessary for me to say anything."

Whereupon he descended from the pulpit and left the mosque.

—TRADITIONAL SUFI TALE

CONTEMPLATION

Not only must we find our own answers, we must also come to understand that sometimes none can be provided, nor would we wish it to be different. Li Po, the classical Chinese poet, asked:

> *"Why do I live among the green mountains?*
> *I laugh and answer not, my soul is serene;*
> *It dwells in another heaven and earth belonging to no man.*
> *The peach trees are in flower, and the water flows on."*

Isn't that a lovely answer?

RESPECTABILITY

In dwelling, live close to the ground.
In thinking, keep to the simple.
In conflict, be fair and generous.
In governing, don't try to control.
In work, do what you enjoy.
In family life, be completely present.

When you are content to be simply yourself
and don't compare or compete,
everybody will respect you.

—TAO TE CHING (CLASSICAL TAOIST TEXT)

One day Djuha arrived at a banquet in his usual rags, only to be turned away at the door. After changing into his costliest clothes and saddling his mule, he returned to his host's house looking like a man of substance. This time the servant welcomed him respectfully and seated him near the guests of honor. As Djuha reached for a piece of roast meat, his sleeve happened to slip down into the food. "Pull back your sleeve," whispered the man sitting next to him. "No," replied Djuha, "that I shall not do!" Then, addressing his sleeve, he said, "Eat, my sleeve, eat and take your fill! You have more right to this feast than I, since they respect you above me in this house."

—TRADITIONAL SUFI TALE

CONTEMPLATION

The Hindu God-incarnate Krishna was, by conventional standards, a most dis-respectable character. He was mischievous and improper. One day when the lovely milkmaids were bathing, the impish Krishna made away with all their clothing.

Yet Krishna, the vagabond, the musician, remains sincere in his call to devotees of spirit. You must, as another divine personality Jesus insisted, leave your father and mother (the respectable life) to follow him.

When Krishna seductively played his flute, many of the respectable cowherds' wives awoke and came running to the woods. They danced with him all night!

There formerly lived a king who had three fair daughters. He married them to three dukes; but unhappily all their husbands died in the space of one year. The king, being made acquainted with this circumstance, would have had his daughters marry again, and calling the first into his presence, he said: "My dear daughter, your husband is dead; I will therefore unite you to another." But she would by no means consent and assigned for it this reason. "If I marry again, I should love my second husband equally with the first; perhaps more, or it might be less. This ought not to be; for my first husband possessed my earliest affection—my virgin troth. Therefore the second ought not to be loved so well. But I might love him more, and this would increase the evil: on the other hand, if I loved him less, there would exist only contention between us. So that I resolve never to be espoused again." The king, satisfied with what he heard, called another of his daughters and proposed the same thing to her as to her elder sister. She replied, "My lord, I also decline this matter. For should I comply, it must be either for riches, or power, or beauty. Now of riches I have quite enough; my friends are sufficiently numerous to defend me; and as for beauty, I do not believe there was so beautiful a person in the world as my late husband. Therefore I too resolve upon a single state." The king then applied to the third daughter, and she gave the following reasons for refusing his request. "If," said she, "I marry, my husband must desire me either for my beauty or my wealth. Now it cannot be for the former, because I am not beautiful; then it must be for the latter, and true love never existed that was founded upon mercenary feelings. When wealth flies, love flies with it. Therefore I would on no account marry again. Moreover, the Sacred Writings say that a husband and wife are one body but two souls; therefore the body of my husband is my body, and the converse. Every day I visit the sepulcher of my deceased lord, and he is ever present to my mind. For all these causes, I determine to remain as I am." The king, pleased with the virtuous resolutions of his daughters, solicited them no more.

—*GESTA ROMANORUM* (CLASSICAL CHRISTIAN TALES)

Those who follow this path, resolving deep within themselves to seek Me alone, attain singleness of purpose. For those who lack resolution, the decisions of life are many-branched and endless.

—BHAGAVAD GITA (HINDU SACRED TEXT)

CONTEMPLATION

We are surrounded, nay, inundated by choices and options. Foods, books, possible mates, vacation destinations, universities, etc. . . . A strong spiritual person does not let herself or himself become distracted. Select what is right, and stick resolutely by your choice. There's much power to be gotten through this —and it will last.

PRAYER

◇

If I pray to you with my heart,
You know it and are gracious unto me.

—TRADITIONAL BORAN TRIBAL PRAYER (EAST AFRICA)

◇

I listen to the prayer of every supplicant when he calls on Me.

—QUR'AN (HOLY BOOK OF ISLAM)

◇

Always let a man test himself: If he can direct his heart, let him pray.

—TALMUD (JEWISH SACRED TEXT)

◇

For the Great Spirit is everywhere and hears whatever is in our minds
and hearts.

—TEACHING OF BLACK ELK (LAKOTA, NATIVE AMERICAN)

◇

I know that words of prayer which serve a good end
Are successful before you.

—AVESTA (ZOROASTRIAN SACRED TEXT)

◇

Pray ceaselessly.

—PAUL'S FIRST EPISTLE TO THE THESSALONIANS
(CHRISTIAN NEW TESTAMENT)

◇

Of all the prayers of the heart, the best prayer is the prayer to the
Master to be given the grace of properly praying to the Lord.

—ADI GRANTH (SIKH SACRED TEXT)

◇

To be visited with the blessings of the kami (deities), one must first direct one's mind wholeheartedly to prayer.

—RECORDS OF THE ENSHRINEMENT OF THE TWO
IMPERIAL DEITIES AT ISE (CLASSICAL SHINTO TEXT)

◇

Every son and every daughter of a family ought with their whole mind
to make fervent prayer for the Pure Land of Buddha.

—SMALLER SUKHAVATIVYUHA SUTRA
(BUDDHIST SACRED TEXT)

◇

Turning to the summit
For provision of nourishment
Brings good fortune.

—I CHING (CLASSICAL CHINESE TEXT)

◇

If powerful men and women
could center themselves in Tao,
the whole world would be transformed.

—TAO TE CHING (CLASSICAL TAOIST TEXT)

◇

Om.

—SACRED HINDU PRAYER CHANT/SOUND

CONTEMPLATION

*"Dear God, I think about you sometimes even when I'm not praying." So says
young Elliott, in* Children's Letters to God, *and he speaks for us, too.*

*This solstice day gives us a lot to think about. For people in the north, it is
the day of least light, when we may feel our darkest and most cynical. For those
in the south, it is the day of most light, and the potentially disturbing sense
that the best has come and only shadowing will follow.*

What can we do? Pray.

*Prayer, author Marianne Williamson shares, "reconnects us with our Source."
And as reconnection (*religere, *in Latin) is the root meaning of* religion,
prayer must be the heart of our religion. Go to the heart. Pray.

DENSITY

If a thousand suns were to rise in the heavens at the same time, the blaze of their light would resemble the splendor of the supreme spirit.

O Lord your presence fills the heavens and the earth and reaches in every direction.

Filled with your terrible radiance, O Vishnu, the whole creation bursts into flames.

—BHAGAVAD GITA (HINDU SACRED TEXT)

Those who are wise will shine like the brightness of the heavens and those who lead many to righteousness like the stars forever.

—BOOK OF DANIEL (HEBREW SCRIPTURES)

CONTEMPLATION

Astrophysicists say there are black holes, stars that become so dense that nothing, not even light, comes from them. Are you a black hole or a living star?

LAUGHTER

A time to weep and a time to laugh.

—BOOK OF ECCLESIASTES (HEBREW SCRIPTURES)

What is the Buddha, what is wisdom, what is the bodhisattva, what is revelation? All the components are by nature empty. Thus those who seek enlightenment are to be laughed at.

—WRITINGS OF SHANTIDEVA
(CLASSICAL BUDDHIST TEACHER)

A lover was telling his Beloved
how much he loved her, how faithful
he had been, how self-sacrificing, getting up
at dawn every morning, fasting, giving up
wealth and strength and fame,
all for her.

There was a fire in him.
He didn't know where it came from,
but it made him weep and melt like a candle.

"You've done well," she said, "but listen to me.
All this is the decor of love, the branches
and leaves and blossoms. You must live
at the root to be a True Lover."

        "Where is that!
Tell me!"

"You've done the outward acts,
but you haven't died. You must die."

When he heard that, he lay back on the ground
laughing, and died. He opened like a rose
that drops to the ground and died laughing.

That laughter was his freedom,
and his gift to the Eternal.

—WRITINGS OF RUMI (SUFI MYSTIC AND POET)

CONTEMPLATION

"A keen sense of humor helps us to overlook the unbecoming, understand the unconventional, tolerate the unpleasant, and outlast the unbearable." This from the Reverend Dr. Billy Graham. The poet Pablo Neruda put it this way: "Laughter is the language of the soul." We know that Sarah, the matriarch of the Jewish people, laughed at the angels. Buddha laughed, too—real big belly laughs, so it is said. Go ahead, laugh; the angels and the universe will still be there. And you'll feel a whole lot better!

MAGIC

◇

During his youth the Laughing Buddha lived in a monastery at Feng-hua in the province of Chekiang. Even when eating or sleeping, he carried a bag with him, and for this reason the people called him the Monk with the Bag.

Once upon a time the deity of fire descended to the temple, which in a short time he reduced to a heap of ashes. There being no money with which to rebuild it, the abbot ordered the Monk with the Bag to collect offerings.

The monk set off with his wooden fish clapper and his bag, and one day he arrived at the house of a widow. She was the owner of a large mountain covered with trees, which had not been felled for more than one hundred years. They were very big now, and the monk begged the widow to give him a bagful of them. Thinking that the monk was making a joke, because, after all, a small bag will not hold many trees, she gave him permission at once.

The monk engaged a few workmen, cut down all the trees on the mountain, and slipped them into his bag. It was extraordinary to see large and small trees vanish into it without a shadow of them appearing inside.

The widow was horrified when she heard the news and rushed off to the mountain, but every tree had been cut down, and there was nothing left but the branches that had been cut off. She thought to herself, "Until now I have lived from the sale of these trees, but with them all cut down, I shall soon die of starvation." She knelt down before the monk. "Don't kneel down. I know what you are thinking, but you will have your trees again in three years," he said to her with a smile.

She only half believed his words, but three years later the mountain was really covered with trees as big as before.

Whither did the trees go? The monk had conjured them away to a small well in the temple. Now that the building materials were ready, he did not need to collect any more money but returned to the temple to supervise the workmen. The temple was to be made bigger than before, and since the time allotted for building was very short, no carpenter was willing to undertake it. The monk had to appoint the magician Lu Pan.

Lu Pan ordered his pupils to take the wood out of the well, but they were careless and overlooked one beam, which was to serve as the center pillar. The monk wanted to test Lu Pan, and kneeling down before him, he asked if the building material was sufficient. "Just right," answered Lu Pan, "not too much and not too little."

The work began. When it was almost finished, Lu Pan found to his horror that one beam was missing. Although he calculated again and again, he could not get it right. Having already said that there was sufficient wood, he did not dare ask the monk for any more. The only thing he could think of was to make the center pillar out of the chips of wood that had been scattered about, and wonderful to relate, it could not be distinguished from a real one.

The monk secretly admired the skill of Lu Pan, and Lu Pan the magic of the monk. Thus the great task was finally completed.

—TRADITIONAL CHINESE BUDDHIST TALE

CONTEMPLATION

Is magic afoot in your life? Each act of magic begins with a step, builds with faith, and concludes with delight. This day, make magic.

ANOINTING

And thou shalt take the anointing oil, and anoint the tabernacle, and all that is therein, and shalt hallow it, and all the vessels thereof: and it shall be holy. And thou shalt anoint the altar of the burnt-offering, and all its vessels, and sanctify the altar: and it shall be an altar most holy. And thou shalt anoint the laver and its foot, and sanctify it.

And thou shalt bring Aaron and his sons unto the door of the tabernacle of the congregation, and wash them with water. And thou shalt put upon Aaron the holy garments, and anoint him, and sanctify him; that he may minister unto me in the priest's office. And thou shalt bring his sons, and clothe them with coats: And thou shalt anoint them, as thou didst anoint their father, that they may minister unto me in the priest's office: for their anointing shall surely be an everlasting priesthood throughout their generations.

—BOOK OF EXODUS (HEBREW SCRIPTURES)

CONTEMPLATION

Anointing, in ancient times, was a rare event, saved only for the most sacred things and people. Aaron, the original High Priest, was the first in Jewish history to be anointed. Many Christians believe Jesus, as the direct spiritual descendant of Aaron and the actual descendant of the anointed King David, to be the Messiah, the Christ, the anointed one, promised to the world. Jesus had no official worldly christening, only that of the Holy Spirit.

What if, from this day on, we all accept anointing?

MASTERMINDS

◇

Two monks were arguing about the temple flag waving in the wind. One said, "The flag moves." The other said, "The wind moves." They argued back and forth but could not agree.

The sixth ancestor said, "Gentlemen! It is not the wind that moves; it is not the flag that moves; it is your mind that moves." The two monks were struck with awe.

Wu-Men's Comment

It is not the wind that moves. It is not the flag that moves. It is not the mind that moves. How do you see the Ancestral Teacher here? If you can view this matter intimately, you will find that the two monks received gold when they were buying iron. The Ancestral Teacher could not repress his compassion and overspent himself.

Wu-Men's Verse

Wind, flag, mind move—
all the same fallacy;
only knowing how to open their mouths;
not knowing they had fallen into chatter.

—MUMON-KAN (CLASSICAL ZEN BUDDHIST TEXT)

CONTEMPLATION

The two chattering monks finally got a mindful from their master. Master Jesus frequently did the same with his witless and argumentative disciples.

Perhaps it was in these interactions that Jesus discovered this truth: "Wherever two or more are gathered; there I [the Christ-spirit] am."

Isn't it marvelous what brilliant ideas and insights come from group meetings and meditations?

You be mindful of this and seek good company.

REINCARNATION

◆

When Death first entered the world, men sent a messenger to Chuku, asking him whether the dead could not be restored to life and sent back to their old homes. They chose the dog as their messenger.

The dog, however, did not go straight to Chuku but dallied on the way. The toad had overheard the message, and as he wished to punish mankind, he overtook the dog and reached Chuku first. He said he had been sent by men to say that after death they had no desire at all to return to the world. Chuku declared that he would respect their wishes, and when the dog arrived later with the true message, he refused to alter his decision.

Thus, although a human being may be born again, he cannot return with the same body and the same personality.

—TRADITIONAL IBO TRIBAL STORY (WEST AFRICA)

CONTEMPLATION

Jewish legend has it that as each new child is born, an angel comes to kiss it. The kiss is one of forgetfulness so that the child and the adult she or he becomes will retain no knowledge of previous existence, place, or circumstance.

What a blessing! Considering how attached and distracted we are to and by this life, the one we're actually living, we'd be completely discombobulated by a connection to others.

Stay focused. Live this life.

DANGER

The time of testing the fledglings had come, and so the flock of crows assembled in the forest. To determine whether these youngsters were ready to fly alone, and thereby be accepted into the company of their elders, the young crows were required to prove their wit and wisdom. This day there were three to whom this question was put: "What, in this lower world, is the thing to be most dreaded and terribly feared?"

The first fledgling answered: "An arrow." The august body of examiners flapped their wings *hata-taki,* signifying their concurrence. The young crow's father puffed with pride.

"You are one of us," the chief examiner proclaimed, and turned to the second youngster. "And what is your response?" he commanded.

The second fledgling said, "I believe the archer himself is more to be feared than the arrow he shoots, for without the archer the arrow could no more cause hurt than this branch I now occupy." The crow elders cawed in approval and the father stood proudly by.

"Most right, most right," the high judge intoned. "You, too, are accepted."

"What do you have to tell us?" he demanded of the last of the three.

The fledgling spoke up: "Neither who answered is right. The archer who holds no skill is the one that chills my blood and causes my feathers to rise in fear."

The assembled elders were astonished at this answer and momentarily fell silent. Then the chief queried, "How do you explain this?"

"Because," the youngster declared, "when one hears the proficient archer pull back his bow and prepare to shoot, one has only to flit to one side or the other and the arrow aimed so well at its target will surely miss it. But with the bowman whose skill is lacking, one cannot say whether it is best to remain still or fly, for this archer's arrows may bring danger in either case."

Now hearing such understanding and wisdom from one "just out of the shell," they bowed to him, and the head crow, sensing his own leadership in danger, flew forthwith to a distant land. The flock appointed the wise young crow as their new leader.

—CLASSICAL JAPANESE TALE

CONTEMPLATION

This can be a dangerous world, with many, skilled and unskilled, aiming for you. Be aware that this is so, and in your spiritual life keep away from those who may do you harm. This will afford at least some protection and respite.

PERMISSION

On the fast day of Tisha Ba'Ab, a sick Jew went to see the rabbi in order to get his permission to eat, for he was afraid his health would suffer if he didn't. But, as he entered the rabbi's house, he was struck dumb with amazement when he saw the rabbi enjoying a hearty lunch.

"Rabbi," he faltered, not at all sure of himself, "I'm a sick man—do I have to fast today?"

"What a question!" replied the rabbi, his mouth full of roast duck. "Of course you do!"

For a moment the petitioner stood in bewilderment, not knowing whether he was coming or going. Finally he scraped up sufficient courage to ask, "Pardon my impertinence, Rabbi, but how can you order me to fast when you yourself are eating?"

"I wasn't fool enough to ask the rabbi," replied the rabbi with a grin, and went on with his lunch.

—TRADITIONAL JEWISH TALE

CONTEMPLATION

Some of us are yet unconvinced that we have complete permission to live in this world.

When we get involved in spiritual practice, we carry over this attitude. You ask yourself, should I meditate for an hour or for thirty minutes in the morning? Never mind that the kids are clamoring for breakfast and you only have thirty minutes of free time. "I'll go ask my teacher," you think. And off you go.

Get over this foolhardy compulsion. Give yourself permission to experiment and experience. From this will come expertise and confidence. When you really need specific permission, you'll be much more qualified yourself to give it.

GARDEN

Ibrahim, the gardener, was asked by his employer one day to bring him some pomegranates. Ibrahim dutifully brought a number of them, but they all turned out to be sour.

His master declared, "You have worked in my garden for many years now, and you still can't tell which pomegranates are sweet?"

Ibrahim said, "I am employed to grow these fruits, not to taste them. How would I know which are the sweeter?"

The owner understood then that Ibrahim, the gardener, was no other than the Sufi master Ibrahim ben Adam.

—TRADITIONAL SUFI TALE

The world is a garden,
The Lord its gardener,
Cherishing all, none neglected.

—ADI GRANTH (SIKH SACRED TEXT)

Remember, it is forbidden to live in a town which has no garden or greenery.

—TALMUD (JEWISH SACRED TEXT)

CONTEMPLATION

At the end of a year, gardens lie quiet and dormant. Nothing stirs in the soil; no bursts of color or obvious growth are visible; no buzzing of enterprising insects is heard.

You, too, may feel sluggish or perhaps apprehensive about the coming year.

You must look to yourself as a master gardener does. Where there are signs of upward struggle for life or incipient greenness, give your blessing.

Your garden is always one-in-the-making.

STORYTELLING

◇

The Baal Shem Tov, may he be remembered, used to go to a certain place in the forest whenever he faced an especially difficult situation. There he would light a fire and pray, and whatever needed to be done was done.

After the Master of the Good Name died, his successor followed in his footsteps, and he, too, went to the very same place in the forest. He said: "We cannot light the fire anymore, for we don't know the Master's way with it, but we can say the prayer." And whatever he asked in prayer was, as before, done.

This generation passed, and the pious Rabbi Moshe Lieb went to the woods and said, "The fire we are unable to light, and the prayer is gone from our minds. All we know is this holy place in the forest, and that will have to do." His prayers also came to be.

In the fourth generation Rabbi Israel of Rishen no longer made the journey to the holy place. He stayed at home, for as he said, "The fire we cannot light, the prayer we don't know anymore, nor do we remember the right place to go. All we can do is tell the story."

And that, too, was quite enough.

—TRADITIONAL JEWISH TALE

CONTEMPLATION

The universe itself is a story yet unfolding. Every religion is a good and well-told story. Every person, as well, is a story in process of creation. What's yours?

SPIRITUAL TREASURY

At the Interfaith Seminary, our Interfaith Minister ordainees and I have been blessed to discover and cherish many precious books and source materials. The following list provides a sampling of titles that have proven edifying, inspirational, and enlightening to us. I pray you will find them so as well.

Armstrong, Karen. *Muhammad*. New York: HarperCollins, 1992.

Beversluis, Joel, ed. *A Source Book for Earth's Community of Religions* (rev. ed.). Grand Rapids, MI: CoNexus Press, and New York: Global Education Associates, 1995.

Dass, Baba Hari. *Sweeper to Saint*. Santa Cruz, CA: Sri Rama, 1980.

Eliade, Mircea. *Essential Sacred Writings from Around the World*. San Francisco: HarperSanFrancisco, 1992.

Fadiman, James, and Robert Frazer. *Essential Sufism*. New York: HarperCollins, 1997.

Hebrew Scriptures. Various versions.

The Holy Bible. New International Version. Colorado Springs: International Bible Society, 1973.

The Holy Bible. King James Version.

Jordan, Michael. *Encyclopedia of Gods*. New York: Facts on File, 1993.

Kolitz, Zvi. *The Teacher*. New York: Crossroad, 1982.

Mabey, Juliet, ed. *God's Big Instruction Book*. Oxford, England: Oneworld, 1996.

Pennick, Nigel. *The Pagan Book of Days*. Rochester, VT: Destiny, 1992.

The Qur'an. Trans. M. H. Shakir. Elmhurst, NY: Tahrike Tarsile Qur'an, 1988.

Smith, Huston. *The Illustrated World's Religions*. New York: HarperCollins, 1994.

Subramuniyaswami, Satguru Sivaya. *Dancing with Siva*. Concord, CA: Himalayan Academy, 1994.

Walker, Barbara G. *The Woman's Encyclopedia of Myths and Secrets*. New York: Harper & Row, 1983.

Wilson, Andrew, ed. *World Scripture* (Project of the International Religious Foundation). New York: Paragon House, 1991.

Ywahoo, Dhyani. *Voices of Our Ancestors*. Boston: Shambhala, 1987.

For more information about the Interfaith Seminary and the activities of Interfaith Ministers, please contact:

Interfaith Seminary
136 Swift Street
Santa Cruz, CA 95060

or

Association of Interfaith Ministers
838 East 218th Street
Bronx, NY 10467

ACKNOWLEDGMENTS OF PERMISSION

The author and publisher gratefully acknowledge the following for granting permission to use copyrighted material which has so enriched this book.

Great devotion and diligence has been put into the effort to trace copyright holders; because great preponderance of the excerpts included in this book come from traditional (and often ancient) sources, this mission has proven to be challenging indeed.

We ask for your forgiveness if any unintended omissions have occurred. Further, we welcome hearing from any omitted copyright holders and will be pleased to make all appropriate acknowledgments in future editions.

Jason Aronson Inc. Excerpts from **THE CLASSIC TALES: 4,000 YEARS OF JEWISH LORE**, by Ellen Frankel. Northvale, NJ, 1989. Reprinted by permission of the publisher, Jason Aronson Inc., Northvale, NJ.

Bahá'í Publishing Trust. Excerpts from **BAHÁ'Í PRAYERS**, by the Báb, Bahá'u'lláh and 'Abdu'l-Bahá. Copyright 1954, ©1982, 1985, 1991 by the National Spiritual Assembly of the Bahá'ís of the United States. 1991 edition. Reprinted with the permission of the publisher, The Bahá'í Publishing Trust, Wilmette, IL. Excerpts from **THE KITÁB-I-'IQÁN: THE BOOK OF CERTITUDE**, by Bahá'u'lláh. Copyright 1931, 1950 by the National Spiritual Assembly of the Bahá'ís of the United States. 1994 reprint. Reprinted with the permission of the publisher, The Bahá'í Publishing Trust, Wilmette, IL. Excerpts from **GLEANINGS FROM THE WRITINGS OF BAHÁ'ULLÁH**, by Bahá'u'lláh. Copyright 1939, 1952, © 1976 by the National Spiritual Assembly of the Bahá'ís of the United States. 1994 reprint. Reprinted with the permission of the publisher, the Bahá'í Publishing Trust, Wilmette, IL.

Bear & Co. Excerpts from **MEDITATIONS WITH MEISTER ECKHART**, by Matthew Fox. Santa Fe, NM, 1983. Reprinted with permission from *Meditations with Meister Eckhart,* by Matthew Fox, Copyright © 1983, Bear & Company, Santa Fe, NM.

Columbia University Press. Excerpts from **THE BOOK OF LIEH-TZU**, translated by A. C. Graham. Copyright © 1960, Columbia University Press. Reprinted with the permission of the publisher.